Blithfield Hall
A Country House Saved

Dedicated to Caryl Ernest, Sixth Baron Bagot
Blithfield is still here because of him

First published in 2011 by Redcliffe Press Ltd. Revised edition October 2011
81g Pembroke Road, Bristol BS8 3EA
T: 0117 973 7207
E: info@redcliffepress.co.uk
www.redcliffepress.co.uk

© Nancy, Lady Bagot
ISBN: 978-1-906593-86-5

British Library Cataloguing-in-Publication Data
A catalogue record for this book is available from the British Library

Designed by Stephen Morris, smc@freeuk.com   www.stephen-morris.co.uk

Printed in the Czech Republic via Akcent Media

Blithfield Hall
A Country House Saved

Nancy, Lady Bagot

 redcliffe

Blithfield Hall

Contents

ACKNOWLEDGEMENTS 7

1   SYDNEY TO LONDON – 1938   9

2   GROWING UP IN AUSTRALIA   31

3   CARYL   49

4   CARYL AND NANCY   58

5   THE HEIRLOOMS   83

6   THE EXTENDED FAMILY   101

7   THE CORONATION   115

8   THE GOWERS REPORT   134

9   BLITHFIELD – OPEN TO VISITORS   149

10   THE NATIONAL TRUST   179

11   A TRIP TO AUSTRALIA   185

12   CARA AND CARYL   213

13   CARYL AND CARA   221

14   LIFE AFTER CARYL   226

15   KENNETH   235

16   THE GOOD SAMARITANS   239

17   THE PEACOCK FLAT   242

18   THE BAGOT COSTUME COLLECTION 247

19   CARA AND HER MOTHER 256

20   THE DIVISION OF BLITHFIELD 275

21   JOHN FORD 286

22   THE BAGOT JEWITT TRUST AND THE CHANCELLOR 2005 295

     APPENDICES

     A   1860: Blithfield 299

     B   1938: Colonel Saint's Report 300

     C   Letter to Mr Caryl Bagot concerning the Blithfield Estate – the River
             Blythe Water Scheme, 25th August 1938 306

     D   Report re: Proposed Acquisition of Land on the Blithfield Estate by
             The South Staffordshire Waterworks Co 308

     E   Mr Philippe Bagot's History of the Bagots in France 310

     F   Court Case – John Ford 311

     G   The Bagot Jewitt Trust 317

     Index 320

Acknowledgements

I would not have started to write my memoirs if it hadn't been for all the encouragement given me by the elder daughter of one of my oldest school friends, Jean Beresford Grant. Her daughter, Kate Minto Russell, BA, Dip Ed, MHP Ed, Director of Humanly Possible, 58 Barons Crescent, Hunters Hill, Sydney, came to stay with me at Blithfield and helped me with a 'plan of action'. Then the baton was handed onto my friend, Sandra Ann Burgess, BA (Hons), MA, Cert Ed, Historian, who had recently moved with her husband from Stoke-on-Trent to Brittany. Sandra is an authority on the Sneyd family of Keele Hall, Staffordshire, having written several lengthy pieces on the family including her thesis entitled *A Study of an Ancient Staffordshire Gentry Family – the Family of Ralph Sneyd Esq (1723–1793) of Keele, Staffordshire – with a survey of its pre-history* (four volumes, unpublished MA thesis, 1990, Keele University, Staffordshire). The Sneyds of Keele married into the Bagot family on three occasions and the junior branch of this family, which lived at nearby Bishton Hall, were friends and neighbours of the Bagots of Blithfield, especially during the eighteenth century, both the Bagots and the Sneyds having had considerable influence throughout central and northern Staffordshire for centuries. It was as a consequence of Sandra's researches into the two families that we became friends.

I cannot thank her enough, and her husband Jeff, for persevering with my writing and spelling. I am not computer literate, so I have had to rely on postal and telephone services.

After moving from the Hall into The Peacock Flat in 2005, when Gordon Brown's vindictive legislation in regard to trusts was announced and became legal, the flat rapidly filled up with papers and photographs. What would I do without my splendid helper, Rachel Haynes? All the things I can't find she finds for me in a miraculous way! In fact, Rachel helps many of us here at Blithfield, including Mrs Mary Hatherill-Stephenson, a friend, who is an excellent cook and who often sustained me when I was busy writing.

When Caryl inherited Blithfield, some things we thought were disasters turned into tremendous advantages, such as the beautiful stretch of water – our 'Italian Lake' – known as Blithfield Reservoir, belonging to The South Staffordshire Waterworks Company. Her Majesty Queen Elizabeth, the Queen Mother, coming to open the reservoir, brought Christopher Hussey, *Country Life* and John Fowler here, and alerted The Historic Buildings Council to our plight. I don't think Blithfield could have been saved if it hadn't been for all the sensitive help we received, especially from John Fowler, aptly described as 'Prince of Decorators' in Martin Wood's excellent book, from which he has allowed me to quote. I also owe much gratitude to my dear friend, Imogen Taylor, John's devoted Secretary, who is always ready to help me.

I owe a debt of gratitude to an Australian cousin, Wayne R Ford, who is writing the *Ford Saga*. We are both descended from a Staffordshire great great grandfather!

Blithfield has been most fortunate in that there have been two dedicated craftsmen working here, both with a love of old houses: first, Horace Deakin from the Lichfield area and, after he died, Jack Brown from Colton, who has taken over the continuing task of looking after Blithfield Hall.

Old houses seem to need the portraits of families who have called them 'home', and Blithfield has been fortunate in having the firm of Charles Ward, in Derby, to restore the Bagot family portraits. Charles Ward's daughter, Margaret, carried on the business, and I have been very grateful for all the generous help she has given me, both Margaret and her devoted helper, Elsie Smithurst. I have always been able to count on their friendship.

After the Hall and the Old Stables were divided into several houses, my friend, Miss Sheila Wroughton used to drive over from Leek to help me take small parties of visitors around Blithfield Hall, the Church and gardens. These were enjoyable occasions for everyone. Not only did our visitors enjoy visiting Blithfield, but it was deeply satisfying for us showing them something which could so easily have been lost, as so many beautiful houses have been.

Quite recently, Caroline Miller (née Bagot), from Sydney, when touring in France, met a Philippe Bagot in Blois, and was kind enough to send me a copy of what he wrote about the origins of the family in Brittany. This has been included as Appendix E.

My greatest debt of gratitude must go to Mrs Oliver, my history teacher at Abbotsleigh, Church of England School for Girls, Wahroonga, about twelve miles north of Sydney, who gave me my enthusiasm for history in the first place.

I am so happy to have kindred spirits living in Cloister House, and hope all four houses in the Hall will be able to claim the same enthusiasm, because we are all dependent on each other to a certain extent.

My friend, Mrs Thea Randall, BA, DAS, County Archivist, has always been most helpful and encouraging, for which I am most grateful.

I asked Mr John Sansom of Redcliffe Press to publish my book because I admired the sensitive way in which the pictures had been treated in the *Historic Gardens of England: Staffordshire*, and I am delighted with what Mr David Wakefield of Peter Rogers, Stafford has been able to do with my pictures. Also Mr Stephen Morris who designed the book.

Lastly, if it hadn't been for Charlie, Caryl's great nephew, and his wife, Cosy, taking on the responsibility of Blithfield Hall, I would not have been able to write the history of Caryl's and my time here. Charlie also has a great deal of responsibility at The National Memorial Arboretum. May their time at Blithfield prove to be as productive as Caryl's and mine.

Nancy Bagot, 2010

1

Sydney to London – 1938

IN THE AUSTRALIAN AUTUMN OF 1938, MY MOTHER AND I, WITH ONE OF my best friends, were arriving at the Sydney dockyard area of Woolloomooloo, with wardrobe trunks, suitcases and hatboxes. When we reached the Orient Line's *Orama*, moored there, all was purposeful activity, apart from the passengers already on board, who were inspecting those embarking, probably trying to match them with names on the passenger list; also, Sydney had a reputation for beautiful girls.

If it was a good wool year, station owners would be bringing their families to England and the Continent – a trip 'home' was like 'coming out' for English girls – and on this ocean voyage of approximately five weeks, many Australian girls met their husbands. As there was no other way to travel, there would be passengers of all ages on board.

In our case my mother had been to England as a teenager with her mother and sister to meet relatives, and so had my friend, Nancy MacDougall. My mother had decided to bring me to meet my father's relatives as I had finished my education the previous year. Nancy and I had spent the summer holidays on the beach, where her parents had a house at Newport, north of Sydney. There we had met our first boyfriends, John Walsh and Harry Gregory and they were just what was understood by the word 'boyfriend' then. They and many other friends and family had come to see us off – it was a very jolly affair, which became more serious when 'all visitors ashore' was announced; then we had coloured paper streamers and we threw an end to those on shore, as the ship slowly moved away from the wharf and out into the harbour. What looked bright and happy suddenly seemed very sad as the paper streamers snapped and the ends fell into the water.

Nancy, on the beach at Newport

Someone watching this was my future husband, Caryl Bagot, an English widower, whose dearly loved wife had died of cancer the previous year, in a Zurich hospital. After her death, Caryl had gone to stay with his youngest sister and her husband on their small farm in Queensland and he was returning to Aix-les-Bains in France. Not long after our first evening on board, we were sitting at a small table drinking coffee after dinner when a small, dapper, gentleman came up, bowed to my mother and asked if he might join us for coffee, his snow white hair, sun browned skin, and aristocratic features made his looks very memorable, and after that first meeting we met from time to time.

As the *Orama* slowly cruised down the New South Wales coast towards Melbourne, I was struck by the low coast-line, covered with dark green trees. We didn't know anyone in any of the Australian ports, but went ashore. Port Philip wasn't impressive after Sydney Harbour. We took a tram ride in Hobart and enjoyed the open seaside views. Mr Bagot, as he was always called by us, had gone with a party to the summit of Mount Wellington, and as we were sailing through the Great Australian Bight, towards Adelaide, he joined me at the ship's rail, looking out towards the

In the surf

South Pole. Mr Bagot confided in me that one of his party the previous day had asked if he had a pen to lend her, as she wanted to write her name on the Mount Wellington Monument! Having been very strongly repri-manded for carving my name on my desk at school − I must have read in one of my father's *Strand* magazines that Winston Churchill had carved his name on a desk at Harrow − I knew this was something to be regarded with horror; but, when he told me some Australians were drinking Crème de Menthe before dinner, I hope I was able to cover up the fact that I had never heard of it, although my cousin, Monica Clifford, had taken me to the Australia Hotel in Sydney once and treated me to a Rum Crustas! As plenty of seagulls were wheeling about, we got onto firmer ground, when Mr Bagot wondered if there might be an Albatross among them, and suggested we went to the library to look for a picture of one in a bird book.

We, my mother, Nancy and I went for a drive in Adelaide and at Fremantle, the last Australian port, we drove into Perth, noticing black swans on the Swan River − not unusual as I had never seen a white swan.

Having left Australian waters we were making for Ceylon and getting used to shipboard life. We had already had to get used to salt water baths, finishing by pouring a tub of fresh water over oneself. The weather was getting hotter now and awnings were being put up on deck, games were arranged, and quite often it was time to play off a heat, almost like being back at school. We had lunch on deck and there were dances every night.

We became friendly with a young Englishman, Ian Hay, who had been at Cambridge and was travelling with his father.

One evening Nancy said to me, 'Ian's father tried to kiss me!' We were very innocent. Mr Bagot told me he had never kissed another woman while he was married to his wife. I said, very surprised, 'I should hope not'. Mr Bagot, with a laugh said, 'Some men do you know'. He also asked me if I believed in God, 'Of course' I said at once. 'Clever little girl' was his reply.

Nancy and I enjoyed the swimming pool and sun-bathing as we were well-tanned after summer months on the beach at Newport; however, I had to retire to our cabin with heat stroke as we neared Colombo and, while lying there, I noticed how the sun shining on tropical waters reflected on the ceiling of the white painted cabin and shining brass fittings. I was told Mr Bagot was anxiously asking after me each day. I recovered enough to go ashore and have a meal of curry, which I didn't like, but I enjoyed the drive to Mount Lavenia. Not long after leaving Ceylon we had reached Aden, hot and dry, we didn't go ashore, but watched small boys diving for coins and bought leather goods which were brought on board. My mother said 'Aren't you proud to be a member of the British Empire?' As we sailed slowly through the Suez Canal, a little girl pointed out a balloon descending 'Look Daddy, it is coming down in someone else's garden'. Her father said, 'A typical English remark'.

Some passengers went ashore at Suez to see the pyramids, riding on camels, we bought a few leather goods which didn't last long, but soon we were in the Mediterranean and the sea was quite as blue as we had been told to expect, even more so.

We went ashore at Naples and I ate octopus, which was like eating rubber. Soon Mount Etna made sure we knew a volcano was there, but Villefranche was so beautiful we had never seen anything like it, and Mr Bagot took us ashore for the day. First we went for a drive along the Upper Corniche Road, and I would have been happier if the driver had kept his hands on the steering wheel instead of waving them about and turning round to talk to us. Mr Bagot took us into the Casino at Monte Carlo, Nancy and I were under age, but as we came nowhere near to breaking the bank, or winning anything at all, it didn't matter.

Mr Bagot was getting off the ship at Toulon, the next port. He said he was going to Aix-les-Bains to 'take the waters' and recover from working on his sister's farm in Queensland.

After Toulon, we realised the author, Axel Munthe, had joined the ship at Naples. It was said he was blind; however, he asked me to go with him to the cinema and explain the Mickey Mouse films to him while he sat holding my hand.

I think Sir John Hay and his son left the ship at Toulon and travelled by train across France, which must have been delightful in the early spring.

The Rock of Gibraltar was what we expected, but rather sinister, being so close to Spain which was just getting over a bitter Civil War. However, the Spanish coast looked peaceful enough from the ship.

Soon we were docking at Tilbury, a depressing place and so was the train journey to London; looking into the backyards of small, working class terraced houses, with their outdoor privies wasn't how Nancy and I had visualised our entry into the capital of our great Empire.

The Cumberland Hotel was where most Australians headed for and it was reassuringly surrounded by shops – in other words Oxford Street – and it wasn't long before we were finding summer in England more like the winters we were used to and were out buying coats and skirts. My mother and I met my father's family for the first time when we visited them at Boxmoor, my grandmother, seeing my name in my raincoat, Nancy Spicer, said 'That's my name', her two daughters, my aunts, Kitty and Dora, were with her. She looked beautifully dressed and cared for, but was beginning to lose her memory.

It wasn't long before my mother decided to move out of the hotel as Nancy and I never seemed to be on time for breakfast, and she soon found a very nice furnished flat in Chatsworth Court, Earl's Court – again, an area where Australians seemed to gather.

Then we went to Australia House to get tickets for various events. We went to Westminster Abbey, St Paul's Cathedral, the Tower of London and the Royal Mint. We watched polo at Roehampton and, of course, Trooping the Colour.

Nancy's stepfather, who was in London, took us to the Temple Church and Guildhall, and afterwards we had lunch and walked in the City. I still haven't forgotten how uncomfortable my shoes were! The day we went to the Tower of London we quarrelled over who should give the Yeoman of the Guard, who was our guide, our last sixpence, so we had to walk to Harrods where my mother was waiting to meet us for lunch. She took pity on us and we went back to Chatsworth Court in a taxi.

Ian Hay asked us to lunch at his house and took us to a theatre to see *French Without Tears* and also to see *A Midsummer Night's Dream* in Regent's Park. He and a friend took us to Cambridge, and we went to see Ian's sister's horse win a first prize at Olympia.

It was a really warm sunny day when we went to see Trooping the Colour. The Queen arrived in an open carriage, with the two young princesses. There was such a crowd we didn't see a lot of the marching and were surprised when some of the soldiers toppled over, as did some people around us, as we didn't think it was very hot. I wrote to tell Mr Bagot in Aix-les-Bains about it and said 'I don't suppose you've seen it'. To which he replied 'I am so glad you saw the Trooping of the Colours, but I'm afraid you missed the absolute perfection as my *old regiment, the Irish Guards, were not in it this year!' This remark was qualified by the asterisk explaining: '(*War time only, as I would never have been allowed on Parade in a bear-skin. It would have amused the troops too much!)'. Caryl was my height, 5'5" – such a height within the Irish Guards hardly qualifying during peace time. On the back of the letter he wrote 'I hope you have stopped growing'. (I had already told Caryl in my last letter that I had just celebrated my nineteenth birthday.)

Next a post-card came from Caryl (he had persuaded me to drop the 'Mr') from Trouville-sur-Mer – 'I have managed to get really burnt black, sun and seabathing, I am not sure that white Australia will have anything to do with me!' However, he said he had decided to come to London and hoped to see us, if we weren't busy all the time.

He came, brought my mother a bunch of red roses and took me out to lunch at Bray in a taxi, with the hood down – luckily it was a perfect day for two sun-lovers.

Caryl's eldest sister and her husband came up from Devon and were staying in London: we had a tea party in the garden of Chatsworth Court. Caryl said to my mother 'What are you going to do with the girls, you can't sit here in London?' My mother said she didn't feel able to organise a visit to the Continent as none of us could speak a foreign language. All three of us were delighted when Caryl offered to organise a tour, acting as our courier, he booked passages in the *Queen Mary* for us as she was stopping at Cherbourg on the way to New York. Caryl confessed years later that, as he waited for us at Waterloo Station, he wondered what we would look like. He needn't have worried, we were wearing our new coats and skirts and our luggage looked impeccable, all thirteen pieces, including hat boxes. We joined the *Queen Mary* at Southampton, Nancy and I rushed to see as much of the ship as possible leaving my mother and Caryl, the latter just getting over a throat infection, to sort our luggage out from that going to New York, which they did, just leaving time for a restorative champagne cocktail before reaching Cherbourg.

Caryl asked us to be his guests for the week we spent in Trouville-sur-Mer, as the hot sunny weather was perfect for swimming, Nancy and I started swimming towards England enjoying shark-free waters. However, very soon a boat came out and rounded us up, the crew warning us about strong currents in the channel. In the evenings everyone seemed to be 'doing the Lambeth Walk'. Caryl took us to the market, and another day was spent at the races in Deauville, the prettiest race course I have ever been to.

From Trouville-sur-Mer we went to Paris, where everything seemed wonderful – the shops, of course. Caryl bought me a cream umbrella, which I still have, my mother thought it very impractical. We visited the Louvre, Notre-Dame, Versailles and the Folies Bergère – I will always remember how beautifully the various scenes were done. We had dinner on the banks of the Seine, where an artist drew a portrait of Nancy and me. Caryl took us to a tea *dansant*, he never danced but young men came and asked us. When they brought us back to the table where Caryl was sitting keeping an eye on us, he would ask us if they had danced nicely and then pay them. One day as Nancy and I were walking up the Champs-Elysées she said 'I believe that Egyptian we danced with is following us', so we hurried back to the hotel!

From Paris we went to Montreux, visited the castle of Chillon and saw the dungeon where the prisoner was kept. The mountains, lakes, rivers, countryside were all so beautiful, but I never liked going up mountains in a funicular and looked at the floor of the vehicle rather than the view, until we got onto firmer ground!

Caryl's dearly loved first wife, Margaret, had died of cancer in a hospital in Zurich a year before and he wanted to go there, also because my mother wished to consult an eye surgeon. She was advised to have some small cysts taken from her eyes, which was done, and I remember her telling me how kind and sympathetic Caryl was. Caryl told me he had thrown all Margaret's jewellery into the river as he did not want anyone else to wear it.

From Zurich we went to Interlaken, it was here that Caryl got a large brown envelope from London. He came to me with it, looking distressed, saying 'All the lovely old houses in England are going, I'd like to show this to you sometime, it might be of interest to you one day'. I had not seen any country houses in England and had never heard of Blithfield, so I didn't show much interest: besides it was time to get ready to go up the Jungfrau, and I heard no more about Blithfield until almost a year later.

When we went into Germany the train was full of German troops, it was 1938 and Prime Minister Neville Chamberlain was flying to see Hitler. The soldiers said to Nancy and me 'We can all speak English, why can't you speak German?' Rather frightening, but we had a fascinating voyage ahead of us down the Rhine, and visited the beautiful Cologne Cathedral before returning home to England where the mood was more, 'How long have we got before war?' rather than 'peace in our time'.

My friend, Nancy MacDougall, returned to Sydney with her step-father, and my mother and I went to visit Aunt Esther, one of my grandmother's younger sisters. She had been a nurse in Sydney Hospital when an Englishman, Henry North Grant Bushby, was taken there after becoming ill on a journey to Japan. The family story was that he thought he had died and was in heaven, being looked after by an angel – Aunt Esther, who was very beautiful. They were married in 1896 at St George's, Hanover Square. Aunt Esther's mother-in-law was Lady Frances North, whose ancestor was the Prime Minister, Lord North. In the reign of George III, Lord North wrote to Sir William Bagot, just before the general election of 1780 as follows: 'It being His Majesty's intention to

Aunt Esther, Mrs Henry Grant Bushby

require your attendance and council, in The House of Peers'. Thus Sir William Bagot Baronet became Lord Bagot.

Aunt Esther, a widow in 1938, was living with her unmarried daughter, Dorothy Bushby, at Portland House, Rodwell, Weymouth, Dorset. Portland House (now a National Trust property) had been built in the 1930s by Aunt Esther's eldest son, Geoffrey Bushby, who died of peritonitis in 1935. I was told it had been built in the style of a Spanish house to follow the lie of the land, which on the Bill of Portland slopes sharply towards the sea. One entered on the bedroom terrace, walked downstairs to the living rooms and out onto the garden terrace, the views from most of the rooms being out to sea. Aunt Esther was large, friendly and kind, she moved about slowly, loved her little Pekinese, which were her excuse for not going anywhere as they could not be left. Dorothy wasn't there at that time, but was always very critical of everyone, apart from a Bushby or a North! Our invitation told us exactly when to arrive and when to depart,

The photograph Nancy gave her grandmother before leaving for England

and I got a new dressing gown out of our stay as my old one wasn't considered good enough to go to Portland House!

We stayed at the Vanderbilt Hotel in Earl's Court, and Caryl, who had been to see his sisters in Devon returned about the same time and stayed at the Rembrandt Hotel, not far from the Brompton Oratory, where he must often have gone with his first wife, Margaret, who was a Catholic. Although he seldom mentioned her to me, he did say there had been a wonderful Remembrance Service in the Oratory for the Irish Guards at the end of the First World War.

Almost as soon as we were in London again, Caryl suggested taking me to the Motor Show, where to my surprise he bought a beautifully made small Rover car, all real leather and mahogany, for £300. Caryl told me he had an early French car, a *de Dion-Bouton*, when he lived in Calcutta and, on going to get his licence, when asked to turn the car around, the two Sikhs sitting at the back got down, one standing at the front and the other at the back, lifted the car up, with Caryl in it, turned it around and Caryl drove off in the opposite direction.

I had an Australian driving licence, not much more than a year old, which I gained when driving my parents' large American Dodge car. It was like driving a lorry — one had to 'double de-clutch' each time the gear was changed, so it was obvious I would need a lot of instruction before venturing to drive in London traffic. Caryl arranged for me to have lessons from the British School of Motoring and was rather horrified when, after returning from a lesson, I said I had seen a dress I liked in Harvey Nichols' shop window! A driver from the School of Motoring drove us to Devon where we stayed with Caryl's favourite sister, Gladys, and I went for my driving test in Barnstaple — quite a stiff test on those hills, but I did pass.

One of our first outings, when we returned to London, was to see Wormley Bury House, which belonged to the Bushbys, and where my grandmother, had stayed with her two daughters, my mother and aunt, in 1908, soon after Aunt Esther's marriage. When Caryl and I visited Wormley Bury, the house had been rented by Major Pam for some years, but he bought it from Mr Bushby in 1931. Caryl introduced himself to Major Pam and told him of my relationship to Mrs Bushby, they welcomed us with open arms, but when Dorothy heard of it, she was very cross and said we should have asked Aunt Esther's permission.

We had some pleasant outings to cousins of Caryl's – the Murray family. Walter Murray had been brought up at Blithfield Rectory, where his father, The Reverend Douglas Murray was Rector for many years. His wife was a granddaughter of Bishop Bagot. Walter and his wife, Evelyn had a son and daughter, Donald and Pamela, who were about my age.

Caryl was very anxious to show me his school, Radley College, near Oxford. He told me his Coat of Arms was decorating the cornice of Middle Hall – this was an honour prefects had. When we got to Radley the school was closed, however, we 'effected a burglarious entry' through an unlocked window – I was nineteen and Caryl was sixty-one – and we were caught coming out! During this time my mother was seeing her mother-in-law and two sisters-in-law. One, my Aunt Dora, was married to The Reverend Alfred Harris, who had been Curate to The Reverend Bernard Douglas Shaw. Mrs Shaw before she married was the Hon Louisa Bagot.

Caryl persuaded my mother not to return to Australia before the dreaded English winter, he said he would ask his sister, Gladys, to travel by sea to the south of France, and the three of us would drive to Nice in the new car and spend the winter in a hotel at Cimiez, on the outskirts of Nice, where Queen Victoria used to love to stay towards the end of her life – the Riviera must have been like a breath of fresh air to her.

Driving through France towards the Mediterranean, either in spring or autumn, was always a delight and we settled into the Alhambra Leospo Hotel in Cimiez very happily, meeting 'Glad' as soon as she arrived.

There was a Russian princess staying at the hotel, who called herself Madame Rossignol (the French for a nightingale) as she had escaped from the Communists. I often sat and talked, and smoked, with an Indian princess of my own age, whose husband was studying at Oxford. She had a nurse with her looking after their baby son.

Many of the fashionable Paris shops had branches in Nice and Monte Carlo, where I went with Caryl and his sister, and paraded many beautiful clothes in front of them, some of which Caryl bought for me. The Jean Patou black net evening dress and several others, now in the Potteries Museum were bought then. Caryl would often take me to dinner at the

Nancy, her mother and
Caryl in Switzerland

Hotel Negreso on the Promenade des Angles, when a cabaret was included, and we went to the ballet in Monte Carlo. One of Caryl's oldest friends from Radley days was staying nearby and occasionally joined us at the opera in Nice. The first opera I saw was *Carmen*. I loved the music and the excitement of it, which was a very good introduction to opera, and I was wearing the Jean Patou black net evening dress.

One of the most delightful places for luncheon was a restaurant at Beaulieu, with a splendid view out to sea and of the snow-capped mountains behind. There were tennis courts at Beaulieu, where the old King of Sweden used to play, partnered by the leading lady French player, Madame Langlan.

Once the owner of the hotel where we were staying, the Alhambra Leospo, Monsieur and Madame Leospo, took us to luncheon in one of the grey stone mountain villages, at a special restaurant they knew of. The villages looked as if they were a part of the mountains and had hardly changed since the middle ages. Madame Leospo said Caryl spoke French like a Frenchman.

Instead of having breakfast in my room each morning, I joined Caryl for breakfast, usually in the garden. On Christmas Day 1938, we were sitting in the garden and Caryl gave me an enchanting little diamond watch, presenting me with a card, on which was written the following equally enchanting words:

> My Darling Nancy
> I give you this little watch
> as a small token of my appreciation
> of your sweet sympathy, and as a souvenir
> of all the many happy carefree days we have
> spent together that it will, in future, record only hours of
> joy and contentment to its owner, is the
> hope and prayers of her
> always devoted
> Caryl.

You may be sure that watch was seldom off my wrist. Caryl must have known I was quite unsophisticated, and if I thought he had marriage in mind I might take fright, as he was so much older. He was very wise.

Early in the New Year we met some Norwegians, who persuaded us to go up into the mountains behind Nice with them. Caryl had never skied, but I had been with a party of school friends to Mount Kosciusko. The slopes in these mountains were much steeper and those I couldn't avoid I went down on my backside. I found The Battle of Flowers easier to cope with and great fun. This takes place each spring and was an event Queen Victoria was said to enjoy enormously when staying on the Riviera. I remember floats, beautifully decorated with pretty girls and masses of flowers, passing through the streets, with everyone throwing flowers in all directions. At night there was a fancy dress ball, the colours to be worn in 1939 were green and gold. I had a Russian costume, Caryl a Mexican and Glad, a green and gold dress. The Mayor was probably told I came from Australia, so I won a prize and a kiss on each cheek.

My mother was having French lessons and had made friends with an elderly American lady. She had decided to go back to England to stay with Aunt Esther, and had given permission for me to go with Caryl and Glad for a tour in Italy.

We called on a friend of Glad's, who was staying in Alassio just over the border. Our next stop was Pisa, where we marvelled at the leaning tower, but we found Rome very cold – the hotel we stayed in had marble floors; however, we were out every day visiting the Vatican, St Peter's and art galleries in the Villa Borghese. I surprised Caryl and Glad in one gallery by asking what a hermaphrodite was. Glad took me aside and explained.

I don't know if we could have gone to see where Joseph Severn nursed Keats until he died – one can now visit the house. Caryl's friend, The Reverend Hew Severn, had been engaged to Glad. Hew went to South Australia to serve as a 'Bush Brother', which meant his being away seven years and Glad married another.

We all enjoyed Florence more – that was where I began to take a real interest in art. I loved the Donatello bronzes, the Cathedral doors, the blue and white Della Robbia and the paintings. Caryl bought me a miniature of Raphael's Madonna of the Gold Finch – still one of my most treasured possessions. I love the furniture decorated with a variety of semi-precious stones found in Italy, some table tops looking like a flower painting. The walk across the Ponte Vecchio was always enticing, with its fascinating jewellery shops. Such beautiful country surrounds Florence and the drive into Sienna was lit by flares as we arrived after dark.

Dear Glad had learned an Italian sentence before we left for the Italian tour 'Please Seignior, could you tell me where the Cathedral is?' When we arrived in Milan, Glad was saying this whilst some Italian youths had their heads in the driver's window, saying 'Nice English girl'. Anyway, we found our hotel, the Cathedral and Leonardo de Vinci's famous mural of The Last Supper, which at that time was in need of restoration.

We had tickets to hear Gigli sing in the La Scala Opera House. Sadly, Gigli was indisposed, but the opera was enlivened by some charming little ballets, during intervals in the opera.

We drove through Verona and by the shores of Lake Garda. Nearing Venice, the land became flat and marshy, and leaving the car in a large multi-storey garage we transferred to a gondola. Slowly gliding down the Grand Canal I felt as if I would like to spend the rest of my life there in that enchanted place.

Since leaving Nice all the Cathedrals we visited had areas such as altars draped in black cloth because it was Lent, so to visit the Basilica of St

Old photograph of the Hall

Marco on Easter Sunday morning was a revelation. The interiors seemed enveloped in a golden glow. The altar piece, the Pala d'Oro, glowed in the soft light of thousands of candles and the mosaics reflecting this light. The great cross, lit by hundreds of candles, hangs low in the centre of this wonderful place.

Whenever I visit Venice I always like to pay my respects to the Tetrarchs, a porphyry group of four male figures embracing, thought to be four emperors brought here from Syria. They stand between the Basilica and the Doges Palace and in spite of their very large swords, they look rather frightened of this modern world.

It was when we were in Venice that Glad said to me 'You ought to marry Caryl'. To which I replied, 'I don't want to get married'. I didn't say 'I don't want to marry Caryl'. Until I met Caryl I had never really felt free – first school, then Domestic Science College, I loved my ponies of course, going to gymkhanas, holidays at the beach, surfing, and latterly tennis parties, but knowing Caryl had given me a taste for a wider world. Little did I think I would tell Caryl I couldn't live without him only six or seven months later! While we were staying in Venice, Mussolini marched into Albania.

From Venice we made our way back to Nice where we met my mother, who had arrived from London, and waved Glad off on her way back to England by sea.

We were in Aix-les-Bains for my twentieth birthday at the end of May and Caryl had twenty beautiful pink roses sent to my room. To me, Aix-les-Bains means sitting under an arbour covered with wisteria, entwined with yellow banksia roses, a lake sparkling in sunshine and mountains capped with snow.

Soon we were back in Paris, staying at the Oxford and Cambridge Hotel, and went to the opera – by then most people felt only a miracle could save us from war. When we got back to London, after being away for about eight months, barrage balloons were floating above Hyde Park and trenches being dug.

I told my mother I wanted to stay in London and drive an ambulance. I didn't know my mother had asked my father to come to England to take us home. He started out, but only got as far as Ceylon before war was declared – so very sad for him as he hadn't seen his family in Boxmoor for thirty years, and he died of pneumonia, after a hernia operation three years later.

The Murray family wanted Caryl and me to stay with a cousin of Caryl's and Walter Murray's, known as Uncle Ernest (in other words, The Reverend Ernest Bridgeman, Prebendary of Lichfield and Rector of Blymhill, not far from Blithfield), so Caryl hoped to drive over to Blith-field with me.

Uncle Ernest's house had not been modernised, but it seemed to be well-staffed, and well-run. It was here I met a hip-bath for the first time – I didn't know if I was supposed to stand, or sit in it. There were oil-lamps and candles and a smoking room, which Caryl and I made use of. I was taken with Pamela and Elizabeth, Walter's daughter and her friend, to see Uncle Ernest's pig, and we went in his old-fashioned car to visit some of his parishioners.

Then one day we drove over to Blithfield. There were coal-mines between Blymhill and Blithfield in a wild area known as Cannock Chase, where Queen Elizabeth I used to hunt, but the country around Blithfield was a picturesque dairy farming area. The Hall remains hidden from view until turning a bend in the drive, this low grey building, with its turrets and battlements suddenly appears looking as firmly rooted in the ground as any of the old oaks nearby.

I drove to the backdoor, which seemed to be in use. It is under a colonnade. We were shown into a rather dark passage by the butler. There were dozens of bells along the wall with the names of various rooms under them. We went through the Drum Hall, where a large drum stood, which had been used to announce meals. There was also a yoke the gardener used to bring two buckets of water from a well in the garden. This water was considered to be purer than the water from the well in the house – nevertheless the drinking water was first put through a Minton Filter, which also stood in the Drum Hall. There was a water tower in the garden and water was pumped up from the Mill Pool to fill it, then it flowed into the Hall through lead pipes.

We were taken up the very neat backstairs to the apartment where Gerald, Fifth Lord Bagot lived in two rooms. His main living room was hung with a particularly fascinating late eighteenth-century Chinese wallpaper (see page 153) with a green background. But Gerald, whose one great love was horses, had cut pictures of race horses from papers and magazines and pinned them to the wallpaper with drawing pins. I could sympathise with that then as my favourite picture at home was of the famous Australian racehorse, Phar Lap.

I found Gerald a charming courteous old man, who would say 'thankee' for 'thank you' and 'perty' for 'pretty'. He had led a rather extraordinary life. Gerald told us he had lived in the Arizona Desert for a time, where his nearest neighbour had been an outlaw. He had spent some time in the Argentine training polo ponies. He allowed two elderly sisters, the Misses Bedfords, to live in the garden cottage because he had been in the Argentine with their brothers. It had previously been the head gardener's cottage. Gerald's niece, Mabel Arden Howarth Booth was staying with him. She was tall and looked rather formidable, although later we became good friends.

We were taken to the Conservatory, where we were to have tea. To get there, we went through the Library, a rather dark room with a barrel-ceiling and oak panelled walls painted green, each panel outlined in gold with a gold 'rosette' in the centre. It smelt of cedar and old leather books and felt very old, quite different from the Chinese room. The elaborately carved oak great staircase (down which we descended to reach the Great Hall) made one wonder about the age of the oak trees, for which Bagot's Woods were famous. It was said that oak from these woods was used when the liner *Queen Mary* was built. Entering the Great Hall, the largest room in the house, is always a surprise, with its three tall windows, looking onto a central courtyard, around which the house is built. It is a very light room and the Regency Gothic plasterwork, which the second Lord Bagot got an Italian craftsman, Francis Bernasconi to carry out, has made it one of the most notable rooms, certainly in the county, if not in the country.

Mabel Arden asked me what I thought of this room, which as I had never seen one like it, I didn't know what to say. As it had been colour washed grey in Victorian times, I thought it rather depressing, however, I am sure I didn't say so. The Conservatory, although it had dark green walls, had an area with a glass roof and large doors opening into the garden and tubs of flowering plants. Walking from the Great Hall into the Conservatory was another surprise, much more cheerful, and I am sure the tea helped! Afterwards, we went into the L-shaped Drawing Room, its dark red walls covered with pictures. The shutters were opened so that we could see better and either Gerald or his niece must have wound up the music-box, which was standing on a desk near the windows. The music-box was in the shape of a circular dance floor, beautifully carved and painted figures mounted on bristles danced sedately around when the music plays a plaintive tune (see page 65). I had the feeling I was being drawn into another age, it seemed to be a lament for the passing of a home much loved by generations of Bagots. Blithfield hadn't housed a family since before the First World War – it seemed to me I was being asked to save it, but a reservoir was to be made, and the Hall itself was to be sold to The South Staffordshire Water Company. Caryl had not spoken of Blithfield to me since the day he received the letter from London, when we were staying in Interlaken the previous summer.

As we were leaving, Gerald suggested our driving across Blithfield Park and into Bagots Park, which had belonged to the Bagots since the eleventh century. We might see the herd of 'wild goats' which lived there, having been presented by King Richard II (according to family tradition) after he had enjoyed hunting in the Park during the twelve days he had spent in Lichfield in Christmas 1397.

Bagots Park, surrounded by Bagot's Woods, looks completely different to Blithfield Park, covered by bracken with ancient stag-headed oaks dotted about. It looked as ancient as the oaks, and very remote, perhaps that is why it was chosen as a practice bombing range at the beginning of the Second World War. It was here that a young Australian RAAF pilot, Flying Officer Edward Bagot, who was stationed at Hixon Aerodrome, was sent to practise bombing. He wrote to Lord Bagot and was invited to visit and was intrigued by all he saw.[1] Alas we saw no goats on that visit.

At that stage I was just a tourist from Australia, who was thoroughly enjoying life and didn't want to get married. Never in my wildest dreams would I have thought I might be living at Blithfield (or that I would want to), which was sold to The South Staffordshire Waterworks Company anyway.

We drove back to Blymhill to get ready to join Caryl's cousin the following day for a tour in Scotland. Caryl's cousin, Olave, Lady Brooke, lived with her husband and their son in London; her husband, Rear Admiral Sir Basil Brooke, GCVO, was Equerry to the King. They were very kind to us and Olave had arranged this visit to Scotland. We were to meet her at a relative's cottage, where she was staying in the mountains near Penrith.

We left Uncle Ernest at Blymhill on a lovely sunny morning, but as soon as we entered the industrial areas of the Midlands and the North, the sun disappeared and the air got foggy or smoggy as we call it in the North. I am thankful it is not like that now. When we came out of the area near the Lake District it was a fine sunny day, this made a lasting impression on me. We found Muriel Castle's cottage where dear Olave was waiting for us, and a delicious tea, finishing with raspberries and cream. Caryl thought one of his raspberries was bad so attempted to throw it out of the window. Unfortunately, the window was shut and we just sat there watching the raspberry sliding down the glass! We all burst out laughing. Something unforgettable – much more amusing than the smog!

When we visited Holyrood Palace, Olave used one of her favourite phrases 'Drive on dear', which because of Basil's position as Equerry, I was able to do and we were taken on a private tour of the Palace. The main thing I remember being shown was a little glass bottle, where Mary Queen of Scots was said to put her tears.

We stayed at a hotel not far from Balmoral and went on to another charming small hotel by the lake of Menteith. As Olave's family, the Cunninghame Grahams, owned land there, they had a rowing boat ready for our use. It was a warm August day so I can say I have swum in the brown peaty waters of this lake. Some of Olave's family are buried on a small island in the lake, the most notable being her uncle, Robert Cunninghame Graham — because he had Spanish ancestors and spent a great deal of time in South America he was known as Don Roberto.

We were on our way to see Don Roberto's nephew, Admiral Sir Angus Cunninghame Graham and his wife, Patricia, who lived in a most attractive house called Ardoch, near Helensborough. We had a picnic on the lawn, from where we could see ships passing up and down the Clyde.

Olave was staying with her brother and sister-in-law and we were to go to London the next day. As Caryl wouldn't think of staying anywhere with me unchaperoned — strange to think of it nowadays! — he got a local man to drive the Rover to London — a long drive with no motorways. We asked the driver if he knew the way and he replied 'Oh yes, I've got my *Phillips Atlas*'.

When we got to London it was apparent that war was not far off, my mother had booked passages for us on the *Empress of Britain*. I told Caryl and he booked a passage too — he wanted to go to see his sister in Queensland anyway. We had only been at sea two or three days, bound for Montreal, when war was announced, and sailors were painting the portholes black.

It was at this time that the first ship was sunk in the Atlantic, the SS *Athenia*, carrying a number of children to America for safety. My poor father didn't know which ship we were on until my mother could send a cable from Montreal.

When we got to Canada we were making for Vancouver across country. One ship a month sailed for Sydney from Vancouver. The weather was lovely and so were the autumn colours, we went to Banff and then Lake Louise, where the intense blue waters of the lake seemed almost unreal. We took a coach trip through a National Park, where I saw a small brown bear, and then boarded a train for Vancouver, sleeping in the bunks which were turned into seats during the day. When travelling through The Rockies, sitting in the observation carriage at the end of the train, the views were magnificent. All this time I had been sending post-cards to Caryl to let him know where we were, so we were able to meet again in Vancouver. My mother hadn't given any indication of her plans, so Caryl hadn't booked a passage on the next ship to leave for Sydney.

Early one morning we had to get up and get dressed, leaving our room and luggage, we were taken to the ship by taxi, put on board and our luggage brought to us. I wasn't allowed to send any messages to Caryl as I wasn't twenty-one. My mother had booked me into first class and herself into second class. I made friends with a very nice English couple, Mr and Mrs Alexander, and wrote letters to Caryl, which I was able to post in Honolulu.

Although my mother must have felt very relieved to have parted Caryl and me, it turned out to be the best thing possible from our point of view, because I became quite determined to marry Caryl as soon as I was twenty-one.

Next stop, Fiji – never before or since have I seen policemen with red Hibiscus stuck in their hair! The ship stopped in Auckland for a short time and I saw a penguin in the harbour.

Next stop, Sydney, where my father was waiting to greet us after fifteen months away, also my cousin, Monica Clifford, and friends, Nancy and Marjorie MacDougall. My luggage was taken to my grandmother's house, where I was very happy to stay and my parents went off together.

Note

1 See Nancy, Lady Bagot, *The History of the Bagot Goats* (Keele Graphic Services, 23 September 2007, p 4.) Edward's photograph appears later in this book, on page 207.

2

Growing up in Australia

I WAS BORN IN MY GRANDMOTHER'S HOUSE AND HAVE OFTEN SAT IN THE stuffy drawing-room feeling very bored with the uninteresting conversation of the 'grown-ups' and watched the sad, sweet expression on my grandmother's face as she pretended to listen, carefully, to all that was said. She was so deaf she couldn't hear anything unless I shouted in her ear, and I wanted to throw my arms around her neck, to feel her hair tickle my nose as I shouted in her ear that they were all talking nonsense, and would she please tell me a story about her childhood in the bush. Although my cousins and I knew most of her stories by heart, we always listened with great interest when she re-lived incidents in her past life.

My grandmother, Constance Maud Mary Stericker (née Ford) must have been about fifty when I was born, but my grandfather, Thomas Edward Stericker, died of pneumonia after only eight years of marriage, leaving my grandmother with two small girls, the younger, my mother, only four years old.

Through my grandmother's long life, these children and later their children, were her sole interest, the deafness, which gradually became worse after my grandfather's death had a good deal to do with this, and also with her wishing to live alone. On very rare occasions when she entertained, either my mother or my aunt had to be at her house, called Shirley, to help her.

On summer afternoons when the waves of heat and the high pitched noise of locusts had died down, I would help her water her small garden, lying in peaceful exhaustion and taking great delight in pointing the nozzle of the grey rubber hose to the sky, and watching silver drops of water float softly onto the parched brown grass. But first the garden had

Nancy was born at her
grandmother's 'Federation' house

Doris and Ida Stericker in
London 1908, aged 16 and 14

to be watered – the long flower bed by the verandah with its old fashioned
roses, sweet smelling Madonna lilies, usually harbouring a good many
ants, and blue hydrangeas.

Then the flower bed under the drawing-room windows, with its bright
red salvia and fuchsias, pale blue love-in-the-mist and forget-me-knots;
here, if no one was looking and the windows were shut, they might be
watered too, producing a drumming sound!

Next came the round beds with more roses, and on the sunny side of
the house, the spotted tiger lilies and white arums, also what we call the
Chinese lantern tree. Most gardens had a slatted wooden fern house.
Maiden hair fern grew here, where there would sure to be a large green
frog, but you had to be careful not to step on a snake.

The red brick 'Federation' house (circa 1900) was built close to the
main road leading north from Sydney through the bush. The garden in
front of the house was hemmed in by rows of camphor laurel trees, with
shiny green leaves, the young leaves looking as if they had been polished.

In spring the locusts, encased in brown armour like shells, crawled from holes in the ground, up the rough trunks of the trees, where they waited helpless until their tough shells split across the back. They then emerged, like brightly coloured and rather clumsy dragonflies, yellow, green and black, the males 'singing' endlessly throughout the day if sunny, in a high pitched single tone, which could be felt vibrating against the eardrums and seemed to add to the heat.

A wattle stood in a corner of the garden, with heavy laden golden yellow branches, drooping amongst the violet blue bell shaped flowers of the jacaranda, their fallen blossoms mingled on the ground seemed a reflection of those above.

When the garden had been watered to my grandmother's satisfaction, we would sit on the hard wooden garden seat on the verandah, with brightly coloured butterflies hovering in the warm air and the smell of the wet garden about us. In a loud voice, which she couldn't hear, my grandmother would begin one of her stories, her round face alight with simple pleasure and goodness.

'Did I tell you about the drought on the Lachlan, when Jessie was a baby?' she would say, and I would shake my head vigorously. 'Well, there had been no rain for several years and all the sheep were dying, poor things – not a blade of grass for them to eat. The river was so dried up, only a few muddy pools and dead fish were to be seen. But we did have plenty of water from the artesian bore, do you know what that is? It is an underground river really. I remember the funny old man who came with a forked stick cut from a Willow tree – a divining rod they call it – and he walked up and down for a long time, holding the stick out in front of him with both hands. Suddenly it moved and he said "Dig here you will find water."'

'The men dug for days, father and my brother, Syd, helped them. Such a deep hole – they had to be let down into it by a rope. One afternoon, they were all grumbling, and saying they didn't believe there was any water there, when BANG – a tremendous explosion,' (she would fling her arms in the air with obvious enjoyment) 'water spurted out of the hole shooting out the man who had been digging. He did get a fright! But he wasn't hurt'.

Granny would then continue telling me of her childhood. 'I cried when my dear little pony died', she said, 'he was a Timor pony that my uncle had given me. Cream coloured, with a darker mane and tail, and a dark streak running down his back. They come from the island of Timor to the north of Australia. My brother, Syd, had one too. We were the only ones that liked riding; father would never let me ride astride though. But I used to jump all the fences, and Syd used to come to fetch me from school and we'd ride home together'. 'I never went away to school like Esther and Gertie as I had to help mother look after the younger children' she would say rather sadly, but brightening again she would say 'I always liked children, there were nine of us altogether, and I was the second eldest daughter. The school-master was a Cornish man and I remember he always called me Cornstance. I liked Geography best, and never thought I would visit some of the places I saw on the map in the school-room'.

'What did you say dear? Were there any blackfellas or convicts there? Yes, but the blackfellas never attacked us, because father was good to them and would never shoot one. Their lubras used to do the washing for mother and they would grin at us, showing all their white teeth: but I never liked them. They were always going bush too, and disappear for weeks, turning up again as though nothing had happened. Yes, I've seen some convicts too, poor fellows: although father had more working for him. But one day we got an awful scare, we heard that Ned Kelly, (it was actually Ben Hall) and his bushrangers were coming. They used to ride about with kerosene tins over their heads, and they'd cut two holes in them so they could see. We had one of those long brick ovens outside, where the bread was baked and mother put us in there. They made her give them some food, and went away again. Cousin Nellie, was in a Mail Coach that was held up by bushrangers. All the men had to get out: but, I am forgetting about the drought. It was terrible seeing all the cattle get thinner and thinner and then die. It broke poor father, he never went back to the land. When there was just one horse left alive, he said we must pack up everything we could in the buggy and go and stay with our cousins – a branch of the Ford family, who lived at Forbes, thirty miles away. I never thought we'd get there. The poor half starved horse could only go very slowly. Father, and we older children had to walk most of the way, while mother and Jessie Beatrice, who was a tiny baby then (born 26th June, 1877 at Bedgerebong) rode in the buggy. We had to camp by the roadside at night, and one day there was a bushfire raging on either side of the road. The horse, terrified, had to be led, the hot air scorched us, the smoke made us choke and our eyes smart: but we had to go on. What a journey that was! We were so tired when we reached our cousins' house we could hardly stand, and dirty too. They were so kind, we stayed there for months. Father did go back to the homestead once: but only the brick foundations and some twisted metal lying among the black ashes remained. It had been burnt to the ground'.

My grandmother told me she had a small box with pieces of gold in it that she had picked up and that sometimes, when fence posts were taken from the ground, there might be strands of gold sticking to them. It was the time of the Gold Rush, so bushrangers held up coaches travelling between Bathurst and Sydney, hoping they would be carrying gold. She said, 'There was a lady travelling in one of the coaches held up, who felt the man sitting beside her drop something on the floor, which she kicked under her long skirt. Ladies weren't made to get out of the coach. It turned out to be a bag of gold. The Ford Coach Company was owned by granny's uncle'.

Some of the names of granny's family and friends living in or near Bathurst, were Janie Peachy, Polly Cummins and the Rottons. Granny would say 'They're all dead and gone long ago'.

After the drought the family went to live in, or near, Sydney. My grandfather was born at Kingston-upon-Hull and was sent out to Sydney to introduce Australia to Reckitt's Blue, so I suppose that is where he met granny. I know they lived in Stanmore, where my mother and my aunt were born, and he was a Churchwarden at Enmore. My grandfather had bought some land about twelve miles north of Sydney, the climate was supposed to be healthier there, and my mother's elder sister had asthma. The name of the place is Warrawee, which means 'My home' in the Aboriginal. After my grandfather's death my grandmother built the house there and her mother and the two girls went to live with her there. I was told my great-grandmother was descended from Huguenots. Her parents left County Louth in Northern Ireland to emigrate to Australia, and my

1920: the Spicers' new house. Uncle Pat, Clive, Aunt Doris, Nancy's father, Nancy,
Monica and Jack

great-grandmother was born at sea, off the small island of St Paul, near
Madagascar.

As my grandfather's family and one of my grandmother's sisters, Aunt
Esther Bushby, lived in England, she must have decided to take her
teenage daughters to visit England in 1908. They stayed at Wormley Bury
House in Hertfordshire with the Bushbys and their young family. Uncle
Harry taught them to skate on the lake by pushing a chair in front of
them. That visit must have made a deep impression, because my cousins
and I were brought up according to what Aunt Esther would do, or would
not do.

Another family my grandmother and her daughters stayed with was
the Borretts at Cransford Hall in Suffolk. They spent a 'never to be
forgotten' Christmas there, and the Borretts' handsome son, 'Bunny' was
often mentioned. Mr Borrett was a solicitor in a firm that looked after the
Bagot estates. It was Mr Borrett who suggested they should stay in the
Isle of Wight for part of the winter as they were feeling the cold and

suffering from chilblains. They also went on a tour of English cathedrals, I remember a small metal 'Lincoln Imp' and hearing of a really frightening storm in Oxford. Mrs Borrett was Jenny Rygate from Sydney, a great friend of Aunt Esther.

Was it Uncle Harry who suggested the Sterickers did a continental tour? Although they couldn't speak French, they stayed in Paris, and then went to Venice, where the weather was so hot granny had to take her money belt (containing sovereigns) off and put it in her bedside cupboard. Unfortunately, when she left the next morning she forgot it but, luckily, the hotel manager was honest and she got it back. Darling granny re-lived this episode very vividly!

Both my Aunt Doris and my mother married Englishmen, and my grandmother gave them a part of her land on which to build houses.

My Uncle Pat, Patrick Wigram Clifford's family, had gone from India to New Zealand, and then he had come to Sydney.

My father, Francis Aldborough Spicer, had been born in Boxmoor, Hertfordshire, and gone first to South Africa, and then to New Zealand, before coming to Sydney, where he married a Miss Hall and had a son, George John (later known to us as Jack). When Jack was three years old his mother died and my father met my mother at a boarding house called Lynton in north Sydney, popular with English people. My mother was staying there with my grandmother, working in a Voluntary Aid Detachment, looking after returned soldiers and no doubt helped to look after Jack. They were married towards the end of the First World War in 1918 at St Paul's Church, Wahroonga. I was born in 1919. My three cousins, Monica, Clive and Lucy (four years younger than me), lived in the house between our house and our grandmother's.

When I was very young I remember my uncle and aunt coming to our house with Monica and Clive on Sunday evenings and my aunt playing the piano, and my mother the violin, and our singing hymns. Later, nothing seemed so happy – it must have been the time of the Great Depression.

I was always a shy child, my parents weren't happy so I wasn't, or thought I wasn't. If my cousins hadn't been living next door I wouldn't have seen many children.

I remember my mother having to go into hospital for an operation and she didn't seem at all well for a long time afterwards. My father lost his job in the Depression, so it was my grandfather's Reckitt's money we depended on.

There was a paddock behind our house and a lawn tennis court as well as a paddock behind the Cliffords' house. Monica and I kept our ponies in the paddocks and we had a Jersey cow, also pretty little bantam hens and a beautiful cock – they had a cage but often roosted in the trees.

I realise now what a pivot my grandmother was, we often stayed with her if it suited our parents. My memories of those nights were of gas lamp lights that had to be lit, and a plate of fruit, with a fruit knife by my bed, when I woke in the morning.

During the day Clive (he a year older than me), Lucy and I often played in granny's fruit trees, each choosing a tree and then inviting each other 'to tea'. There were the usual apples, pears, plums, peaches, apricots, loquats, oranges, mandarins, persimmons, quinces and nectarines. Granny used to pick the persimmons before they were ripe to stop the flying foxes getting them and they were put on a shelf in her rather dark larder. Their shiny orange skins brightened the larder, and we were allowed to go and choose a ripe one to eat.

Clive and I spent a fun afternoon once in granny's camphor laurel trees, where he put an old purse of his mother's on a long string, then hurled it into the middle of the road. Not many cars went along the road, but most stopped to pick up the rapidly disappearing purse. The police soon stopped that game!

If it rained a small stream flowed through our two paddocks, and we played a game of 'trading' using pieces of wood for boats and tying 'goods' on with string, guiding them to ports with sticks. Sometimes a large pond would form and once I was dared to jump into it, which I did unhesitat-ingly. I was not popular when I got home. Our closest neighbours, often joining in this game, were Margaret and Berta (Bunny) Knox, whose father was a master at Knox Grammar School opposite our houses.

Another game which required skill and camouflage was 'Indians' – this was usually played in the bush, preferably bush which had been burnt in a bushfire, which helped with camouflage. Once we picked up Anne and Mary Williams, who lived in a charming W Hardy Wilson house in Fox

Valley Road. They had long plaits of fair hair, almost white, which I believe had just been washed so needed quite a lot of camouflage. The idea was to reach the one person standing up without them seeing you. I wonder if Mrs Williams recognised her daughters when we delivered them home, we didn't wait to see!

When Clive's parents had a tennis party their guests had to leave their cars neatly parked outside my grandmother's house on the main road as only a long strait drive led to the Clifford's house. For Clive, this was too much of a temptation, he would choose one and wearing one of his father's hats would drive his younger sister, Lucy, and me, wearing our mothers' hats, around the area, much to the astonishment of any motorists we passed.

Clive went to a sheep station near Wagga Wagga, as a jackeroo, after he left school, and it wasn't long before he wrote home to tell the family he had taken the 'Mare' of Wagga's daughter out to a dance!

Clive's young life would have fitted him for what was to follow – he joined the RAAF, and trained as a navigator to fly in a Lancaster Bomber. In March 1942, they were shot down when laying mines in the Atlantic, to prevent the German Submarines sinking so many of our ships.

My father was a friend of Mr Bradfield, the Chief Engineer for the English firm of Dorman Long, which was building the harbour bridge, so we had very good seats for the opening in 1932. New South Wales had a Labour Government and no one liked the Labour Premier, most people thought Jack Lang was a Communist, and didn't at all like the idea of his opening the bridge. My brother, Jack, was at Sydney University and was there in the University Training Corps. The Australian Light Horse were lined up, and just before Jack Lang was to cut the ribbon, an officer in the Light Horse, Captain de Groot, rode forward and slashed the ribbon with his sword. I am sure there was clapping and cheering, but the gallant Captain was dragged off, the ribbon tied up and cut by Jack Lang with a pair of scissors. Everyone was buzzing with excitement over the brave way the bridge had been well and truly opened!

The granite for the pillars came from the south coast near the Victoria border. Mr Bradfield must have told my father about it because we spent a camping holiday there one Christmas at Mourya, a beautiful beach – it

A bush picnic

is still as lovely, although there is a small airport there now.

My parents bought a heavy open-car, presumably to take camping, but it wasn't the most suitable to take on the drive to Bobbin Head, a favourite picnic spot by the Hawkesbury River. The road, a series of hair-pin bends, required the driver to manoeuvre the car backwards and forwards around the bends. At the first bend, my mother said 'I'm not staying in the car' and got out, and so did I, so we were better able to shout 'stop, stop' as the car got near the crumbling edge of the dirt road. It was as a result of buying this car and learning to drive that my mother was able to drive me to Eldinhope, a pre-school or *kindergarten* as we called them, run by two Miss Hookes in their large Victorian house in Wahroonga. The front of their house faced Burns Road, a street with a number of large houses and gardens, not near a main road. Eldinhope had a long narrow drive at the back of the house, opening onto Water Street. Mothers took it in turn to ferry their small daughters to school, mostly to the back of the house. We were told not to run down this drive. I did one day and fell into a puddle, much to my distress I was made to change into one of Miss Hookes' long brown dresses with a bone collar. It was at

Jack, Nancy's mother and Nancy (with paper parasols)

Eldinhope I learned most of the arithmetic I can remember, like the tables, and by no means all of them. Some of the friends I made at Eldinhope have been friends all my life, such as Jean Grant.

By the time I was nine or ten I went to Abbotsleigh, I could walk there and back, taking my lunch with me. The headmistress, Miss Everett, and I were new at the same time. She was tall, with golden wavy hair, bright blue eyes and lovely complexion. She spoke beautifully (I think she came to Australia from England). I always remember her reading the lesson from *The King James Bible*, of course, at Assembly each morning, but I don't have happy memories of our first meeting. I was put in too high a class, and because I couldn't understand what was being taught, did things to make the other girls laugh; in other words, I was thoroughly disruptive. One morning, Miss Everett came and took me to a lower class, which put a stop to my showing off, but my mother wasn't happy about it.

I didn't at all like the mathematics teacher, Miss Allen; she had a stern face with small dark eyes. I got nowhere with mathematics, and as it was holding me up with other subjects I was allowed to give it up. My mother complained about my spelling, but Miss Everett just said 'It's fashionable

Nancy riding Victor

not being able to spell', and I seemed to be more and more fashionable.

I liked Sunday evenings best when we had prayers, and Miss Everett would read to the older girls in Read House after I became a boarder. I have a letter Miss Everett wrote me in January 1960 from her house in Fox Valley Road. I had written to congratulate her on an honour she received from Her Majesty the Queen. At the end of the letter she wrote 'I think Lord Bagot is charming and the happiness of you both was delightful to see. It radiated warmth to our little gathering'. (We had called to see her during a visit to Australia.)

My cousin, Monica (four years older than me) and I often rode with other friends, who had ponies, into the bush. There is nothing quite like an early morning ride in the bush, the smell of eucalyptus, and as the sun got hotter, the sound of locusts, drumming in one's ears.

Sometimes we would pretend to be Knights of the Round Table, carrying 'black boys' for spears, these were the huge seed heads of the xanthorea plant, which often grew to five yards tall. Monica would be King Arthur leading the Knights. Other times we might collect tadpoles in jam jars from a creek, and take them home where we would watch them grow into frogs.

A favourite ride was to Christmas Bell Common or to 'Lover's Leap' near St Ives, where gymkhanas were held, and there was a disused race-course in the direction of Fox Valley Road. We could race around, and near to it we found a cleared space, surrounded by rough wooden benches, where men would play 'two up', we wrote in the sand 'Police, you are discovered' and hurriedly rode off!

My great friend at Abbotsleigh (and later for life), before I went as a boarder, was Jean Grant. She and I chose a paddock and rode there on our ponies quite frequently to observe everything we possibly could that was happening and make a record. This was a school nature study project we really enjoyed. It was amazing how much of interest we found in a cow pat!

Monica stayed with a friend once or twice on a station near Bourke. She brought back a joey (a baby kangaroo) after her first visit, and a sulphur crested cockatoo another time. He pecked everyone except Lucy. If anyone was playing tennis and missed a shot, he would call out 'You're a duffer!'

Any of my friends who had ponies lived by Mary Grant Bruce's *Billabong* books. We all wanted to be like her heroine, Nora, a twelve year old, who was independent, adventurous and decisive! We all wanted to rescue our father's black faced sheep from the bush fire, like Nora and to have a brother like Jim, who had a friend like Wally, and, of course, to live on a station like Billabong.

Mary Grant Bruce wrote thirty-eight books in the *Billabong* series, producing the last in 1942. She was born in Sale, Victoria, in 1878, and died in England in 1958. MGB Angus and Robertson published her biography, *Australia's Best Loved Author*.

If I went out with Miss Cassie Cains, who had a riding school, we would go further afield to Bobbin Head, bathing costumes in our saddle bags. A fire would be made and a 'billy' boiled and chops cooked. I have never forgotten the feeling of excitement when my pony started swimming as we crossed a part of the Hawksbury River. My greatest ambition was to own a riding school like Cassie Cains.

Gymkhanas took up a great deal of time – first, deciding what events to enter. I usually entered Best Girl Rider, or Best Pony. Monica would enter the Open Gallop – very brave of her for unless one was in the front a hail of stones would be kicked up in one's face. The only protection worn, more for the sun, was a felt hat in winter or a khaki cotton hat in summer.

Ponies were very well groomed, but we had to ride to the gymkhanas, sometimes several miles away. Once I rode with two friends through French's Forest to their beach house at Newport, about twenty-five miles away. As it was winter and the beach empty, we could gallop along it, near the surf where the sand was hard, and even into the surf.

The Cliffords had cousins, the Hayters, who had a sheep farm on an island, off the coast of New Zealand. When I was twelve or thirteen, Adrian Hayter came to stay with the Cliffords; he was on his way to England to train at Sandhurst, and then join the Gurkha Regiment. My cousin, Monica, was a lovely fair haired, blue eyed girl, of fifteen or sixteen, and I am sure Adrian must have been delighted by her – they played a lot of tennis.

When the time came for Adrian to join the P&O liner that was to take him to England, I was asked to go to see them off. Aunt Doris was one of my godmothers.

We were to have a picnic on Manly Beach before going to the docks. I was very conscious of my appearance – dark straight hair, on which I was wearing my school hat, quite a lot of puppy fat, clothed in a short sleeved cotton dress, black wool stockings and black lace up shoes. It wasn't very warm on Manly Beach that day, and there was sand in the sandwiches, but the ship was splendid. When 'All visitors ashore' was announced I wondered if it would be possible to stow-away. The next time I boarded an ocean liner the circumstances were very different.

I must have been about thirteen when I became a boarder at Abbot-sleigh. I was very worried at the thought that some of the girls in the sleep-out might not have started periods. We didn't talk about such things, but when it happened I wasn't reconciled until my mother told me that even the Queen (Mary) had to put up with it.

The girl sleeping next to me, Sandra Jaques, was younger than me, she became my friend for life. Her mother's dog, a Maltese terrier looked like a toy sitting on her trunk, but it was very much alive! Her mother lived in Double Bay. Sandra (or 'Sandy' as I called her, and I was 'Spice') loved to come home with me and ride my pony.

Both my mother and my aunt had been at Abbotsleigh, a large Church of England girls' school, about a mile from where we lived, and my two cousins were also educated there.

I grew to like being a boarder and did my best work then, gaining honour prizes over three years. The prizes emphasised my connection with England, first, *The Tower of London*, second, *Jane Eyre*, and last, *Kim*. I spent the holidays crying about *Jane Eyre*.

I loved history (English mostly), taught by Mrs Oliver, English, taught by Miss Lamplough, and botany, taught by Miss Austin, who had taught my mother. I also liked physiology, but definitely not mathematics!

Prize day at Abbotsleigh was held towards the end of December, in a large marquee put up on the Oval, and decorated with pink flowered Christmas bush, *cerato petalum gummiferum*, and blue hydrangeas.

Miss Bynon, our little Welsh choir-mistress, had us practising 'The Blue Danube', which we sang and swayed to. The boarders wore their Sunday best white silk dresses and everyone bobbed when receiving a prize from the presenter, usually the wife of a bishop or a governor.

Unless one of my friends (mostly the MacDougalls, who also became lifelong friends) invited me to stay with them at the beach, I never seemed to be doing anything in the holidays, and I used to get fits of depression. I was often really very unhappy as a teenager – I found lying on my pony's back, with my arms around his neck was a comfort and he seemed to understand.

My cousin, Monica Clifford, had been taken to England by her aunt, Miss Lucy Clifford, who lived in New Zealand. She had been presented to the uncrowned King Edward VIII at a Garden Party in 1936 – the only one he had, and I am sure all the girls must have been very disappointed, as Monica said he had his head turned most of the time talking to Mrs Simpson, who was standing behind his chair.

Aunt Esther had had Monica to stay, but the Sterickers were the most hospitable – Monica stayed with them in a castle in Scotland. I am sure she had more than one proposal of marriage on that trip. She and I used to go to our grandmother's garden with rugs and cushions and our favourite books, in 1936 they would have been Lin Yutang's *The Importance of Living*, and Rabindranath Tagore Gitanjali's *Song Offerings*. Certainly no sex magazines! I was enjoying PG Wodehouse books and *The Strand*

Monica's presentation to
Edward VIII, 1936

Magazine my father bought to remind him of England. We were far
enough away from our own houses to be out of earshot of our mothers'
requests and as our darling old grandmother was stone deaf, she was probably unaware of us.

My mother took a course in dressmaking during the time of the Great
Depression when my father lost his job and he took a course in account-
ancy. I have always enjoyed embroidery, canvas work, and dressmaking.
For the canvas work I have to thank Aunt Esther, she used to send pieces
of her unfinished work to us and I was the one who liked doing the work,
chiefly because of the colours. My mother liked very different colours –
pinks and blues – whereas I liked yellows and greens, coral, apricot and
crimson.

The first evening dress I was allowed to choose for myself was made of
'shadow' taffeta, containing all these colours. When I was wearing it I felt

happy and confident. I had left Abbotsleigh by then and was going to spend a year at a Domestic Science College at Kirribilli – the college consisting of two Victorian houses with gardens stretching down to the north shore of Sydney harbour, not far from the new bridge. It was run by the two Misses Stenhouse sisters from New Zealand. I am sure my going to this college, the first year after I left boarding school in 1937, was my grandmother's idea, and she probably paid for me to go there. Many of the girls had been at Abbotsleigh and my friend, Nancy MacDougall was also enrolled. We were taught to do everything in a very methodical way – I am afraid many mothers were not happy to be told their methods were not correct! To begin with we went each day, by train, for cooking lessons. We were all out on the lawn to watch the new Governor, Lord Wakehurst, arrive with Lady Wakehurst in a large battleship, when Miss Stenhouse came out carrying a very black sauccpan and asking 'Whose carrots are these?' Unfortunately they were mine! It wasn't until I read *The Memoirs of Hermione, Countess of Ranfurly*, written over sixty years later, that I learned the whole family and staff had travelled from England in an ocean liner and Lord and Lady Wakehurst had transferred into the battleship, outside the harbour.

Soon we were boarding, this meant working in each position of a well-staffed house. I started at the bottom as a scullery-maid and Nancy was cook, and I wasn't too happy to see my well-scrubbed floor and clean sink getting dirty. I was always happier cleaning than cooking, but after a week we changed roles, then moved on to be housemaid and parlour maid. I dreaded housekeeping as this meant doing accounts; hostess was pleasant and we all wore long dresses for dinner each evening.

Nancy and I felt to be fashionable we ought to smoke, so, after buying a packet of cigarettes we had a try in our bedroom, quite soon collapsing onto our beds, we felt so dizzy.

There was a small ferry crossing the harbour to the main part of Sydney, leaving from the bottom of the garden, and as we were addicted to Laurcl and Hardy films, also the wonderful Ginger Rogers and Fred Astaire films, I am afraid we too often hopped on a ferry – our usual lunch, a banana milkshake, cost 6d. We were the only two not to gain a Certificate at the end of the year. However, I could hardly have had a

Ruth Church,
Lola Little
and Nancy
Spicer on the
oval at
Abbotsleigh

better education for my future life.

I spent most of the 1937 summer with my friends, the MacDougalls, at their Newport beach house and don't remember any talk of going for a trip to England in the New Year.

Some boys of Nancy's and my age had, like us, recently left school, so we met them on the beach and in the surf on most days. It was innocent company, surfing and sunbathing, and going to dances at the Surf Club. Having recently read a book about the dangers of the mouth of the Hawkesbury River, I realise how easily our young lives could have been cut short then. Nancy and I and our two friends, Harry Gregory and John Walsh, decided to hire a rowing boat on the Pittwater side of Palm Beach and row to the other side of the Hawkesbury for a swim on one of the beaches there. As soon as we noticed the weather changing we decided to get back. The waves were getting larger and larger and Nancy and I had to warn the boys when an extra large wave was coming. They had quite a struggle to reach the shore.

My mother must have been saving all through the Great Depression to take me to England — being thoroughly Australian I wasn't very keen about travelling, my friend said 'I don't want to go abroad, Australia is the best country in the world'. In the end, it was agreed that Nancy MacDougall, whose step-father was travelling to England shortly after us, should travel with my mother and me.

3

Caryl

CARYL'S FATHER, THE REVEREND LEWIS RICHARD CHARLES BAGOT, WAS Rector of East Bradenham, in Norfolk, where Caryl was born on 9 March 1877 and baptised the same day. His grandfather was Rector of Castle Rising, also in Norfolk, and his great-grandfather, besides being Rector of Blithfield and Leigh, in Staffordshire, had been Canon of Worcester, and of Windsor, and Prelate of The Order of the Garter, Bishop of Oxford, 1829, Dean of Canterbury, and Bishop of Bath and Wells in 1845. Caryl's mother was the daughter of The Reverend Henry Jodrell and grand-daughter of Admiral, Sir Charles Napier, KCB. Caryl always loved sea voyages and travelling, which he must have inherited from Charlie Napier.

In 1879, Caryl's father was introduced to the Vicarage of Stanton Lacy in Shropshire, close to Ludlow, almost on the racecourse. Caryl's older sister had been born at East Bradenham, like Caryl, but his two younger sisters, Gladys and Enid were born at Stanton Lacy.

The Vicarage had a great advantage from Caryl's point of view, the little River Corve flowed through the grounds so he was able to practise fly-fishing from an early age. It became a life-long skill and enjoyment. The Windsor Clives, owners of Oakley Park at that time, allowed him to fish in the Teme, which flowed through their land.

Caryl and his sisters must have had a very happy childhood, because, in later life, when I knew them, they never stopped talking about Stanton Lacy. If Caryl hadn't inherited Blithfield, I think we might have bought the Old Vicarage and been very happy there.

Although Caryl had been at a small school in Montreux when his parents were staying in Switzerland, his first school was at Malvern Link, so the train must have taken him through some of the most beautiful country in England, from Ludlow to Malvern, and later, to his public

Caryl aged 11 in a sailor suit   A prefect at Radley

school Radley College near Oxford, which he entered in Michaelmas Term, 1891, as a junior scholar. By the time he left in 1896 he was a prefect and in the cricket XI and also the football XI. In addition, he acquired five prizes for classics, English, French, Greek and Latin and mathematics. It has been said Radley's mark on a boy will be indelible.

Caryl was brought back to life for me as I read Christopher Hibbert's book *No Ordinary Place. Radley College and the Public School System 1847–1997*.[1] 'There was a good spirit in the school' quotes Hibbert at the beginning of Chapter 15, Firm Hands 1880–1896.[2] 'In the dormitories, the curtains of the cubicles were replaced with sliding doors which were opened each morning after a perfunctory knock by a servitor bearing the traditional can of what was – or was at least supposed to be – a modicum of hot water'.[3]

'Radley's guests were justified in concluding that the school, compared

Cricket on the lawn at The Vicarage, Stanton Lacy, Shropshire

with similar places, was a pleasant and tolerant place. The boys were not only polite but had a reputation, unusual in their kind, of being clean. Certainly most of them were neatly dressed; indeed, it was suggested that more interest was taken in clothes than was altogether desirable'.[4] It would seem that 'ready-made suits were frowned upon'.[5] Hibbert reports that the prefects were 'allowed to wear turn-down collars then in fashion, the less privileged being required to retain their single stick-up collars', and goes on to say that the small boys 'had to wear Eton collars'.[6] Whilst commenting upon the buildings and new structures within the college, Hibbert describes the 'walls of Hall,' as being 'formerly decorated with Prefects' banners', but adds that they were later 'ornamented with shields bearing their families' coats of arms'.[7] Hibbert also reflects upon appearances, stating that good looks were 'extremely important' at Radley, 'quite as important as they could be at any girls' school. They were almost as important as prowess at games or on the river, or as good birth'.[8] The 'consecration of the new Chapel was celebrated on Gaudy Day, 29 June, 1895',[9] whilst guests regularly 'commented upon the good behaviour and friendliness of the boys' and 'the well-mannered attentions of the masters'.[10] Radley was

Caryl in Calcutta

also 'celebrated for its parties, outings and junketings'[11] – Caryl never lost his appetite for these. He was always popular for his quick wit and sense of humour, and he had the endearing gift of being able to laugh at himself. Wherever Caryl was, there was a happy atmosphere.

Talking of Radleians, Hibbert quotes comments made by the Warden, who reported that there was 'a charm about so many of them, an ease of manner and kindliness of temperament' which, the Warden conceded, 'people find attractive'. 'But the best Radleians', he continued, have 'always been quite steely and competitive under that charm of manner...'[12]

Instead of going to university, Caryl was sent to live with a family in Paris. I have sometimes heard people in France say 'he speaks French like a Frenchman'. Then he went to learn to speak German in Heidelberg – he must have been bored there, because he and another young man went out one night and amused themselves by breaking street lights. They were put in prison and Caryl's father had to pay £500 to get him out! Perhaps that is why he didn't go into the Diplomatic Service.

Caryl's mother had a good friend living in the Manor House at Stanton

Caryl, 1916. Irish
Guards, 2nd Battalion,
Great War

Lacy, Mrs Ralli. Two Ralli brothers started the firm of Ralli Brothers in
the early nineteenth century and Caryl first worked for the firm in
London and then in Calcutta, which is where he met his first wife,
Margaret McMenemy. They were married in 1911 when she was only
seventeen and must have returned to England during the First World
War, because Caryl was serving in the Second Battalion of the Irish
Guards, known as the 'happy' battalion.[13]

A platoon had crossed the rivulet Broembeek on 12 September 1917
and disappeared. Patrols had gone out, however, the Brigadier was not
pleased with what had been done, so, on the night of 14 September, 'out
went another patrol', 'under Lieutenant Bagot, with intent to reconnoitre
"the river that wrought them all their woe." They discovered what every
one guessed – that the enemy was holding both river-crossings, stone
bridge and duckboards, with machine-guns. The Battalion finished the
day in respirators under heavy gas-shellings'.[14] The guards were waiting to

Margaret Bagot (née McMenemy), 1916

be relieved by the First Coldstream, a big gun barrage was firing onto the far side of the Broembeek, so everyone was completely amazed and delighted when, on 16 September, Sergeant Moyney turned up with the remainder of No 3 Company's Platoon, missing since 12 September. They had some rations and a bottle of water each and had to keep as quiet as possible. The enemy didn't know where they were exactly, nor how many there were hiding in a shell hole in Ney Copse. When the enemy were within 25 yards of Sergeant Moyney he ordered his men to attack, he then gave the order to 'charge through the Germans to the Broembeek'.[15] 'They were bombed and machine-gunned as they floundered over to the swampy western bank;' while he covered their passage with his one rifle.[16] Sergeant Moyney was awarded the Victoria Cross.[17]

'The total losses of the tour' (on the far side of the rivulet) 'had been – one officer missing (Lieutenant Manning), one (2nd Lieutenant Gibson) wounded; one man wounded and missing; eighty missing; fifty-nine

Caryl with sisters and Margaret at Dawlish Warren

Margaret, Caryl, Ysolde, Gladys at Widecombe Moor church

wounded and seventeen killed. And the worst of it was that they were all trained hands being finished for the next big affair!"[18] Passchendaele!

Zero hour on 9 October was 5.20 am, 'which gave light enough to see a few hundred yards'.[19] 'The Welsh Guards relieved in the late evening, and by eleven o'clock the whole Battalion was safe in Dulwich Camp with an amazingly small casualty list. The only officer killed had been Captain Hanbury. Lieutenants Close and Bagot were wounded and also Alexander and Father Browne, these last two so slightly that they still remained on duty'.[20]

Caryl said his batman thought Caryl had been hit in the head because he had 'spun around', but he was hit by a piece of shrapnel in the left hip. I don't know how long it took for him to get to London, but he was taken to Fishmongers' Hall. A nurse came to give him a bath, but he didn't want to be disturbed, so she simply picked him up and took him off.

One of the few things Caryl told me about his time in the Irish Guards was that he could never find his way, anywhere. Having seen pictures of the devastation in Rudyard Kipling's *The Irish Guards in the Great War*, I am not surprised.

Caryl and Margaret attended a very moving Remembrance Service for the Irish Guards at The Brompton Oratory before returning to Calcutta, and Caryl went on working at Ralli Brothers for several years, until he resigned in 1932 and returned to England.

William, Fourth Lord Bagot died in December 1932, leaving no direct heir to the title and the Bagot Settled Estates. His brother, Walter's son, should have succeeded him had he not been killed aged nineteen, whilst serving as a Second Lieutenant in the Welsh Guards, on the Somme at Ginchy in 1916.

The heir was an elderly kinsman born in 1866, who had been living abroad for most of his life. No one seemed to know anything about him.

Caryl and Margaret went to stay with one of the Trustees, Sir Francis Newdigate at Arbury Hall, perhaps thinking Gerald, the heir, may no longer be alive and that Caryl would be Lord Bagot. However, after about three weeks, Gerald was discovered training racehorses outside Paris. He had spent many years in South America, training Polo ponies, was not married, and had no children, so Caryl, though only ten years younger than Gerald was heir presumptive.

Caryl and Margaret, having no ties, decided to spend their time travelling, India, China, New Zealand, where they enjoyed fishing, the USA, the Andes, France and Switzerland. Caryl's parents were both dead by the 1930s, but I am sure he and Margaret must have visited Ludlow and the parts of Shropshire where Caryl grew up. Also, Southern Ireland, where Margaret's family came from, and spent some time with two of Caryl's sisters in Devon. Caryl's favourite sister, Gladys, or Glad as he called her, had a small beach house on The Warren, at Dawlish in Devon, where they could bathe and sunbathe.

I don't know when Margaret first began to feel unwell, but she died of liver cancer in Zurich in August 1937. Caryl was devastated and went to stay with his youngest sister, Enid and his brother-in-law, at their small farm in Yandina, Queensland, eighty miles north of Brisbane, near Nambour. He spent the summer there helping with the farm, deciding to return to Europe the following April.

Notes

1 Hibbert, Christopher, *No Ordinary Place. Radley College and the Public School System 1847–1997* (first published by John Murray (Publishers) Ltd, 50 Albemarle Street, London, W1X 4BD, 1997).

2 *Ibid*, p 120.

3 *Ibid*, p 121.

4 *Ibid*, p 128.

5 *Ibid*, p 128.

6 *Ibid*, p 136.

7 *Ibid*, p 121.

8 *Ibid*, pp 141–142.

9 *Ibid*, p 127.

10 *Ibid*, p 127.

11 *Ibid*, p 76.

12 *Ibid*, p 351.

13 Kipling, Rudyard, *His forgotten masterpiece. The Irish Guards in the Great War. The Second Battalion* (originally published in 1923; republished in the UK by Spellmount, Ltd, The Old Rectory, Staplehurst, Kent, TN12 0AZ, 1997), p 153.

14 *Ibid*, p 147.

15 *Ibid*, p 148. For a fuller description of these events see pp 147–148.

16 *Ibid*, p 148.

17 *Ibid*, p 213.

18 *Ibid*, p 149.

19 *Ibid*, p 151.

20 *Ibid*, p 152.

4

Caryl and Nancy

CARYL HAD CAUGHT THE NEXT SHIP LEAVING VANCOUVER FOR SYDNEY, and now he was due to arrive in the *SS Aorangi*. I had last seen him two months ago, before my mother and I left Vancouver.

Monica, Nancy MacDougall and I went to the docks to meet him. Monica only knew what I had told her about him, Nancy knew him as an old friend, and I was full of longing and excitement because I had quite decided I couldn't live without him and wanted to tell him that I would marry him.

He went to stay at the The Australia Hotel and then my aunt and uncle made him very welcome at their house. Uncle Pat was especially pleased to have a companion for billiards, and we soon found our speed, when playing tennis, was no match for his quick wit. Caryl was very fond of my darling grandmother and she of him, and I am sure she persuaded my parents to give their consent to our marriage three months before my twenty-first birthday. Caryl and my father had met, and Caryl wrote to *The Sydney Morning Herald* asking them to insert the announcement of our engagement early in December. As he wasn't sure about getting money out from England he gave me his father's blood stone signet ring, with its goat's head crest to wear as an engagement ring, which I wore proudly, until later when he bought me a lovely emerald ring, my favourite stone and my birthstone. Caryl never wore his father's ring – he would never wear any ring, or even a wrist watch.

After our engagement my aunt rented a beach house at Newport, which was very kind of her. Monica, Lucy and I stayed there and Caryl rented a room in a cottage belonging to an Englishman on the Pittwater side of Newport. By then we had a Ford V8. Every day was spent on the

Nancy and Caryl before
leaving for England, 1942

beach, and although Caryl didn't attempt any surfing, he 'bathed' with the
children in the shallows and loved sunbathing and enjoying the spectacle
of beautiful Australian girls, writing to his elder sister in Devon likening
it to watching a cabaret – he got a sharp reply! (Ysolde and her husband,
Bertram, living on the Devon coast, on the outskirts of Teignmouth, were
being subjected to German Airforce 'hit and run' raids.)

After Christmas, Monica and I stayed in a very nice bed and breakfast
house at Newport. Monica was engaged to John Bowen, who was studying
law and had joined the RAN.

As my parents had agreed to our marriage, Caryl went to see the
Reverend CA Lucas, Rector of St John's Church, Darlinghurst, Sydney,
who knew Caryl's father. The date agreed upon was 1 March 1940. Later
I heard that the fact of our marrying on St David's Day had been noted
in Wales, where, due to Walter Bagot having married the Salesbury

Wedding photograph, 1940

heiress in the seventeenth century, the Bagots used to own a large estate in north Wales.

Monica was my bridesmaid and her fiancé gave me away as, sadly my father didn't come, only my mother and my grandmother came. We went to The Australia Hotel, where a large bunch of red roses awaited me. The wedding ring I chose was an engraved platinum band, small diamonds embedded in about a quarter of it, I now say they represent the twenty-one years I was married to Caryl. The gold ring of Oriental origin, which I also wear, I found here at Blithfield, so I call it my Blithfield wedding ring.

After a few days we started out to drive to Queensland, to Enid and Jack's little farm eighty miles north of Brisbane at Yandina. We had the Ling dog with us – a little West Highland terrier Caryl had given me a few weeks previously. In those days it was really country not far north of Hornsby, with a long, straight, dusty red road ridged like corrugated iron, so one had to drive at a certain speed, otherwise it was a very bumpy ride, as well as a dusty one. The Ford V8 was good for travelling, just a bench seat in front and a 'dicky' behind where we put our luggage. At the back of our bench seat was a comfortable fold where the Ling dog could lie. A child who saw him there asked if he was a pig! Just as well we had a sturdy American car, as neither of us had any idea what to do if it broke down or got a puncture.

Seeing this long straight road, with no sign of any other vehicle, Caryl suddenly said 'Let me have a drive'. We changed places and the next thing he said 'I can't see the road'. He wasn't used to having a large engine in front of him, however, we set off. A cloud of dust appeared on the horizon, and Caryl said nervously, 'There's a car coming what shall I do?' To which I replied 'Keep going, keep going'. He must have put his foot on the brake because the car turned round, Caryl got out shaking and said 'I'm never going to drive again' – and he never did.

We decided to spend the first night in a hotel in Newcastle, but when they heard we wanted to bring a dog in with us that was quite out of the question – dogs were working animals and lived outside. Rather than argue we decided to go on and find a nice country hotel. We drove on, and on, and on, until we came to a small town where there was only one hotel. Caryl asked if we could have tea. The reply was 'Yer tea will be ready at six and if you're not in the dining room by then, the door will be locked!'

We were driving north on the coastal route and hotels seemed to be run for commercial travellers, and it was assumed we would all want to sit together at one large table. Ling was allowed to sleep in the Patterns Room. When we got to the New South Wales/Queensland border, I passed through the 'rabbit proof fence', built to keep the masses of rabbits in New South Wales (introduced to Australia) from swarming into Queensland.

We enjoyed a few days over Caryl's birthday, 9 March, staying in the one hotel at Surfers' Paradise, and having the beach more or less to ourselves. From there it didn't seem far to Brisbane, where we stayed at The Cecil Hotel, near the Botanical Gardens.

Such a happy period. After my Caryl had died, over twenty-one years later, one of my most piercingly painful moments (bitter sweet) was remembering lying in bed watching him shaving and singing, also looking at him on a rough piece of ground outside the hotel, with the little West Highland Terrier on a lead – so unlike any Australians I knew. Roman features, small and neat, brown suntanned skin and white hair, wearing a very bright toweling bathrobe and red leather slippers. I couldn't bear to think I wouldn't see him again, but who knows?

A few days later Enid came to Brisbane, and I met Caryl's youngest sister for the first time. She said she didn't like the publicity Caryl's and my marriage had attracted, and I am sure his three sisters must have been very upset at his marrying someone so much younger.

Jack and Enid's little farm was up a very rutted unmade track, a short distance from the small village of Yandina. The house, like most Queensland houses, was weather-boarded and 'on stilts', a verandah front and back, and a living-room in between. We had two stretchers at one end of the living-room, and Enid had a bedroom at the other end. The back verandah had a 'kitchen' with a fuel stove, at one end and a 'bathroom' at the other end. The lavatory was outside and lighting was by oil lamps and candles. Dear Enid had always adored cats, so not only her cats, but everybody else's cats, seemed to live there. On our arrival Enid's cat flew onto her lap and scratched her, frightened by my little dog, who lived mostly under the house, which was better for him as it was cooler there.

The living-room had signs of an English drawing-room, a round table covered by a cloth, with little pieces of silver on it, which I was happy to clean. Enid grew strawberries and sweet peas, and I enjoyed arranging the flowers. Very often, however, the vase would tip over, as a large green frog had taken up residence, and a number were living in the outside water tanks, which collected our water supply from the roof.

The farm consisted of a number of cows, a bull and a horse, also pigs and 'chooks' (Australian for poultry). The cows had to be hand-milked by Jack and Enid; afterwards the cream was sent to Gympe, where there was a cheese factory. Not far from the house a small river ran through the property, which being near the coast had a good rainfall so sugar cane grew on this coast. When we went by bus (driven by the one-armed bus driver) up into the hills, we saw the little train which collected the cut cane.

Caryl had bought a small farm up there for Enid called Kurcelpa, which she let, so we went with Enid to collect rent from Mr Roberts. On

Nancy as a VAD 1940-42   Clive Clifford, training in Canada, RAAF

the way the bus driver flung papers, etc into kerosene tins, mounted on posts to form letter-boxes!

Everyone seemed terribly poor, and it was such a lonely life. I can see why Enid wanted Caryl to be with her all the time. She and Jack had some English friends, called Midgley, who lived at Budrem. They had a daughter about my age. We all went to the Brisbane Show one day, leaving Caryl and Jack on the farm. Caryl had never had anything to do with farming and Jack was a soldier, not a farmer. He was soon back in his uniform as Recruiting Officer for the area.

I can't say I enjoyed life at Yandina; in fact if it hadn't been for a week or two at Mooloolaba, a most beautiful surfing beach, we wouldn't have stayed so long. There was one boarding house by the beach where we were very comfortable and spent the days and evenings on the beach. It was obvious we weren't going to be much use helping Enid run the farm and we set off to drive back to Sydney, stopping at Warwick and Tamworth on the New England road. Each place we stopped at the news from England was worse, until the last stop before Sydney, near Scone on

30 May 1940 (my twenty-first birthday) and the last evacuation from Dunkirk. Poor Caryl must have been terribly worried and upset; I was upset at having to spend my twenty-first birthday in a small country town.

On returning from Queensland, Caryl rented a flat in Wahroonga House, on the top floor. It was in Burns Road, which I knew well, as some of my school friends lived in that area. The lower part of the road wasn't macadamised so we used to race our ponies there.

The flat was very comfortable and we had the pleasure of entertaining my parents there. To look after us we had a charming girl, Winnie Finch. She and her sister lived in Botany Bay and never married. I kept in touch with her until she died, many years later.

Two elderly ladies lived in the flat under us, and quite rightly didn't like my little West Highland terrier cocking his leg on their garden, so they threw jugs of water over him. Not being very polite to them is one of the many things I regret having done.

I joined a Voluntary Aid Detachment – most of the members were school friends, and we worked part-time, first at the Lady Gowrie Home for Returned Soldiers, who had been fighting in North Africa. The building was erected by a now disgraced financier, who had made a bathroom with a black bath in the middle of the room, black tiles everywhere, and the walls covered with engraved mirrors. Matron made sure it was all polished and shining before we left, and in the drawing-room, now a dormitory, every 'red cross' had to be exactly in the middle of each bed before it was passed.

I don't remember how long we worked there, but life was easier for Caryl and me when I and my friends were told to work at a new Convalescent Home at Wahroonga called Neringa, close to Abbotsleigh, where most of us had been at school. The Sergeant used his false teeth as an ashtray, and was careful to try to stop soldiers swearing when the VADs were about. Another Sergeant, Sergeant Bully, drilled the VADs on the Abbotsleigh Oval, where we had often played cricket and hockey.

The news from England got worse and worse, but the Battle of Britain saved England from being invaded. Caryl and I were enjoying a morning drinks' party at the Grant's house, Maiala, when we heard that Japanese bombers had carried out a devastating raid on Pearl Harbour, both

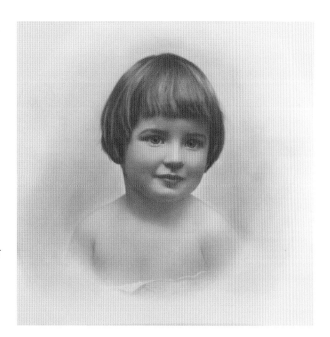

Nancy aged two and a half

'Listening to this music box on my first visit to Blithfield made me feel I was needed here'

The Green Room, where the late-eighteenth
century wallpaper 'brightened the walls'

Goat Lodge

The Bluebell Walk
in the Grove

The courtyard, Blithfield. Taken from a watercolour by John Buckler in the 2nd Lord's
Memorials of the Bagot Family, 1824. Salt Library

The courtyard at Blithfield in 1950

Frances Wolseley setting out from Wolseley Hall for tea at Blithfield

Stebbing Shaw's south west view of Blithfield showing the west end of The Orangery and Blithfield Church, c.1790. Watercolour

Lady Bagot in Coronation robe

Screens passage at the east end of the hall

Ceiling of the Great Hall

The Conservatory, 1956

L-shaped Drawing Room

The Great Hall after John Fowler's 'good wash'

Charlotte Sneyd's watercolour, 1852. Eleanor Bagot with her little dog 'Trip'

Charlotte Sneyd's watercolour of 'The L room at Blithfield', 1852

The Green Bedchamber, 1956

Toy Gallery and Museum of Childhood

Punch and Judy

shocking and a relief – a relief that England and Australia weren't 'on their own', but shocking because we were so unprepared. The big guns at Singapore were pointing out to sea and couldn't be turned round. Japanese bombers sank two British battleships, their troops advanced through the jungle to Singapore, and then they bombed Darwin.

My cousin, Clive Clifford, with the RAAF in England, said in his last letter to me 'Australia seems to be in a bad position just now, it is rotten being over here when we are now all needed at home'. About three weeks after writing this, the Lancaster Bomber in which he was navigator was shot down, whilst laying mines to prevent German submarines sinking our shipping in the Atlantic. My poor aunt – she adored Clive.

Caryl must have been worried about getting money out from England and said he didn't like being away from England at a time like this, so in April or May he booked to return by ocean liner, sailing in convoy via the Panama Canal. But with a flat, a car and a dog to deal with, we couldn't be ready in time. As it turned out, the ship was sunk off the coast of Florida. Fortunately, however, as she was in convoy, no lives were lost, but passengers did lose all their luggage.

When we were ready we went to stay in Monica and John's flat, part of a large house in Turramurra. John was away in the Australian navy. While we were there two Japanese midget submarines managed to get into Sydney harbour. Air raid warnings sounded, Monica got up, turned the lights on and asked Caryl if he thought we ought to go and sit in the trench John had dug in the garden which was half full of water! 'Certainly not' said Caryl, 'go back to bed'. We heard later that guns had been firing across the harbour and an American ship had been sunk.

Caryl had booked passages in a small ship, the *Glendenbyshire*, built to take twelve passengers, directors of a company in Hong Kong. It wouldn't be going in convoy, but she was a fast ship. There would be twenty-four passengers on board, mostly wives of British soldiers taken prisoner by the Japanese in Malaya. It was a sad scene on the little Warrawee Station when we said goodbye to my mother and father; I never saw my father again, for fifteen months later he died of pneumonia.

We spent our last night at The Australia Hotel, where we had spent our wedding night. It was 1 March 1940 and still summer then; now it was winter, June 1942, and we lay in bed listening to the mournful sound of the fog horns coming from ships in the harbour.

We seemed to go quite far south before coming up to the Panama Canal, where there were several British ships' captains waiting for new ships. It was a time when German submarines were sinking ships within sight of the Florida coast.

The Panama Canal is like a series of lakes, linked by canals; sailing slowly through this picturesque area it was hard to believe a war was being waged. We only had one 'Bofors' gun on board our ship. Most of the men did so many hours watch for submarines, and we all wore Mae West waist-coats with lights on the shoulder, to switch on. We kept an 'escape bag' with us all the time. The crew were Chinese, who had been signed on in Hong Kong.

We landed in Belfast after an uneventful trip. Then, as we came across to England, guns started blazing. It would have been too much to bear if the ferry we were in had been sunk in the Irish sea.

As soon as we got to London I sent a cable to my parents, and they put the following notice in *The Sydney Morning Herald*, July 1942:

> Mr. & Mrs. F.A. Spicer of Wahroonga have received a cable from their daughter, now Mrs. C.E. Bagot, announcing that she and her husband have arrived safely in England. Mr. & Mrs. Bagot, who will make their home in England, left Australia by ship and made the journey in 35 days.

We went to The Rembrandt Hotel, where Caryl had stayed when we were in London before. But since so many older people had left their homes and were living in hotels, they were mostly full. However, The Berkeley in Piccadilly could take us, and after a few days we were on our way to Devon to see Caryl's two sisters. As it was July we wanted to enjoy the summer! Olave was in Scotland.

We stayed at The Royal Hotel on the sea front at Teignmouth and were changing for dinner when quite unexpectedly we heard aeroplanes and gunfire. When I went out into the entrance everyone was lying on the floor: it had been a hit and run raid of which there were many. Poor

16 The Gateways, Chelsea, where
Caryl and Nancy (left) lived for
twenty years

Ysolde, Caryl's eldest sister, lived on that coast at Shaldon, near Teign-mouth, with her husband, Bertram. Their house was damaged by a bomb blast, which blew Bertram into the downstairs cloakroom. Luckily, Bertram was not seriously injured. They used to tuck all their ornamental china into the sides of armchairs each night, but although it was all out to be admired, nothing was broken. Admiral Sir Charles Napier's miniature was found later in the garden in a lavender bush.

Glad and her husband, Frank, were living in part of an old Devon farm-house, with a thatched roof. When we went to stay with them, it seemed like another world, watching the wheat being cut by the light of a full harvest moon and being woken in the morning by the orchestra of birds in the thatch. I found the broad Devon accent difficult to understand.

Back in London, Caryl's cousin, dear Olave, Lady Brooke, who had been so kind to us when we were in London before, came to our rescue again, helping us look for somewhere to live. Caryl had no furniture, as he and Margaret hadn't lived anywhere since leaving India. We were looking for a furnished flat in a large concrete block, which was just what most people wanted – old houses weren't good at standing up against a bomb blast.

One day we were walking though Chelsea, along a small private road. On each side were courtyards, surrounded by brick houses, some quite small, but all without cellars or attics. They had small gardens, and there was a fountain in each courtyard. I was immediately attracted by them and said to Caryl, 'I'd love to have one of those houses'. As we had no furniture, he replied 'Perhaps after the war!'

Unable to find a furnished flat, we took the last vacant house. Most of the windows had been broken when a land mine fell on the large block of flats opposite.

The Gateways, as they were called, were owned by an insurance company, so they were responsible for repairs, and Olave Brooke said she would lend us some furniture, an oak gate-leg table and Windsor chairs, which looked just right in our one living room, with its large open fireplace.

The Gateways weren't far from Peter Jones' shop in Sloane Square, and there we were able to buy wartime utility furniture (the bed and dressing table are still in use) and everything necessary for the kitchen.

Before establishing somewhere to live we had to acquire ration books and gas masks, and then, once we were installed at No 16 The Gateways, tin hats for protection, and buckets and stirrup pumps for fire fighting.

Olave introduced me to some of her friends in the Chelsea Red Cross Divisional Office, and I started working with them in the basement of Chelsea Town Hall after buying a uniform at Burberrys.

Miss Milicent Buller was our Divisional Director and I was put into

Detachment 444. Two years later, I was very proud to be made Commandant of the Detachment. It wasn't far to walk to the Town Hall, but Caryl
and I went to north London and Caryl bought a bicycle for me. There was
very little traffic on the roads as only buses and official cars could get petrol.

Working underground we didn't hear much of what was going on in the
King's Road. I and Mrs Legge went home for lunch. Soon after I had
started work there Mrs Legge left to go home at lunch time and came
back saying 'It's a bit heavy out there, I think I'll wait a while'. I thought
she meant rain but no, she meant an air raid, so I waited too!

I went to classes about different gases that could be used by the enemy,
but thank God they weren't. Caryl had never told me about wearing gas
masks in the Great War. It wasn't until I read the 1997 reprint of Rudyard
Kipling's book *The Irish Guards in the Great War, the Second Battalion*, that I
had any idea of what he must have been through; all he said was that he
never knew where he was. I knew he had been wounded; if he hadn't
been, I doubt he would have survived Passchendaele!

On moonlight nights, German planes flew over the Thames, and the
mobile gun, which seemed to be driven around our houses, made far more
noise than the planes. I hate loud noise and couldn't stop shaking and
thought Caryl very unfeeling when he said 'Oh do stop shaking!'

We never went to an underground shelter, but sometimes slept in the
cupboard under the stairs, where there was just enough room – we were
both 5' 5". Miss Buller asked me to go and have typing lessons at a school
nearby, which cost a shilling a term. The machines were large and old-
fashioned, the keys covered with wooden shields. The pretty, fair, very
English looking girl sitting next to me, looking at my book, said 'My name
used to be Bagot'. When I told Caryl, he knew exactly who she was –
Peggy Bagot Chester. If one saw an advertisement for Craven 'A' cigarettes, or a twinset pullover and cardigan before the war, Peggy would be
the beautiful young woman smoking a cigarette or wearing the twinset.
She drove an ambulance through the London Blitz and was still driving
one. We became great friends; she was living near the Town Hall.

Quite a number of people would send donations to the Red Cross,
naming the donation as being from their pets, so now I could type thank
you letters, often starting 'Dear Miss Tibby Toes'. Also, I could type

letters for Miss Buller, who had a saying, 'If you leave a letter long enough, it answers itself'.

During the long winters we missed the sun – the clocks were two hours ahead in summertime, but with having to draw blackout curtains we hardly saw daylight in winter, and I missed my family and friends.

Caryl, not having lived in England, apart from a short time after he was wounded in the Great War, had very few friends, and anyway everyone was occupied. Caryl was asked to be a Fire Officer, but he said he was going to 'Stay at home and look after his wife'.

Not long before Christmas 1943, I got a bad shock – a cable from my brother saying my father had died. Later, I heard he was in hospital having an operation for a hernia, he caught pneumonia, and with no penicillin, of course. This was terrible for my poor mother – she felt very bitter about not being able to get in touch with the surgeon, when she could see my father's life was rapidly deteriorating.

My parents had been wonderful, sending food parcels not just to us, but to daddy's family, his mother and two sisters, to Aunt Esther and Caryl's sisters. The food parcels contained items such as fruit cakes, dried fruit, sugar and butter, tins of ox-tongues, etc. My mother continued to do this, for which everyone was very grateful.

From time to time we practised putting out fire bombs with buckets and stirrup pumps, crawling around on a smoke covered bomb site nearby. Thank heaven we never had to wear gas masks. Unlike the First World War, no gas was used.

Something Caryl and I looked forward to in the summer was going by bus to the club at Roehampton. There was a pool there where I could swim, and Olave often joined us for she, like Caryl, loved sunbathing. Another outing we enjoyed was spending a day at Kew Gardens and Hampton Court.

One day I was asked to take charge of a Red Cross buffet lunch party at its Headquarters in Belgrave Square. I had never been in a kitchen like it before – huge lead-lined sinks and lots of plate racks, all in the base-ment. The luncheon was to be at the top of the house, but fortunately there was a lift and everything had to go up in it and come down again. One time something that hadn't meant to come down was a very cross

BRCS Chelsea Divsion

General – I must have pressed the button for the lift a second before he got out at the top!

When the King and Queen were going to a concert at The Albert Hall I was one of the members asked to go with a Red Cross collecting tin, and was standing near the royal party. Tim Nugent (Caryl's friend from the Great War days) was with them.

I was also out collecting in the King's Road on a grey day in 1944 when the word went round, 'they've landed'. I remember an old soldier, who had been in the Normandy landings saying, 'You won't find many atheists in a landing craft'.

Sadly, Caryl's favourite sister, Glad, who had spent the winter with us in the Riviera, and had been on the spring tour of Italy, died in August 1944. Caryl wanted to go to her funeral, of course, and I couldn't leave my work, so Caryl asked our next door neighbours, charming refugees from Poland, two sisters, one with a diplomat husband, if I could spend the

My Australian friend Paddy Love (née Hemphill). A prefect at Abbotsleigh and WRNS in London

night with them. Their house was a little larger than ours, so they had room for a Morrison Shelter, a steel table with wire round the sides. We all smoked like chimneys and the sisters had hung empty paste jars on the wire for ashtrays, making the shelter look like a large bird cage!

Although German planes came over on most clear nights, we didn't take a lot of notice until a bomb fell in nearby Sloane Avenue, hitting a gas main, and breaking windows, including ours. We were really disturbed that night and didn't get much sleep. Next day we were due to go to the christening of my first god-daughter, Sarah Jewitt, Caryl's great niece. We enjoyed the day away from our broken windows.

I wrote to my mother from No 16 The Gateways, 15 July 1944:

My Dearest Mummy,

A lovely lot of papers, and a letter arrived by ordinary mail yesterday, thank you so much for them, the letter was written at the end of April so it's taken some time to get here. Now I can tell you all about the 'doodle bugs', or flying bombs, just at the moment things are much quieter, and last night we slept in bed for the first time since they started about a month ago. We have put a mattress under the stairs, and have been sleeping there, it's much more comfortable than going to a public shelter, most people in The Gateways stay in their houses.

The Red Cross office is now in another office in The Violet Melchitt Centre, Flood Street, Chelsea. Our office has very large glass windows. The other day my 'boss' was talking to H.Q., on the telephone, when we heard a 'doodle bug' coming, she said 'Would you mind holding on for a minute, a flying bomb is going over.' She got under the large desk, and sitting on the floor, calmly went on with the conversation.

I was one of the youngest members working at Chelsea Headquarters, so from being surrounded by family and friends in Australia, I hardly saw anyone my own age, and suffered from depression from time to time.

The friendship of Hugh and Louise Bagot, and their daughters, Mary and Cynthia, Irish Bagots, who lived in Wimbledon, meant a great deal to us. Our name was in the telephone directory, and quite often people would ring our number and ask to speak to either Mary or Cynthia, then Hugh got in touch with us and invited us to luncheon at The Berkeley Hotel, bringing Cynthia. We became close friends with the family and dear charming Louise invited us to their house in Wimbledon for dinner in the evening on Christmas Day two or three years running. After the war, the family moved to Jersey, but we saw as much of them as possible and I am godmother to Cynthia's daughter.

Towards the end of the war my Aunt Dora, my father's younger sister, a favourite of mine, invited Caryl and me to her younger daughter, Elizabeth's wedding. The marriage ceremony was performed by her father, The Reverend Alfred Harris, Rector of Kew Gardens. Uncle Alfred had started his ministry as Curate to The Reverend Bernard Douglas Shaw, Vicar of The Annunciation, Bryanstan Street W. He was second husband to the Hon Louisa Bagot, sister of the Fourth Lord Bagot.

After leaving Sydney in 1942, my one link with Australia during the war was a childhood friend, Paddy Hemphill. She had been a prefect at Abbotsleigh and was a year or two older than me; her younger sister and brother had ponies so we used to ride together. During the summer of 1940, Paddy and her older sister, Sybil, were travelling to Tasmania, on an

Orient ship, bound for England, 'just for a holiday'. Also on board was an English RN officer, who had been in the Battle of the River Plate. This led to a shipboard romance and they were married in Freemantle. When they reached England, Paddy's husband, Captain Philip Love, RN, was back on duty and Paddy joined the WRNS. As soon as she heard where we were living (her mother and my mother were friends), when she had leave, she came to see us, and sometimes would bring WRNS friends.

Paddy was with us on the day we knew the war in Europe was over. The following day we were going to Blithfield; we hadn't been since our first visit in 1939.

Paddy was in her WRNS uniform and I in my BRCS uniform and we set out with Caryl in the evening just to walk in the crowds. We walked in a river of quietly happy people to Piccadilly Circus, not excited, more satisfied, and thankful, of course.

The crowds gravitated to Buckingham Palace and stood calling for the King. The King and Queen, and the two Princesses, came out onto the balcony and were called for again and again. Very soon the Princesses were also among the crowds, calling!

5

The Heirlooms

THE DAY AFTER THE END OF WAR IN EUROPE WE WERE IN A TRAIN BOUND for Derby. From Derby we travelled in a small local train to Uttoxeter, where Caryl had booked a room for a few days at The White Hart.

The next day, VE Day, Whitehall (who worked at the sawmill) collected us in Gerald's old Vauxhall car. On the way to Blithfield he pointed out Bagot's Woods and he and Caryl discussed where they had been on the line during the First World War. When we got to Blithfield, the stone gate posts at the entrance to the first Courtyard were decorated with two rather moth-eaten Union flags.

I doubt if we would have been invited to Blithfield if Gerald hadn't had to get Caryl's consent to sell the heirlooms, consisting of most of the contents of the Hall. Of course, Caryl had known, since 1938, that Gerald had agreed to sell most of the Estate, and the Hall, to The South Staffordshire Waterworks Company, which was to make a reservoir in the Park, by building a dam across the little River Blythe. Gerald could have been forced to sell the land to be flooded, also some of the surrounding land, but having succeeded to the Title and Estate, towards the end of his life, he not only wanted to get rid of the Estate, but to sell the Hall too, and make some money. Caryl had been told when the reservoir is full the Hall would be uninhabitable!

By the terms of the Settlement, made by the Third Lord Bagot in 1881, the Estate and Hall could be sold without the heir's consent, but the money had to be held in the Bagot Settled Estates by the Trustees, only interest from the capital could be used by the tenant for life. Both Gerald and Caryl were alive when the Settlement was made, but not any future holders of the Title.

Nancy, Gerald 5th Lord Bagot and Paddy Love (née Hemphill), married to Commander Philip Love RN, 1945. Paddy and Nancy, two Abbotsleigh Old Girls

During the war, hardly any repairs could be done to houses like Blithfield, which housed only Gerald, a cook and a housemaid, and couldn't be used as a convalescent home as there were no modern conveniences. Lady Dorothy Meynell, President of the British Red Cross Society in Staffordshire during the war, told me she had visited Blithfield to see if the Red Cross could make use of a part of the house, but she 'hurried away!'

Caryl and I were rather horrified by the state both of the Hall and its contents, and also by the lack of any effective security. As we walked around with Gerald and shutters were opened, letting light into rooms which hadn't housed a family for about fifty years, Gerald said, 'When rain came into the Upper Gallery, and froze in winter, it made an excellent skating rink!' His nephew, Harry, had already warned us to 'take umbrellas if you want to walk around Blithfield in the rain'.

The only things exempted from the sale of the Hall were medieval windows depicting scenes from the Life of Saint John the Baptist. This glass was bought by Sir William Burrell and is now in the Burrell Collection on the outskirts of Glasgow in Scotland.

Caryl had been given a large detailed list of heirlooms by the solicitors and wanted to check it, which didn't please Gerald, he said 'Of course, if there is anything Nancy wants to keep we will keep it'. Next day, when we

South and west
fronts of the
Hall

came again, there was a fierce looking woman with Gerald – Miss
Bedford, who lived with her sister in what had been the head gardener's
cottage. I soon learned not to say anything – if I did it was greeted with,
'Oh that will fetch a good price', or 'That's the wicked Lady Bagot, she
took all the silver and linen from Blithfield to her second husband's
house, she must go'; so, the few things I did want to keep I put into the
rooms where Gerald was living, hoping they wouldn't be noticed. As No
16 The Gateways was only a tiny house and we knew we would never be
living at Blithfield, it seemed only sensible for Caryl to give his consent to
the heirlooms being sold, but as soon as this was done we had no more say
in the matter, although there would be about 3,000 acres, including
Bagot's Park, that Caryl would be responsible for when he succeeded,
whenever that would be. Gerald looked a quite fit eighty year old and he
had permission to live in the Hall for his lifetime.

The Beggar's Oak from Strutt's *Sylva Britannica*, 1882

Next time we came to Blithfield, it was for three days of sales, which were held in the Great Hall. All the more valuable items were to be sold at Sothebys in London.

It was towards the end of September and we decided to stay at The Crown in the centre of Abbots Bromley. Hugh Bagot came to the sales with his eldest daughter, Mary, they also stayed at The Crown.

Looking out of the three tall windows of the Great Hall into the Courtyard, around which the house is built, the ground floor of the building opposite was almost hidden by elders and other weeds.

Poor old Gerald got very cross when a ring of dealers called out 'full of worm', whenever pieces of furniture were brought onto the platform. Suddenly, he himself disappeared, a leg of the chair he was sitting on had come off, and he was on the floor!

I noticed a group of two or three women, who were bidding energetically for the cheaper furniture and rush matting, and I heard someone

"WHEN THE GOATS DIE OUT THE BAGOT WILL BE GONE."

Bagot goats in Bagot's Park 1933

sitting in front of us say 'Look at Lady Shrewsbury and her sister, they look like gypsies'. Also, I heard the auctioneers discussing whether to sell the heraldic figures on the carved oak staircase – thank goodness they are still there.

Caryl bought some yellow painted Sheraton chairs I liked that were in the Yellow Bedroom in the front of the house, and a white painted side-table, which we had painted to match the chairs – the chairs were 'full of worm', but treatable.

Before returning to London, Hugh and Mary joined us for a walk in Bagot's Park hoping to see the famous herd of Bagot goats, but the bracken was almost as high as we were so there wasn't a hope of seeing them.

In October, after the September sales at Blithfield, came the sales at Sothebys in London. It was sad, but interesting, and I began to learn about pictures, furniture, jewellery and silver.

One day, Caryl and I went to Garrards, where Bagot silver and jewellery was stored. I was admiring some silver, which had been cleaned, and the man in charge of the stores said, 'Your silver is much better'. Obviously, he could see we were very far from being experts! However, when it came to jewellery, I fell in love with the emerald ring and brooch, and asked for them to be kept, also the pearls. I couldn't see myself ever wearing the rather heavy looking diamond tiara, or the Stafford Knot diamond brooches, and they would 'fetch a good price'.

The last sale of valuable books and papers took place at Sothebys towards the end of November, but before then Gerald came up to London and came to see us at No 16 The Gateways. He described Blith-field since the sales as a 'great barn of a place'. He wrote to Caryl and asked him to make sure nothing of interest to the county was amongst the books and papers taken from the Library, and said he hoped he would now

The servants' picnic under the Beggar's Oak

be left in peace. He died on 6 April 1946, so Caryl and I were now Lord and Lady Bagot. We had no idea Gerald was ill and it felt very strange. Caryl went to Gerald's funeral and I rode my bicycle to work as usual.

It wasn't long before Caryl had a letter from the solicitors of The South Staffordshire Waterworks Company, informing him they would allow him three months to remove all remaining contents from the Hall, and then he must hand it over to them.

Doreen Bexon, the cook, lived at Blithfield with her husband and their baby son, also Sarah Jackson, housemaid, had lived at Blithfield since going to work for the Fourth Lord Bagot, aged fourteen. They told us Gerald had promised them a cottage in the village, but none were vacant. Caryl said that they should have one as soon as one became available. It was obvious we would need to spend time sorting things out at Blithfield, so we bought a second-hand open car, a small green Singer – lovely driving about on a fine sunny day with the hood down, although Caryl said 'We can't have people throwing their cigarette ends onto us when we pass a double-decker bus'. However, as 1946 proved to be a wet summer, the

Caryl and Nancy with Mrs C Villiers Bagot sitting among the moss grown roots of the Beggar's Oak

hood was hardly ever down.

Before the war, Blithfield water supply was pumped up from the Mill on the Blythe to an impressive castellated water tower in the Grove – then water came to the house via lead pipes. There was, and still is, an old well in the house. Early in 1940 soldiers were camping in The Grove, so the water tower was connected to the main water supply, but Blithfield had no bathrooms or electricity, and no heating other than open fires, so we decided to stay at The Crown in Abbots Bromley, where we had stayed the previous autumn, when the heirlooms were being sold.

Looking back, the heirlooms and sales were a shared interest for Caryl and me, which had started with the Continental tours, before the war, but from the monetary point of view, it couldn't have been worse. The value of land and the contents of country houses were very low; also, when Gerald died, death duty had to be paid on a sum of money, the value of which couldn't be disputed, whereas the value of the heirlooms could have been argued about.

Whenever it was fine we liked to walk from The Crown to Blithfield, where we worked all day and then walked back in the evening. I will never forget the walk across the Park, mostly covered by water now. After walking along Bagot Street, past The Bagot Arms, and along the main road to Uttoxeter until we came to the Bromley Lodges, opposite the drive to Bagot's Park, we turned in through the Lodges and walked along the gravel drive, passing through the Duckley Woods, full of rhododendrons, to the stone bridge, which crossed the Tad Brook over Kitty Fisher's Bridge, with her two small footprints on the balustrade. From there we walked along an

Engraving of William, 2nd Lord Bagot

avenue of beech trees, planted for Queen Victoria's Diamond Jubilee, passing Stansley Wood, where the sawmill stood. The drive then wound down to the Blythe valley and water-meadows, through an oak avenue, leading to Blithfield Mill, still working then. The water-meadows looked like a Constable painting. We soon realised we had inherited a very challenging job. The part of the house where Gerald had been living was still furnished with heirlooms, and although there weren't any horses in the Stables, there were five coaches in the Coach House and large copper vats in the Brewhouse.

The roof of the Hall seemed to be leaking everywhere, so there was dry-rot everywhere – thank goodness we discovered a very damp Muniment room containing masses of folded documents, all carefully labelled by the Second Lord Bagot, who wrote *The Memorials of the Bagot Family* in 1824, some documents dating back to the twelfth century. We got in touch with The William Salt Library in Stafford and Mr Burne and Miss Midgley came to look at the collection. They said if we would take them all out and spread them, unfolded, on the floor to dry they would take them to The William Salt Library and gradually restore them. It turned out to be a blessing after all, to have so much empty floor space, all of which was covered before we had finished.

Our hands got very dirty and I had a recurrence of the previous winter's chilblains. Dear Sarah brought two small cans of water, hot and cold, up to Lady Bagot's Bedroom and Doreen cooked us delicious hot meals. I always enjoyed her steam puddings with marmalade on top, and custard. Sarah brought everything upstairs to the Green Room, where the Chinese wallpaper brightened the walls, just as she had done for Gerald. Mrs Edgar, at The Crown, was a good cook too, so we had an excellent dinner in the evening – very different to what we had been used to in London.

We soon realised it would be impossible to get everything sorted out and disposed of in three months, so we asked the Trustees to start negotiations with The South Staffordshire Waterworks Company, to buy back the Hall and thirty acres of grounds. We had both begun to love the place and felt we didn't want to be the first Bagots to leave it. Because the Trustees had already agreed to the sale to The South Staffordshire Waterworks Company, on Gerald's behalf, it fell to poor Caryl to sign the document on 1 December 1947, without being able to alter anything. When we were still trying to comply with The South Staffordshire Waterworks Company's demand to hand over a vacant property to it, we read in the newspaper about a Museum of Coaches that Sir Garrard Tyrwhitt-Drake was forming in Maidstone. Caryl got in touch, and sent him a photograph of the Travelling Coach in which the Second Lord had crossed the Alps – built in 1824 and painted yellow, it is a very handsome looking carriage and was accepted at once. We were sad to see it suffering the indignity of being towed along the drive behind a tractor to Rugeley station. It arrived safely in Maidstone and was welcomed into the Museum. Later, when Blithfield was given a grant for repairs in 1954 by The Historic Buildings Council, and we were preparing to open the house to visitors, we wanted the coach back, so a deal was struck. Sir Garrard would let us have the coach back if we would give him some Bagot goats for the Maidstone Zoo. To our great joy, the Trustees were able to buy the Hall back from The South Staffordshire Waterworks Company, surrounded by thirty acres, on 2 March 1948. We had asked a member of the Company what it had intended doing with the Hall and he said he didn't know.

Marcia Russell, Margot Bagot, Caryl Bagot and Lucy Clifford on Kitty Fisher's bridge over the Tad Brook

I must admit at that period, when hardly anyone seemed able to see a future for country houses, everyone thought we were mad! I can quite see how anyone brought up in a country house, before the war, couldn't visualise living in a huge house without an army of servants.

If Gerald had considered his successor at all, he probably thought he would live in the Georgian Rectory, which the Second Lord had built for his brother early in the nineteenth century. The Ecclesiastical Commissioners were anxious to sell the Rectory, and we went to look at it. The previous rector was still living in it with his sister. It is a large square house, in a splendid position facing south-west overlooking the Trent valley with Cannock Chase in the distance. The garden, with its two terraces, was quite overgrown, just as the garden at Blithfield. The rooms were large and square, with high ceilings and tall sash windows. The fact that a lawn mower was kept in the oak-panelled library on the ground floor and, amongst inches of dust under the beds, in the main bedroom upstairs, was a stuffed cat, were not the chief reasons I rejected it. I said to Caryl 'I could manage those rooms [where Gerald had been living] at Blithfield, much better than this house'. Blithfield was the sort of house where we could live in a corner and not feel we were in a huge building – no two rooms are alike at Blithfield!

Blithfield Rectory

I suppose the late eighteenth-century Chinese wallpaper attracted me most, in the apartment the First Lord made for his young wife; having been brought up in Australia, the sulphur crested cockatoo and many of the birds and butterflies were familiar to me, but not the masses of blue-bells in the Grove, which I found enchanting (see page 66). The Grove, where the Bluebell Walk is situated, is in part of the garden laid out by the First Lord – it is on a ridge between two valleys, the Trent to the west, with Cannock Chase beyond, and the Blythe to the east, with Bagot's Wood beyond. I am glad the original Blithfield family had the foresight to choose this spot for their home in the eleventh century.

There were still about 3,000 acres Caryl was responsible for, including Bagot's Park and the goats. For a medieval house, it is very light, being built around a courtyard, which, as I described at the time of the sales, was full of weeds, and even more so now. Doreen kept her hens in it, safe from foxes.

I had seen a nineteenth-century picture of the courtyard, during the Second Lord's time, with a fountain in the middle, and decided it must be one of the first things to be restored, so we set about it. I am sure there must have been a special breed of ferocious midges living there, which resented being disturbed. Any fit guests were put to work. My cousin

The Courtyard at Blithfield after the weeds had been cleared, 1948

Monica came to England as soon as possible after the war, and met her second husband on board ship. They were staying at The Crown Hotel with us, when Mrs Edgar told us she had a long standing booking for Whitsun. The weather being especially fine and warm, we decided not to go back to London but to 'camp' at Blithfield. We soon got very hot, hoeing and chopping weeds in the courtyard and decided we must have a bath. There was a drain outside the front door so we put a hip-bath there, brought cans of water and nursery screens – I suppose you could say that was the first bathroom at Blithfield!

When the Second Lord was 'Gothicising' Blithfield in the early 1820s, he was also putting in a number of water-closets, each with its lead-lined tank for water in the attics above. These had frozen in wartime winters, splitting the lead and causing dry rot.

There was a large coal-fired boiler to produce hot air in the main rooms (Great Hall, Library, Nursery, Corridor, Cloisters and Lower Gallery, 'L' shaped Drawing-Room and New Drawing Room), but not in the rooms where we were living. It would have needed an enormous amount of coal, so open fires were easiest, but could only be lit in the few fireplaces where chimneys were not blocked by jackdaws' nests.

When we started living at Blithfield we discovered a large bath set in mahogany panelling in the Young Ladies Room, so it was best to use that as a bathroom. A hip-bath was put in there and cans of hot and cold water brought up each morning from the one fuel stove in the Still Room. Then, at least water could be poured away in the large Victorian bath and didn't have to be carried away. There was a water-closet by the end bedroom (end of the Nursery Corridor) which had a small lead-lined flat sink in it. Carefully painted on the wall above it were the words 'Pour no water down this sink'. The room under the end bedroom was known as the Bath-bedroom, and when a cloakroom was being put in here years later, a small white tiled area was discovered sunk in the ground, which could have been used as a bath. This part of the house, in fact most of the house, is half-timbered.

Old houses are quite noisy at night, floor boards and furniture creaking. I wouldn't stay in the Chinese Room on my own at night, because with only one lamp I couldn't see the end of the room. One of the doors from the Chinese Room leads into Lady Bagot's Bedroom, which Caryl and I used. Another door leads to Lady Bagot's Dressing Room, which we used as a small sitting room. The noise made by mice behind the wainscoting at night was quite disturbing. Once we owned Blithfield, Lord Bagot's Dressing Room was made into a bathroom. Before then, at night, we used to go in convoy to the bathroom in the Young Ladies Room, Caryl leading the way with an oil lamp, Monica and I following with candles.

Although The South Staffordshire Waterworks Company, actually owned the Hall from 1 December 1947 until the Trustees bought it back on 2 March 1948, we never moved out.

Blithfield, for two Australians, was like a fairy castle, a thrilling place. We used to walk along the drive on moonlight nights, just so that we could look back at it in moonlight. Driving towards the house at night, the car lights would catch the glass in a window, making it look as if there was a light in that particular room – we called it the ghost light. One day, Monica and I collected some attractive looking chestnuts, and took them into the Still Room Kitchen, telling Doreen we were going to roast them in the fire. Doreen looked disgusted at our ignorance and said 'You can't roast those, they are Horse Chestnuts'.

At that stage there was a Kitchen and Laundry Wing attached to the north-east of the house – it had been built in the late nineteenth century. Gerald told Caryl and me, on our first visit to Blithfield, how, at the beginning of the war, men came collecting iron 'for the war-effort', and they took all the copper from the Kitchen. Luckily, Gerald kept quiet about the iron balustrade set in stone around the garden between the Orangery and the House – it was painted to look like stone.

The Kitchen and Laundry Wing, with its eye-catching circular game larder, was built onto the north-east wing of the house. The roofs were leaking badly and we were afraid dry-rot could come through into the Chinese Room, so as soon as we owned the house, we decided to demolish this wing, leaving the game larder, part of which had been a dovecote. There were no planners in those days, and there is now a very attractive small garden, where not so long ago non-stop activity must have taken place. I have often said 'Whatever we did at Blithfield turned out to be better than expected'.

Now, sixty years later, I am living in a charming ground floor apartment, in rooms once occupied by Sarah and Doreen. The Steward's Room, under the Chinese Room is my sitting room; a small kitchen next door was the Butler's Room; the Still-Room is my bedroom, with a shower room, etc, where fuel for the wood-stove was kept. This was the room where Doreen used to produce delicious meals and where any water needed, hot or cold, came from. The Housekeeper's Room next door, under Lady Bagot's Bedroom, is a guest room (now my writing room), and the china cupboard opposite has become a bathroom, below bathrooms on each of the two floors above. This apartment, made for an agent in 1971, is called The Peacock Flat.

Caryl was Patron of the Living at Church Leigh – land there had belonged to the Bagots through inheritance from the Aston family, but the handsome church replaced an older disintegrating one in the nineteenth century. Caryl's great grandfather paid for the chancel of the new church when he was Bishop of Oxford, as well as Rector of Leigh. The tiles in the chancel by Pugin and given by Mr Minton display the Arms of Oxford and Bagot.

The chancel has recently been restored by the late Mrs Sheila Halden, who loved the church, and has been a very generous benefactress. When she was Churchwarden, she was careful to see any modernisation was carried out in an appropriate manner and to the highest standards.

The Old Rectory at Leigh, when Caryl and I first went there, was owned by Mr and Mrs Prall, who had not only restored the house, but turned it into a comfortable home for present day living, and encouraged us in our belief that we could do the same for the north-east wing at Blithfield. The Old Rectory at Leigh is unusual in being partly surrounded by a dry-moat. As we walked into the churchyard with the Rector, he asked me if I had faith. When I replied 'I hope so', he said 'Hit the trunk of that tree as hard as you can with your hand'. When I did, the bark felt almost like cotton-wool, as it was a huge wellingtonia.

Parish churches relied on a summer fête and a Christmas bazaar to raise funds. Such occasions were also social events. When Caryl and I went to the meeting for our first fête at Blithfield, everyone knew who had which stall. It seemed to me that everything was home made – cakes of course, the main stall for knitted goods, babies/children's coat hangers and household goods. Also, being near to Stoke-on-Trent, one could get china that wasn't up to standard. (They didn't have 'seconds' then, but that is what they were – usually they were free.) There were also plants, flowers, ice-cream and soft drinks. Caryl half-jokingly asked if we were insured against food poisoning. There would be a hoopla stall and a bran-tub for children. Then there would be children's and adults' sports, bowling for a pig, and kagle – which I liked as I couldn't hold the larger balls, and we didn't want a pig.

At Colton, there was always clock golf, which Caryl usually won. The prize was a packet of cigarettes. Our fêtes were mostly held in July, when it often rained. The empty rooms became very useful, because everything could be moved indoors. Excellent home-made teas were much enjoyed.

During November 1946, Caryl wanted to have my portrait painted and on Gerald's niece's advice, we chose Anthony Devas. He lived not far from The Gateways in Carlisle Square, but his studio was at the end of Flood Street in Rossetti Studios, just down the road from The Remembrance Hall, where the Red Cross Office was located. I had recently bought a full-length evening dress – the silk material covered with red poppies – very pretty. Anthony said 'You always ought to wear dresses like that'. I thought him very charming and handsome. He was kept busy stoking the boiler as I had five sittings in November. I was enjoying reading Osbert Sitwell's autobiography, *Left Hand Right Hand*. I thought the old house 'Renishaw', sounded like Blithfield and was telling Anthony how noisy old houses were at night and about Blithfield.

Caryl asked Colin Agnew, who had been valuing the pictures, to look at my picture. Anthony told me he said 'Pity you didn't take as much trouble over the face as you did over that arm'. Caryl said he thought my wrist was rather thin, and Anthony said 'Your wife has got thin wrists'. Anyway it was accepted for the 1947 Royal Academy and placed in Gallery Number I near a portrait of HRH The Princess Elizabeth, by Rodrigo Moynihan, RA, who Colin Agnew suggested should paint my portrait. We thought he was better at painting men.

After the opening, a Sunday newspaper said people were turning away in disappointment from R Moynihan's portrait of Princess Elizabeth to the bright colours of a Devas portrait of Lady Bagot. The bright poppy dress is now in The Potteries Museum with The Bagot Collection.

Although we were spending most of the summer and Christmas at Blithfield, we went back to No 16 The Gateways soon after Christmas, before the long freeze of that winter. I went back to help at the Red Cross Office in The Remembrance Hall in Flood Street. It always made us very cross when people came along and asked what we were doing – 'The war's over you know'. We were busy helping the WVS (as they were then), taking 'meals on wheels' to some of the poorest areas around the World's End, Fulham, etc. People lived in large blocks like the Peabody Buildings and as there was no coal to be had, the poor older people just stayed in bed. I think the meals we brought them were all they had – each meal cost a shilling. Whenever I was on duty, the pudding always seemed to be steam pudding with golden syrup – as it had to be ladled out, it was diffi-cult not to finish the round without being in a sticky condition.

Sarah and Doreen were having a bad time at Blithfield. The pipes bringing water froze so they had to use melted snow to make a cup of tea. They said snow covered the sundial in front of the house. As soon as a cottage in the village of Admaston became vacant they moved into it. We did have an English couple here for a short time, but no English staff would be willing to put up with the living conditions here, as they were then. Caryl and I did for a short time during the early part of one winter. By the time we had done all the chores it was time to light the lamps again.

A number of Polish officers had been living at Alton Towers during the war. We drove up to see them and that was how we heard of Josef and Tamara Pawlowski, a young couple, who had been used as forced labour in Germany during the war. They seemed quite happy to put up with the lack of modern conveniences. Soon Josef's father came here. He had been fighting with General Anders and he was very happy to work as a gardener helping Elsmore, who couldn't use any mechanical tools. Then Josef's mother managed to get here by some circuitous route, and we were very happy to have the whole family here.

When Josef's father was working on the Archery Ground one day, he saw a man sitting on a garden seat. Thinking it was Caryl he went over to talk to him, but when he got there, the seat was empty. He always said he'd seen a ghost!

We were determined to use the front door when guests visited us, although it was as far away as possible from where we were living. Josef's father had managed to get nearly all the oil lamps working and for our first drinks' party, a string of lamps led from the front door to the Green Room, or the Chinese Room as I liked to call it, because of the beautiful Chinese wallpaper.

Electricity came in the late 1940s and might not have come at all, because the electricity board wanted to put the poles through the garden, which was the easiest way for them. But when I said we would continue with lamps and candles if the supply wasn't put outside the garden, they consented. Electricity made a tremendous difference of course. I had most of the old oil lamps converted to use electricity and also we were able to have electric heaters.

Josef and Tamara were splendid coping with all the dust of ages covering everything during the upheaval of having electric wiring put into the part of the house we were using. It was done by a local firm from Uttoxeter. We had been in London and on our return we were met by the head of the firm, who said he had a surprise for us. To our horror there was a large TV in the Gold Room, which much to his surprise we asked him to take away.

Electricity also made a great difference to the church. At the PCC meeting, advertisements for modern electric light fittings were brought out.

Initially, it was thought that the glass shades, hanging from chains, might be utilized. However, after my suggestion that these might need frequent cleaning, my idea of using the wrought iron fittings, which held the oil lamps and could easily be adapted for electricity, was agreed upon.

The Bagot family always sat in the chancel and during the first few years, Caryl paid for its upkeep and we set about giving it some TLC. The brass chandelier, given in memory of the Third Lord Bagot, was repaired, cleaned, lacquered and re-hung. The candlesticks were also cleaned and lacquered. The tombs and memorials in the chancel and vault are all family related and the vestry was built as a memorial chapel by the Second Lord Bagot.

If my cousins were staying here for Harvest Festival, we decorated the Chancel seats with crab apples and Virginia creeper, and at Christmas, holly. I usually put Madonna lilies in the altar vases and I arranged flowers from the garden at other times. I cleaned the brass memorials and polished the oak, and was pleased to see a beautiful piece of sixteenth century Italian silk needlework, given as an altar frontal, in memory of Daisy, an Irish Miss Bagot, who married Edgar Clare Wigan. This altar frontal was expertly repaired by the Royal School of Needlework. There are also two pieces of needlework by the altar, worked in Italian silks by Caryl's mother.

6

The Extended Family

I DIDN'T REALISE WHAT A PRIVILEGED POSITION I WAS IN AT BLITHFIELD. THE
Second World War had meant the end of a pre-war way of life for many
country houses and their estates and it was thought that Blithfield would
go the same way. However, there were still a number of country houses
around us.

The Earl of Harrowby was Lord Lieutenant of the County, and dear
old Lady Harrowby thought I needed mothering – which I did. 'Now dear,
where are you going to put your cutting border?' The whole garden was
completely overgrown. I had never heard of a cutting border – I just made
use of what was here – willow herb, wheat and barley. I heard a visitor at
the first fête here say, about my arrangements in the Great Hall 'Look at
that – weeds!' Then, after the old gardener had cleared all the bracken and
brambles from the formal garden, between the House and Orangery,
there was the question of what to put in the beds. I thought roses. Lady
Harrowby said 'Yes, but what sort of roses? You had better come over to
Sandon and Frances will show you our Rose Garden ...' – which I was very
happy to do and Frances became a good friend. The rose garden here (see
page 156), as it became, started as a 'job lot' from the Kitchen Garden at
Shugborough, they were old-fashioned roses and had a lovely scent.

Lady Harrowby hoped I might follow her as President of the Staffordshire Girl Guides, I think, and asked me to deputise for her at a parade
and meeting to be held at the Town Hall in Walsall. I had never been a
Girl Guide and was quite unprepared, and rather terrified, as I stood on
the podium in front of the Town Hall with Lady Baden-Powell, who was
to take the salute. However, I was still a Commandant in the Chelsea Red

Lord and Lady Bagot with Rob and Roy. Photograph taken in the rose garden for
Staffordshire Life, 1948

Cross, and was thankful for the time I had spent working there during the
war. When I had to say a few words in the Town Hall, I said 'I must
confess, I am not a Girl Guide'. I heard a loud voice in the background
say 'Not yet!' There was so much to be done at Blithfield, I couldn't take
on any other work.

Our nearest neighbours with a large estate were the Wolseleys at
Wolseley Hall, who were kindness itself. Sir Edric and Lady Wolseley's
children were my age; also my Clifford cousins, Monica and Lucy, were
often staying with us. Edric and Clare had tea-parties in the summer
months and invited all their Staffordshire friends to meet us. We met
Lord Lichfield (The Earl of Lichfield, a widower then) and his son,
Viscount Anson (Patrick, the photographer's father).

The Cavenagh-Mainwarings became special friends – Rosemary, Rafe's
wife, came from South Australia. They lived further away at Whitmore
near Newcastle-under-Lyme, but we met them at Wolseley. Later on
Rosemary's daughter-in-law asked me to be godmother to her daughter,
Tara – Rosemary's granddaughter.

Lady Wolseley, Frances Wolseley, Monica Clifford and her sister Lucy Clifford

Dyonese Haszard, who inherited the Levett Estate when her brother was killed in the First World War, descended from a Bagot/Levett marriage, a daughter of The Reverend Walter Bagot married a Levett. Dyonese was a charming lady, artistic and knowledgeable about Levett and Bagot history. She gave me a copy of Anne Bagot's Diaries and some very finely cut-out pictures of goats in Bagot's Park.

The Wolseleys introduced us to Mrs Fitzherbert, who was living at Swynnerton Hall with her eldest son, Basil, who was Lord Stafford, and his brother, Evelyn (sadly killed fighting in Egypt) and a half-brother, Lord Brougham. They also introduced us to Paddy and Mary Wenger, who took us to a fancy dress party at a moated manor house, Birtsmoreton Court, near Ledbury. The owner of Birtsmoreton Court, Mr Bradley Birt, had a party on 26 December each year. My cousin, Lucy Clifford, Margot Bagot and Marcia Russell were staying with us for Christmas and we were all invited. Luckily, Caryl and I had discovered a large walnut chest full of clothes that had belonged to previous genera-tions of Bagots, so we were able to provide costumes for everyone. Caryl wore Sir Walter Wagstaffe Bagot's magnificent eighteenth-century suit, which consisted of a canary yellow waistcoat and mulberry coloured coat, embroidered with silver, which made it rather heavy. His breeches were

Margot Bagot and Lucy
Clifford, two Australians

Nancy wearing Sir Walter
Wagstaffe Bagot's suit

mulberry coloured and he wore an original wig and black shoes with red heels. On top of it all he put on a duffle coat, recently bought from a wartime utility store. As he never stopped smoking and the wig seemed to be getting in the way, I was afraid he might set himself on fire! I just wore a full-skirted, duck egg green evening dress, but took the hooped part of a crinoline to put on under my skirt on arrival.

Lucy wore a high-waisted Regency dress, with large puff sleeves. Marcia wore the green and gold Russian fancy dress, which had won a prize for me at the Battle of Flowers in Nice almost ten years previously. It suited her especially, as she had long fair plaits. Basil Stafford and Evelyn wore Staffordshire Yeomanry uniforms that had belonged to the Third Lord Bagot. Lord Brougham wore a top coat, with many capes and a top hat that had belonged to the Second Lord, and called himself a 'Highway Man'. Mary Wenger had her own fancy dress, but Paddy, with his Oriental looks fitted perfectly into a Turkish costume and fez, brought back from Constantinople by Sir Charles Bagot. Mary said 'Mr Bradley Birt will hide all his carpets when he sees Paddy coming'.

We went in a taxi from Abbots Bromley, and had some difficulty finding the place. I think Mr Bradley Birt was quite pleased if people found Birtsmoreton Court hard to find. He said 'Did you come through Upton-on-Severn?' One of his guests had answered 'Yes, several times'. We arrived eventually, the Staffordshire Yeomanry officers rather muddy, through having to get out and look for signs, but the short drive, to the bridge over the moat, was lit with flares and with the old half-timbered house reflected in the moat. It was all most romantic. Mr Bradley Birt had worked in the Indian Civil Service, so he had a number of animal skins on the floors. They all seemed to have heads with open mouths – one had to be careful not to trip over them. At 12 o'clock a boar's head was brought in and the old carol sung 'The boar's head in hand bear I, bedecked with bay and rosemary'. We were very tired when we got home about 3.30 am, but we enjoyed Mr Bradley Birt's party for two or three years, and stayed with him once in the summer. Staying in a moated house is almost like being in a ship.

The Twenty-second Earl of Shrewsbury and his wife, with her sister and brother, and their combined families, were living at Ingestre, where

John looked after an estate famous for its expertly run farms. Everything at Ingestre seemed to have been kept in pre-war order. I had heard that Nadine, John Shrewsbury's wife, a Miss Crofton-Atkins, had lived in Devon before she married and that they met on John's twenty-first birthday. The family occupied all the Hall during the war. They were very kind and hospitable, but to go to Ingestre from Blithfield seemed like another world. By the time we started to entertain we did have a bathroom, although the water still came from the old Water Tower in the Grove. No wonder Australians, who stayed at Blithfield, say they will never forget it, especially if we went to Ingestre to see a Victorian Christmas tree lit with real candles. But Ingestre didn't have a peaceful atmosphere! Nadine didn't seem to be still for a minute – one felt it was necessary to be careful what one said. Nadine, who was a practised singer, and an excellent speaker, was inclined to keep asking me to do things for her. 'Oh Nancy, I can't take the chair at such and such a meeting, you'll do it for me won't you?' 'I'm sorry, no, I have never taken a meeting in my life'. 'Don't be silly, of course you can'. Or just before a garden fête at Ingestre, 'Nancy, Tommy Handley can't come and open our Conservative Fête, you'll come won't you?' That was when I realised I would have to go to the Abbey School for Speakers in Westminster and learn to make speeches and take chairs!

It was at the Ingestre fête, after I had 'opened' it, and had been given a lovely bouquet of flowers by the youngest of one of Nadine's pretty daughters, I was encouraged by dear Mrs Mardell, widow of the old butler. She had brought along a number of supporters from our little village of Admaston, which is near the front gates. Mrs Mardell's mother, who used to keep the Post Office in the village said, 'Now there is a Lady at the Hall, Blithfield will be like it used to be'.

Most country villages had a church and each one usually had a summer fête and a Christmas bazaar in order to raise money for the parish. Openers for fêtes and bazaars were much in demand. To begin with, I could hardly manage to utter a word when making a speech, but after attending The Abbey School for Speakers in Westminster, I felt much more confident. We were taught to learn what we would say at the beginning and the end, write it on a card, then write headings for what we

First fête at Blithfield, 1948.
Revd Goodin, Mr Shipley,
Mrs Goodin, Mrs Spicer,
Lady Bagot, Mr Smith, Lady
Brooke and Lord Bagot

wanted to say and string the cards together with a 'boot lace'.

At a fête, the 'opener', if a woman, would be expected to wear a hat and gloves. The incumbent would introduce her and one would hope he wouldn't take the opportunity to list all the things the money raised was to be used for, as that was sure to be what you hoped to say. Then you would thank everyone for their hard work and congratulate them on how well they looked after their church and churchyard, commenting on their history and architecture perhaps. Not too long or there wouldn't be a cake left on the home-made cakes stall. It was usually a happy, friendly occasion, if it didn't rain.

In those days, not long after the war, I wore a hat and gloves when going out for lunch and a long evening dress when going out for dinner, and always went into a room in order of precedence on formal occasions.

We met a number of very nice neighbours at the Ingestre fête. Mr and Mrs Stafford Northcote had a Boys' Preparatory School at Bishton Hall, where a friend of Gerald's used to live, nearer to us than Wolseley. Dear Ben Stafford Northcote looked after us and saw we got some tea. Colonel and Mrs Guy German were good neighbours too, and Guy was a great help to me later.

It was after our first summer at Blithfield, when we were in London

1950 fête at Ingestre. Lady Bagot, above, receiving a bouquet after the opening and with Mrs Lily Atherley, right

during the winter, that I went to Mrs Mears' Abbey School for Speakers at Westminster. I was feeling rather nervous and was the only woman. The others were ex-servicemen, wanting to get into politics. After the preliminaries, we were asked to stand-up, one at a time, and speak for three minutes. Seeing how nervous some of the men were who spoke before me, I felt better, and when my turn came I pretended I was opening a fête. It was very good training and I was also taught how to chair a meeting.

Neighbours nearer to Derbyshire, related through marriage, were the Meynells of Hoar Cross. I was especially fond of Lady Dorothy Meynell, a sister of the Earl of Dartmouth. Although she often stayed at Hoar Cross, I liked to think of her in her charming little Georgian house in Maids of Honour Row, Richmond.

The Chandos-Poles lived in Derbyshire, at Radburne Hall. Gerald Bagot's mother had been a Chandos-Pole, and Gerald had been born at Kirk Langley. Aunt Eleanor had been Caryl's aunt, who he remembered fondly, and Wakey's great aunt.

Shortly after the war Jill and Wakey were struggling with Radburne near Derby. They were able to live in a Victorian wing quite comfortably, but

Fête at Colton, 1953. Mr and Mrs Betson, Mrs Goodin, Lady Bagot, Lord Bagot

the main eighteenth-century hall was not comfortable to live in until after it had been modernised and decorated by John Fowler in the late 1950s.

Caryl and I stayed in the Victorian wing for a Hunt Ball, which was held at Keddleston. It was bright, crisp, snowy weather and very cold. We were quite a large party, so dinner was in the Main Hall, where the only heating was a large fire. We all wore coats, and Wakey's uncle, Guy Sitwell, just returned from Russia, wore an Astrakhan hat. Keddleston made a very splendid setting – much too grand for present day Hunt Balls. The Ladies Cloakroom was in the State Bedroom and Jill found two girls jumping up and down on the State Bed as if it was a trampoline. There was quite a scrum in the Lower Hall waiting for carriages and I heard Wakey's uncle, Guy Sitwell, say 'I do not like ze English, zay are so rude'. However, he got his car before Wakey's car and Evans, the driver, came for Caryl and me. Wakey, thinking Guy would come next and pick him up, tucked us in solicitously and waved us off. Next morning, at breakfast, Wakey, having walked home in soft crisp snow, was much the brightest.

He told us he had telephoned Jill, who thought he was putting the dog out, and by then everyone had gone to bed. His hostess, Tilla Scarsdale, was walking around picking up cigarette ends, obviously anxious to get rid of the last guest, so Wakey set off and having hunted on both estates enjoyed the moonlight walk.

One of my grandmother's Stericker relations, who like my grandfather had been living in Australia, came back to live in England after the Second World War, with his Australian wife. Charles and Kit bought what had been the Dairy of Painshill House outside Cobham. They turned this one-storey 'round house' into the most enchanting place and now, of course, Charles Hamilton's wonderful garden has been restored.

Caryl and I were staying with Kit at the Round House, when we heard our friends, Sir John and Lady Wedgwood were staying at Leith Hill Place, Dorking, Surrey, so we drove over to see them and joined a party of visitors. John made us stay behind and opened a bottle of Champagne to celebrate our first visit. I had introduced them to Jill and Wakey at a dinner party here. They were interested to hear there was a Darwin magnolia at Radburne, planted to mark Erasmus Darwin's marriage with a widowed Mrs Chandos-Pole.

Caryl and I, from time to time, were invited to Sunday lunch at the farm house of our closest Derbyshire neighbours at Doveridge, Sir William and Lady Feilden. Billy always made a point of telling me how brave the Australians were at Gallipoli, which I appreciated as one of my mother's cousins had been shot down on the beach. He said that when he was at a meet of the Meynell Hunt at Blithfield, Sir Harold Nutting said, 'What more could a man want than Blithfield, and to hunt with the Meynell?'

Our first visit to Chillington, the Giffard's ancestral home, took us some time to find. I always did all the driving so I expected Caryl to do the map reading. One of the few things he told me about his time on the western front in the First World War, was that he never knew where he was – certainly, he could never re-fold a map! When we drove into Wolverhampton, I stopped by a man in the street so that Caryl could ask him how to get to Chillington. He hadn't heard of it, so we went on like this for a while. Caryl always said he liked to talk to people 'face to face' – in fact he hated talking on the telephone. We got to Chillington eventually, and I have since enjoyed very many happy visits there.

Apart from Caryl's sisters, who lived in Devon, Olave, Lady Brooke, his first cousin, who lived in London, was the first member of his family I was taken to visit. She was very charming and friendly and when we returned to England from Australia, in 1942, during the war, she was like a surrogate mother to me and a great support to Caryl.

The Copelands were very kind to us and invited us to their China Works in Stoke-on-Trent. We were driven there by Ida (Mrs Copeland), through Hilderstone and over moorland, Rough Close Common. Ida drove as if she were riding to hounds and pointing out places of interest, just like the Frenchman who drove my mother, my school-friend and me along the upper Corniche road from Monte Carlo. I prefer not to look if the driver seems more interested in the view than the road! Both drives were rather frightening, but the China Works was fascinating. We saw men balancing long wooden boards on their heads, and on the boards were unfired pieces of pottery being taken to the bottle-ovens to be fired. The clay objects had to be packed into fairly large oval pottery containers, called saggars, before being put into the oven. We were shown everything except where Gresham Copeland made the glaze. The glaze formula was a secret.

After working, often for generations, making beautiful things, these people seemed to be especially artistic. When we saw a china tea-set being painted with various flowers, we were told an artist went to Mrs Copeland's family home in Cornwall to sketch and paint flowers in the beautiful gardens at Trelissick, now owned by The National Trust.

In the early 1950s, every piece of decorated china had to go to America, to help pay off the war-debt. Only plain china could be sold in this country, so I was simply delighted when Ronald asked if I would like a tea-set decorated with flowers painted in the garden at Trelissick. The set was called London Stone. It was packed in straw and wood-shavings, in a large wooden barrel, and sent to our little house in Chelsea, No 16 The Gateways. At lunch-time, we sat with Ronald and other members of the Copeland firm around a large table. I thought the round china dumb-waiter, laden with vegetables in the middle of the table, practical as well as decorative. After lunch we were taken to the Museum on the top floor of the building, where we saw amazingly beautiful pieces, now in the

Trelissick Mansion near Truro.

Caryl and I were asked to spend a weekend at Trelissick in the spring of 1950 – a perfect time for the garden, especially for the part of the garden called Primavera. We were shown a home movie one evening, with some of Ida Copeland's Italian relatives ballet dancing in the Primavera Garden.

I always liked the Potteries people – they were so pleasant and friendly, rather like Australians. When we were having dinner with Ronald and Ida at their house called High Chase in Little Haywood, before going to a dance, Ida said she hoped we didn't mind going out with 'Potteries people'. I was surprised and rather embarrassed. Ida was MP for Stoke-on-Trent at one time and such a dear, kind person, as was Ronald. One of the nicest compliments ever paid to me was when Ida said to Caryl, 'She's such a homemaker, isn't she?'

Caryl's cousin, Olave Cunninghame Graham, married Sir Basil Brooke, an Admiral in the First World War and ADC to the Duke of York, later to King George VI and Treasurer to the Queen. Olave and Basil were friends of Lord and Lady Vernon, so when dearest Olave came to stay at Blithfield, as she did each year, I drove her over to Sudbury to have tea with her friend, Lady Vernon – both widows by then. Basil and Olave were great friends of Sir Howard and Lady Kerr, who were living in the Dower House in the town of Melbourne, Derbyshire. Howard was Comptroller to Henry, Duke of Gloucester and had been with him when he was Governor General of Australia. We had lunch with Howard and his wife, Christina, on the day Staunton Harold was opened as a Leonard Cheshire Home. Howard had to use all his diplomatic skills, plus a good deal of port, to persuade two celebrities to jointly perform the 'opening ceremony'. One had been asked, but had another appointment, so another was asked and accepted, then the first celebrity said he could do it. Howard's sister, Marie Kerr, who owned Melbourne Hall, was preparing to open it to visitors, so she had made a Drawing Room and a Dining Room in what had been Staff Quarters. The Dining Room had a small balcony and Howard suggested it would be ideal for a dwarf violinist. We went to many delightful entertainments at Melbourne, one of the most memorable to celebrate the restoration of the beautiful wrought iron Gazebo by Robert Bakewell of Derbyshire, called the 'Bird Cage' in the eighteenth-century garden, which was in the style of Le Notre. Marie kindly invited us all to luncheon, when Robin and Annette Bagot from Levens were staying with us. Melbourne, an ancient home, feels welcoming, friendly and delightful – like its family.

I much enjoyed the friendship of a daughter of close friends of Marie. Her parents had died young and Marie had given Jo Dorehill a flat in the attic at Melbourne, which gave me the idea of making a flat for my daughter Cara in the attic here many years later.

On one memorable occasion, I had been invited to dinner by Marie about ten years after Caryl's death, when she had a friend from Sydney staying. He and I were the only two guests who didn't play bridge, so we sat talking until after 12 o'clock, when the others were ready to leave. A friend and I, who lived near Burton-on-Trent, through which I had to pass, had agreed to drive in convoy as far as possible. We got into our cars and started them up, but they wouldn't move. Then we noticed they each had a flat tyre. My friend Steve Anson, who lived at Catton, got a lift home, but because Blithfield was much further away, I had to stay the night and wait for my tyres to be made safe. They had been punctured by a dart, presumably by youths from the town. The event might have had very unpleasant consequences if my tyres had gone down when I was only half way home. Another guest, who had left earlier, knew nothing about it until he found his car with flat tyres in the garage next morning. There wasn't a sound from Marie's beautiful dalmatians!

We were able to invite friends to a unique entertainment – the Abbots Bromley Horn Dance. The reindeer horns, which have been carbon tested and dated to the eleventh century, are kept in the church at Abbots Bromley, in the care of the Vicar. Every year, after a short service about 8.30 am, the dance begins, visiting various places by tradition, usually arriving at Blithfield between midday and 1 o'clock. The first time we saw the dance, Caryl and I were waiting to welcome the Horn Dancers to Blithfield early in September 1946. The morning was misty with a promise of sun later. We heard a rhythmic sound of metal being tapped and then we saw the tops of reindeer horns appearing from the mist in the valley. The Horn Dancers had walked across the Park, carrying the horns on their shoulders, and crossed the Blythe at Blithfield Mill. There was no reservoir then. No one had come to see them, like the crowds that come nowadays. The ancient dance was a serious occasion – it felt as if we were back in another age. Jim Fowell, the leader, carried the heaviest horns. There are six horns, three brown and three white, and during the dance they move forwards towards each other as though attacking and then back, and then weave in and out. The hobby horse comes next, snapping his jaws, followed by the bow and arrow. Afterwards comes the man (dressed as a woman and called Maid Marion), followed by the fool (jester), and then the boy with a triangle, who we heard first.

During the first two or three years we were at Blithfield, I could see the dancers needed new clothes, which I was very happy to get for them, and again, years later, when the dancers needed new clothes, this time the many friends, who had been coming each year to see the dance, helped to pay for them.

My friend, Sheila Wroughton, arranged for the Derby University Textile Department to weave the material for the breeches with the old pattern of oak apples and leaves. We are immensely proud that this ancient dance comes to Blithfield each September, on the first Monday, after the first Sunday after 4 September. More and more people from many parts of the world come to see it.[1]

Note

1 If you wish to know more about the Abbots Bromley Horn Dance, Jack Brown has written a booklet, which is available from The Cottage, Colton, Rugeley, Staffordshire, WS15 3LA, England.

7

The Coronation

▼

KING GEORGE VI AND QUEEN ELIZABETH WERE MUCH BELOVED, NOT only did they take over when Edward VIII left the country, but they didn't desert their people during the war. When our King died it was a real loss to his country and it felt like a personal loss, especially to all who had been with him and the Queen and his family in London during the war. All the shop windows I saw were draped in mourning. We didn't go to the funeral but listened to the very moving scene on our radio.

Olave Brooke had taken Caryl, her daughter-in-law and me to a Buckingham Palace Garden Party to be presented. I remember Princess Elizabeth saying to Olave 'I don't think you've met my Philip yet'. Her engagement had recently been announced. Another year, as I had been presented, I was able to present my cousin, Lucy Clifford. Lucy always found it impossible to keep any sort of time. She had been to the hairdresser in the morning, and when we were almost ready to leave, to my horror I found she was washing her hair. We must have managed to get there because the first person we met was the daughter of the Presbyterian Minister in Wahroonga.

Caryl and I met the Wigans through Gerald's niece, Arden – Cecily or Daisy, as family and friends called her, was an Irish Bagot, a cousin of Walter Bagot in Adelaide, she and her elder sister had married two Wigan brothers. Daisy's husband, Edgar Clare, known as Jimmy, was the same age as Caryl, but he lived to be 103. He was to become a godfather to Caryl's and my adopted daughter, and both Daisy and Jimmy became very dear friends. In the spring of 1952, we had decided to join them for a holiday in Cyprus. We couldn't leave at the same time and were to meet at Athens airport. We flew via Nice and Rome and spent a few days in Athens, arriving at the airport. The Acropolis, flood lit for the first time

Lady Brooke, Lord Bagot's cousin. Widow of Admiral Sir Basil Brooke, Comptroller to the Duke of York and Treasurer to the Queen. Later GVCO, and ADC to King George VI

since the war, seemed to be floating in the air. As we drove to the King George Hotel, the taxi-driver told us that most of the tarmac roads had been paid for by wealthy Greek ship-owners, and as we walked about the city during the next few days, Athens seemed more like a large country town. Opposite the hotel we were treated to a display by the Royal Guard (known as the Evzones) in front of what had been the Royal Palace, more like a ballet, both in uniform and marching steps. It was our first visit to Athens and we made the most of our time visiting the Acropolis and Athens Museum.

We met Daisy and Jimmy at the airport, but Daisy didn't seem to be talking to Jimmy; apparently Jimmy had collected all their luggage and put it behind Daisy, who had stepped back and fallen onto it, which wouldn't have been so bad had she not recently been vaccinated for smallpox, as I had. When we got into the little plane taking us to the northern part of Cyprus, Jimmy was told to go and sit up in the front and Daisy sat with us – he didn't seem to mind!

We stayed at The Dome Hotel, Kyrenia, which was full of English people. Sir Philip Brocklehurst, from Swythamley Park in North Stafford-shire was there on honeymoon with his second wife. They said they wanted to tour Cyprus on donkeys. Many of the pretty little cottages in the town were owned by English people and there was an English Club by the old castle on the coast. Further inland the real wizard's castle in the mountains, used by Walt Disney as the setting for the residence of Snow

Lady Brooke presented Nancy and her daughter-in-law Bunty to the King and Queen at the first garden party after the war

Nancy was then able to present her cousin Miss Lucy Clifford a few years later

White's wicked stepmother, had been home to Berengaria, wife of King Richard I, Coeur de Lion.

The Troodos mountains were beautiful and full of wild cyclamen – the sudden glimpses of the blue blue sea reminded us that we were on an island in the Mediterranean. One day we went to a deserted beach and saw a small boy playing a pipe – I couldn't help looking to see if he had cloven hooves.

We had decided to return by sea and land, so caught an Italian ship, sailing for Venice, which meant sailing through the Corinth Canal – so narrow it felt as if you could touch the land on either side. There was quite thick fog in the Adriatic and whenever the fog horn blew, if the Captain happened to be sitting in the Saloon with us, he would raise his hands and eyes in a despairing gesture, which was anything but reassuring. It made us wonder if anyone was on the Bridge! Thankfully the fog cleared before we reached Venice. There is nothing quite like entering Venice by sea in the spring, the atmosphere is what I call 'Mother of Pearl'. Soon we were in a gondola gliding into the entrance of the famous Danieli Hotel, and that evening we dined on the rooftop, eating our favourite Italian meal – scampi – and then zabaione.

We travelled by train to London, where we met Walter Bagot and his younger daughter, Betty. They had recently arrived from Adelaide. Walter, a cousin of Daisy's, was of the Nurney Irish branch of the family. As a leading architect, he had been asked to build a house in Adelaide and to take the Grand Staircase and linen-fold panelling from the Tudor house, Beaudesert on Cannock Chase in Staffordshire, which had been built by the Paget family and had been their main home since the time of Henry VIII. The head of the family, The Marquess of Anglesey, decided to demolish Beaudesert in the mid-1930s and live in the house they owned, Plas Newydd, on the Isle of Anglesey, so this staircase and panelling can now be admired in a very different climate.

During this summer of 1952, I had a very kind letter from the Dowager Lady Bagot, Lily, asking if I would like to have her Coronation robes, which she had worn to the Coronation of King George VI and Queen Elizabeth. I told her I would love to have them, and we met for lunch at a rather gloomy hotel in Welbeck Street. Caryl and I had not met Lily, who before her marriage in 1903 to the Fourth Lord, 'Billy', was Lilian Marie, daughter of the late Henry May of Maryland, USA. However, the marriage hadn't lasted and they separated after a year or two. Lily was tall and good looking – she gave me a photograph of herself wearing the Coronation robes. She said to me 'You are so lucky to have such a nice husband' (with which I heartily agreed); 'when I wanted new curtains for the Drawing Room at Blithfield, my husband told me that these curtains were good enough for his mother, so they are good enough for me'. Lily lived in Hove with a companion and we never saw her again. I know she was a friend of King Edward VII, who I believe tried to mend the marriage. As a Roman Catholic she wouldn't contemplate a divorce.

Jill Chandos-Pole's baby daughter was born towards the end of November in 1952, and she asked me to be a godmother, also my Australian friend, Paddy Love had had a little daughter. We went by train to see Paddy and her baby in hospital. Poor Caryl, I cried all the way home. I had been going to see doctors and gynaecologists, but somehow felt that I wasn't going to be able to have any children and was so upset I couldn't bear to speak about it. I did have an early miscarriage, and darling Caryl went out and bought me a beautiful singing bird box I had admired in a jewellery shop in Bond Street.

At the beginning of 1953, Coronation year, Peers were told they would have to ballot for a seat in Westminster Abbey and we weren't lucky, but we would be able to have tickets for seats in the Peers' Stand, close to the entrance to The Abbey. Then later we were told we could have two seats in The Abbey, as some Peers preferred to sit in the Stand with their families. My gynaecologist, Doctor Sara Field-Richards, said it was my compensation prize.

Lily Bagot had given me the name of her Polish dressmaker, so I set about finding her and asking her to alter the lace slip to go under the kirtle. The train hooks onto the back of the kirtle. Mrs Kulczycki had trained under Hartnell and from then for many years, she made nearly all my clothes. Quite a lot are now in the Bagot Collection in The Potteries Museum, including our Coronation robes, some jewellery and the singing bird box. Caryl didn't need to worry about his robes, they were here, in immaculate condition, having been made for the Second Lord Bagot from

Lord Bagot in Coronation robe

silk velvet and real ermine.

There was one other Australian Peeress in The Abbey, who I didn't know – Lady Gifford. When Caryl and I reached The Abbey, as I walked towards the chancel, feeling as if I was in a dream, I realised Caryl, walking on my right, slightly behind me, was doing the Guards' Slow March. I wrote a descriptive letter to my mother about the Coronation and can't do better than include it here.

Blithfield,
24 June, 1953
My Dearest Mummy,

I have made several attempts to write this letter and hope I shall be successful this time. Since the Coronation there hardly seems to have been time to breathe. We went to cocktail parties and gave one ourselves, went to the Derby, Trooping the Colour, and the Antique Dealers' Fair, then to Portsmouth for the Naval Review, which we saw from the aircraft carrier <u>Perseus</u>; thank goodness it didn't rain for once, although it was very cold. Next to us was Sydney, looking very smart, but the Italian Training ship, a replica of Nelson's Victory, looked lovely, and it was thrilling to see her manned, the sailors standing on the yardarms. Unfortunately, we couldn't stay on board for the illuminations and fireworks at night; however, we were very glad to reach home about midnight, as we wanted to go to Ascot next day. Again, spoilt by rain, but we enjoyed it. Drove here, last Saturday, and were delighted to find the drive finished, one simply floats over it now, and the reservoir looks fuller than ever.

Thank you so much for your 'Coronation Flight' letter, Mummy dear, which I shall keep, and for yours and Lu's airletters.

I'm so glad you heard all the Service so well, wasn't it exciting? London before the Coronation felt, I thought, just as it did before V.E. day. Lots of people had said they intended to keep well away from London until it was back to normal; what a lot they missed! London was the centre of the world.

About a week before the Coronation the ugly wood and tubular steel stands were rapidly being painted, and decorated; all along the route buildings and streets were being transformed. Everywhere private houses became gay, with flags and decorations. But often, the gayest of all would be some little back street, in a poorer part of London, which the Queen would not even see.

The general theme of the decorations was of a Medieval Tournament, bright colours, Coats of Arms and gay flags and pennants. The stands in Parliament Square, especially, gave this impression, with their lovely azure blue, upswept awnings. Berkeley Square looked delightfully pastoral, decorated with deep rose-pink garlands. There were even nightingales in cages and no-one can now say they haven't heard a nightingale sing in Berkeley Square because mechanical nightingales sang all day, and all night too, I expect! Eros looks much better in his golden cage, but the large pink Tudor roses, decorating Regent Street, weren't very inspiring. Whitehall could perhaps have done with more of the cleverly decorated standards, topped with models of Life Guards cuirass and plumed helmet. The Mall, spanned by graceful arches, decorated with the Royal Coat of Arms and crowns, is lovely and, when lit at night, looked indeed a triumphal way for a fairy queen. No wonder it was thronged with people every night. After the heat of the previous week Coronation Day dawned cold and grey; my heart sank when I looked out of the window at about 4.30 a.m. The poor people who had been camping on the pavements all night, and in some cases for two nights, must have had a miserable time, but no-one seemed to mind. My hairdresser told me she was at Hyde Park Corner; she said she and her friends played cards all night and kept the cold out with brandy, and that she wouldn't have missed it for anything. However, there was no time to worry about the weather, as I had to have breakfast ready for four by 5 a.m. Luckily, when the car arrived to take us to The Abbey it was fine, although there was another heavy shower as we drove along the embankment, in slowly moving lines of cars. Occasionally one caught glimpses of brightly-coloured uniforms or velvet robes. Everyone looked serious and purposeful, obviously concentrating on getting to their seats in good time!

We were deposited at about 7.15 a.m. at the Peers' Entrance, next to the Royal Entrance, and at the side of the newly-built annexe. Rover scouts helped us out, and I noticed the high Government stand opposite, a sea of faces.

Just inside the annexe was a wide passage, where peers and peer-esses were waiting before walking through the Abbey to their seats. On the left of the passage was a cloakroom, for peeresses, large looking glasses lining the walls, so there was no excuse for a crooked tiara or a train not properly hooked on. The annexe was lit by an enormous pinkish glass window, filling the whole of the end wall space, and carpeted with blue. It looked bare and empty then, but must have been crowded and colourful enough later, when the Royal Processions started to form up.

A Gold Staff Officer took charge of us, and we stepped through the Great West Door of the Abbey. It was an Abbey transformed and almost unrecognisable, more like some magnificent theatre – ahead stretched the new blue carpet and on either side tiers of seats rose to the vaulted roof – the only place where one seemed to notice the familiar grey stone. These seats, already filled, were draped in front with rich delphinium blue and silver brocade, patterned with wreaths of oak leaves and, in the centre of the wreath, a rose thistle, shamrock or leek and the whole surmounted by a crown. The more subdued colours of the Nave accentuated the glowing colours of the Chancel. How wonderful the first glimpse of the Chancel was! After passing through the Choir, we mounted the gold-carpeted steps to the 'Theatre'. Here for the moment everything seemed to be gold. The gold carpet stretched right up to the gold and white altar cloth, and on the altar the wonderful gold plate glowed in the soft light of candles – then one's eyes were caught by another magnificent array of gold plate on the long grey flat-topped tomb directly below the Royal Gallery. Gold brocade draped the fronts of the tiers of seats here but the colour scheme returned to blue again in the Transept. In the middle of the Theatre or space between the two Transepts, on raised steps, stood the elegant gilded Throne, upholstered with a deep rose-red brocade and decorated with the Royal Coat of Arms, embroidered back and front. It could only have been meant for a Queen. Beyond this Throne in the centre of the Chancel and just in front of the High Altar stood the historic Coronation Chair. The Peers sat in the South Transept and the Peeresses in the North. The chairs, raised so that everyone could see over those in front, were covered with blue velvet and decorated with E.II.R. in gold. We are delighted we can buy them. They should look very well on the Great Stairs. In front of the Peers' seats stood three large crimson-covered chairs for the Royal Dukes. As the seats in the Transepts filled, so the colour scheme changed from blue to crimson and white; the effect of all that soft rich crimson velvet and white ermine (or perhaps I should say white fur) massed together was very striking – what a pity the robes must be kept only for Coronations! The Peeresses especially, sparkling with the most wonderful jewellery I have ever seen, and all wearing long white gloves, were an enchanting sight. I wished I was a Peer and could look at them instead of at the Peers! Caryl said, when the sun shone on the Peeresses at one moment during the Service the whole of the North Transept blazed with diamonds.

A pity it did not make us feel a little warmer! But there was a bitterly cold draft and the long velvet trains were soon being used as cloaks. I was kept busy putting my neighbours' trains around their shoulders.

We all sat in order of precedence. I was no. 245. Lady Hawke was on my left, Lady Suffield on my right, with Lady Kenyon beyond. They all had very old heirloom robes, lovely silk velvet and real ermine, but they were terrified of their splitting! There was nowhere to put anything, except on the floor at one's feet, and I was very nervous in case I kicked my coronet, and it rolled down under the chairs in front.

On every chair was a large card with the name of the occupant, and two books, one the Order of Service, and the other containing the names of all the people in the various processions. I've sent you one of the latter but Caryl left his Order of Service book behind, he said it fell under his chair, and he couldn't bend to pick it up, as his coronet was too big and kept falling off! We both took Horlicks Malted Milk Tablets, and Caryl put his into a special pocket he'd had made inside his robe, but the robe is so voluminous and the space to manoeuvre so small he was never able to find his pocket again. After hearing stories of the discomfort of sitting next to a man wearing his sword and spurs I was thankful peers and peeresses were separated. Although we were in the Abbey from soon after 7 a.m. until about 3 p.m., when we walked across to the House of Lords under a covered awning, for lunch, it didn't really seem a long time, everything was so entrancing, and I felt quite sad when it was over. Then I realised I was tired, cold and hungry.

But I was so glad we'd arrived in good time, it was such fun watching the others arrive. Lady Hawke on my left, such a sweet person, looks very young to be the mother of six children, all daughters! Lady Suffield and Lady Kenyon, both quite young, were saying what a strain the long wait would be for smokers, and Lady K. turned to Lady S. and said 'Do you smoke?' An oldish person, sitting in front, turned and looked at us in horror: 'You're not going to smoke here, surely!' she said. We reassured her, but later on, I had great difficulty trying to stop laughing when her coronet would slide about on her head in the most alarming manner every time she moved. Once or twice she only just managed to save it. However, she was not the only one, by any means, who was having coronet-trouble. They are awfully difficult to fix on securely; they fit behind the tiara, and some hook theirs onto the tiara. Some had long pins, but they were obviously meant for the days of long hair, piled on top. My hairdresser advised me to sew a small hair comb in the front of my coronet, and I pushed it into my hair as I put it on. Husband-spotting seemed to be one of the main amusements, and a conversation rather like this went on behind me: 'I think I can see my husband, he has a very round face', and someone else said 'I should be able to see mine, he has a bald head which shines.'

One of the youngest peeresses must have been Lady Stafford, whose wedding we went to last Summer; she sat just in front of me. Nadine Shrewsbury, wearing her beautiful diamond necklace and tiara, was one of the last to arrive, and we heard afterwards that, when their coach reached Whitehall the horses refused to face the crowd, and they had to go on by car to the Abbey. I also saw Tilla Scarsdale, Lady Lothian, and the young Duchess of Devonshire, who must have been very proud of her son, playing his part as Page to his grandmother (Mistress of the Robes) so beautifully.

From my seat I looked down on the Throne, but could only see a little of the Royal Gallery and the back of the Coronation Chair. However, I could see the processions coming up through the choir stalls, and the Queen of Tonga sitting there, eyes alight with interest and excitement. She wore a rose-pink robe, and a headdress looking rather like two tall knitting needles with a pink feather between; it made her appear to be about 10ft. tall. Someone told me the carriage she rode in had to be strengthened, as she weighs over 20 stone! The poor little Sultan, riding in the carriage with her, was quite overwhelmed, and obviously longed to put the hood up, to protect himself from the rain and cold.

Caryl, from his side, also looked directly down onto the Throne, he could see the Coronation Chair well and almost up to the High Altar. Dorothy Meynell (Lady-in-Waiting to the Duchess of Gloucester) told me she was behind a pillar, and could see nothing, but everyone agreed it was so wonderful to be in the Abbey, actually taking part in the service, it didn't really matter whether one saw it or not. There can be comparatively few in the Abbey who saw everything in such detail as did those watching on television, and it must have given millions of people a completely new idea of the true meaning of the Coronation. Cameras and microphones were well camouflaged. I did not see the sign of a camera, and only noticed two small microphones under the front leg of the Throne and one (I think) on the back of the Coronation Chair. It seemed we had not been waiting long before members of the Royal Family started to arrive. The Duke of Edinburgh's mother in a complete contrast to all the richness and colour, in her soft grey Sister of Mercy habit. The Princess Royal so dignified and the charming Duchess of Gloucester with her two boys in kilts walking one on either side. Then the Duchess of Kent with the young Duke and Princess Alexandra, both the latter looking a little self-conscious. Princess Margaret – her deportment faultless – looked lovely in her shining white dress. And last, but most gracious and captivating in her manner, the Queen Mother. The train-bearers managed the long purple trains beautifully, folding them as yards of material are folded in shops. Then putting the folded train over the owner's arm, and with a graceful curtsey going to their seats. Poor old Princess Marie Louise, however, became very flurried, snatched her train from the train-bearers before the latter had time to fold it and bundling it over her arm started up the stairs to the Royal Gallery, train dragging behind. Then to the intense surprise of everyone, while we were waiting for the Queen's procession, what should appear but four women in white overalls with brooms and carpet-sweepers, who proceeded to sweep the gold carpet round the Throne – the carpet did not look to be in need of a sweep, and would, I think, have been much better left alone. However, all was now ready for the Queen's procession, which was heralded by the harsh, rather eastern sound of the trumpets and the boys' voices breaking into the lovely anthem 'I was glad when they said unto me we will go into the House of the Lord'. They shouted 'Vivat Regina Elizabetha' as soon as the Queen had moved through the Choir Screen.

As the head of the procession wound slowly round the Throne and up into the Chancel, one seemed to be back in the Middle Ages. The church dignitaries in their richly-embroidered robes, the heralds' tabards glowing with colour, the peers in their crimson robes. I felt I might have been watching a coronation procession taking place hundreds of years ago and it gave me a wonderful feeling of continuity. Also, another thing that struck me was the fact that everyone looked so at home in their various dresses, as though they always wore them, even the Pages. The Lord Chancellor was a striking figure in black and gold barred robes with a full-bottomed wig and when later he had to put his coronet on, on top of the wig, he looked exactly like a man in chain mail, although this illusion was rather spoiled when turning full-face one noticed he was wearing horn-rimmed spectacles. Although the procession moved so slowly, it was difficult to pick out the various people and I found, too, I was concentrating on the spot where the Queen would first appear. When she did appear, one noticed no-one else. Sometimes, almost hidden by the two supporting Bishops, she moved very slowly, seeming to float along, so lightly does she walk. The full skirt of the beautifully-embroidered coronation dress fell in shining stiff folds which swayed slightly and she wore the circular diamond tiara often seen in pictures of Queen Victoria. She looked so lovely and serenely dignified. What a lovely complexion she has! Her pale skin seemed to glow. Then I noticed the six Maids of Honour in their embroidered and shining white satin dresses, all moving so gracefully, and with such perfect timing they might have been ballet dancers.

The age old Service began and I noticed how soft and yet very clear the music and the voices sounded. First the Archbishop, presenting the Queen to her people. Did you hear the peers' great shout 'God Save Queen Elizabeth' louder than all the others?

Then we heard the Queen's clear soft voice making her responses and solemn promises. I thought of you and all the millions of people who at that moment were listening to those words, just as we in the Abbey were, and I could hardly believe I was really there.

The Queen seemed to be inspired and there could be very few of those listening millions who did not pray for her and wish her well, with all their hearts.

There was a moment of intense excitement when the Queen was crowned with King Edward's Crown, a forest of white arms went up all around one as the peeresses put on their coronets and in a moment the scene in the two Transepts which had been bright before became brighter still with thousands of coronets.

Then I could see the Queen again as she slowly walked towards the Throne, wearing the shining gold robes and carrying the Orb and Sceptre; the crown looked very large on her small head. Some of the newspapers, commenting on her putting up her hand to straighten the crown after the Duke of Edinburgh had paid homage, said he unbalanced it when he touched it but it seemed to me the Queen moved her head slightly for the Duke to kiss her cheek and I expect that unbalanced the crown.

The peers paying homage had been well-rehearsed, and managed the difficult feat of walking down the stairs backwards in their trailing robes very well. John Shrewsbury did it particularly well. Each time the Queen took the hands of those paying homage between hers I noticed the heavy gold bracelets gleaming on her wrists: 'the bracelets of sincerity and wisdom.'

I shall never forget the perfect beauty of the whole service, the colour and the richness of it all, its timelessness and solemn significance. How lovely, too, the boys' unaccompanied voices sounded, singing 'O taste and see how gracious the Lord is.'

All too soon, it seemed, the Queen's procession began forming up, slowly winding around the gold and rose Throne and down the steps into the Choir Stalls. Once more one was waiting for the Queen to appear and once more noticing no-one else until she was out of sight. Now she was wearing the wonderfully-jewelled Imperial Crown and

Staffordshire Society
Coronation Ball. Lord Bagot,
President, greeting guests with
Lady Bagot, in the County
Buildings, Stafford

carrying the Orb and Sceptre, her long deep purple train, edged with
ermine and embroidered with gold, spread out behind her; she slowly
moved out of sight as we all sang 'God Save the Queen.'
With lots of love from us both, dearest Mummy.

Your affectionate,
Nancy.

Three years later when the Hall opened to visitors, the letter was printed
so that they could have copies and I found I was much in demand for
talks, dressed in the Robes! What impressed me was the way the Peers
looked as if they wore their Robes everyday and were not dressed in what
would, on any other day, appear to be fancy dress.

1953 brought about a complete change for Blithfield. The building of
the reservoir during the last six years had turned what had been the
peaceful scene of the valley of the River Blythe, with Blithfield Mill in the

Lady Bagot saying 'goodbye' to HM Queen Elizabeth, The Queen Mother

middle, and water-meadows on either side of the river, into what looked like a battlefield. We felt rather sorry for ourselves and couldn't visualise the little river filling the valley. Then, coming home from London one day, there – like magic – filling the valley – was a beautiful blue lake sparkling in the sunshine.

Caryl was asked by The South Staffordshire Waterworks Company, if we would allow the Company to use the Great Hall for the Luncheon Party it proposed giving, to entertain HM Queen Elizabeth the Queen

Mother, after she had opened Blithfield Reservoir in October of that year. Of course, we were delighted, and Caryl asked if the Company would agree to pay for the redecoration of the Great Hall and also if it would tarmac the drive, which had suffered from use by American soldiers, who were camped in the Park practising road building during the war.

A friend brought Christopher Hussey, editor of *Country Life* to see Blithfield and we asked him who he thought we should get to redecorate the Hall. He immediately said John Fowler. Daisy Wigan had told Caryl that John Fowler, of Colefax and Fowler, was very expensive, and when we called to see him at 39 Brooke Street, every time he mentioned anything, Caryl would say 'Yes, but how much is that going to cost?' I don't know why, because The South Staffordshire Waterworks Company was paying. (I noticed he held a cigarette holder with a cigarette in it which looked as if it was alight, but it wasn't.) His office window overlooked a pretty courtyard with a leafy catalpa tree in it, and all around us were beautiful materials, wallpapers, carpets, lamps and furniture, etc. It was like an 'Aladdin's cave'. I also noticed he had a long suffering, charming secretary. Mr Fowler, John as he became later, said he would come to see the Great Hall, which he did, and asked if he could have a bucket of water and a scrubbing brush. He knelt down by the fireplace, pushed back his spectacles onto his forehead and proceeded to scrub a small area of the wall, getting up he said 'You know, all this needs is a good wash!'

I said to him, when I tell people that the Great Hall was half-timbered before Francis Bernasconi's plaster Gothic decoration in 1822, they say 'What a pity it was altered'. He said, 'What fools they are', and we spent the rest of his day here dashing about the house, trying to see as much as possible. I was just as excited about it as he was, and I couldn't have had a better teacher.

Men from the local building firm in Abbots Bromley carried out the 'good wash' with a lot of scaffolding and dozens of packets of Vim – a cleaning powder – getting back to the original pale biscuit colour, and removing the ginger varnish from the oak doors and window frames. The result just lifts one's spirits every time you go into the room.

When HM Queen Elizabeth the Queen Mother was lunching with us, after opening the reservoir, she said, looking about her, 'I am quite used

Lady Bagot planting a 'Bagot' oak opposite the 'Bagot' oak planted by HM Queen
Elizabeth, The Queen Mother

to this sort of decoration' – similar work having been carried out at Royal
Lodge, Windsor. Most of the guests were invited by The South Staffordshire Waterworks Company. Our chief guest, who stayed here of course,
was Caryl's cousin, Olave, Lady Brooke, whose late husband, Rear
Admiral Sir Basil Brooke, GCVO, had been Equerry to the King.

Her Majesty's Lady-in-Waiting was a friend of Olave's and Her
Majesty's Private Secretary, Sir Oliver Dawnay had had a Bagot marriage
in his family, so it was an especially friendly affair. Of the sixty-four guests
sitting down to luncheon in the Great Hall, seventeen were our friends.

Lady Katharine Seymour said in her letter to me 'I am to say that
Queen Elizabeth was so pleased and touched by all the preparations you
had made, prior to Her Majesty's visit, and also how pleased she was to
have seen your lovely home'.

Sir Oliver said in his letter of thanks to Caryl that 'Her Majesty was so
very pleased to have the opportunity of seeing your lovely home and her
visit to you made the happiest of interludes in a very busy day!'

Lady Bagot, President of the Staffordshire Society, 1977, at the Silver Jubilee Dinner held at Blithfield Hall, and attended by members of the Sealed Knot Society

I had asked Sir Edric Wolseley's youngest son, George, to take a film of HM Queen Elizabeth the Queen Mother when she came out of the house after lunch, with my movie camera, which he did. Her Majesty went at once to speak to the Members of the Mothers' Union and Women's Institute, waiting in the entrance courtyard. She then stepped very neatly over the side of a cattle grid, into the Park, to plant one of the Bagot oaks, which is now following tradition, and has grown into a large sturdy tree. Shortly after HM Queen Elizabeth the Queen Mother left for another engagement, I planted the oak tree opposite and Caryl planted another oak sapling, to the west of mine. So ended a very memorable day, one of the many days on which we felt glad we hadn't deserted Blithfield.

8

The Gowers Report

▼

AFTER HM QUEEN ELIZABETH THE QUEEN MOTHER'S VISIT, CHRISTOPHER Hussey asked if *Country Life* could write an article about Blithfield, and in October 1954, the first of three excellent articles by Arthur Oswald appeared. *Country Life*'s veteran photographer came to take the photographs. He stayed in Abbots Bromley and we gave him a china cupboard on the ground floor to use as a dark room. Tissue paper screened the windows in the Chinese Room, which faces south and if anything wasn't perfect it had to be done again. Before his work was finished we were going to London and left the photographer, standing in the Park in front of the Hall, head under a black cloth, waiting for the clouds to be right, with the cows advancing towards him to investigate this strange object!

The Gowers Report, brought out by Mr Attlee's Labour Government must have saved hundreds of country houses after the war. We knew if we were lucky enough to get a grant to repair Blithfield, we would have to open the house to the public, and three quarters of the house was empty. Nevertheless, Caryl went off, armed with the *Country Life* articles, to see The Historic Buildings Council.

Our architects, David Evelyn Nye and Partners, reported as follows:

> Lord Bagot's family is one of the oldest families existing, they have been in continuous residence at Blithfield since 14th Cent. (at Bagot's Bromley since 1086) though the present house dates from 16th Cent. there are still signs of the earlier medieval period. The house, together with the stabling, orangery, church and parsonage form a composite and interesting group of buildings, which I am of the opinion should be preserved on historical, as well as architectural, grounds!

North-west front of Blithfield Hall. Michael Burgher's illustrations from Dr Robert Plott

We were very grateful to get a substantial grant from The Historic Buildings Council. 1955 must have been the busiest year for the old house since the second Lord decided to give Blithfield a romantic Gothic dress in the 1820s.

The Stafford firm of Sandy undertook the work, which started with the roof. Tiles were taken off and put back; lead was taken off and replaced – sadly not by the old lead, but by new; some flat roofs were covered by copper, whilst nearly all the many chimneys were stuffed with jackdaws' nests. I remember watching from my bedroom window, a jackdaw picking up a stick and flying towards the house, next minute the stick came down the chimney. Most chimneys had to be partly taken down and built up again.

Indoors, the trouble was dry rot. The little Paradise Room in the sixteenth century front part of the Hall, had to have a completely new oak floor. In the 'L' shaped Drawing Room, to the west of the Great Hall, a

The Great Hall c.1500

sixteenth-century stone fireplace was discovered behind the present one.

When the extent of the old oak roof, above Bernasconi's elaborate Gothic work, was discovered, I asked Mr Robert Meeson to do a survey of the roofs and the following is part of what he wrote:

> R.A. Meeson.
> Two Early Roofs at Blithfield Hall, Staffordshire, and their significance.
> Part of a medieval moat around Blithfield Hall remained open until c. 1769 when it was filled up to provide a site for the New Drawing Room at the S.W. corner of the house. (Bagot 1824. 143) Although there are projections at two corners of the house its fundamental plan is four ranges set around a central rectangular courtyard – an arrangement which probably reflects the size and shape of the moated platform.[1]

Towards the end of the year our thoughts turned towards what we could

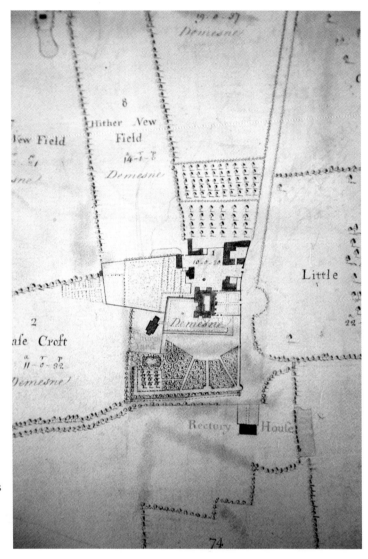

Edward Lawrence's
1724 map

put into the rooms that we hoped people would want to come and see.
We also concentrated upon how the rooms should be redecorated, which
would happily involve us with John Fowler again. From the beautiful
bright Great Hall, already transformed by John, one entered the West
Wing of the house. The first room – the Conservatory – with dark green
walls and brown woodwork, grained to look like oak, was gloomy in spite
of the garden end having a glass roof and large windows. I decided to
make it as much like Charlotte Sneyd's watercolour picture of the room
as possible – her picture was painted in 1850 (see page 71). John suggested

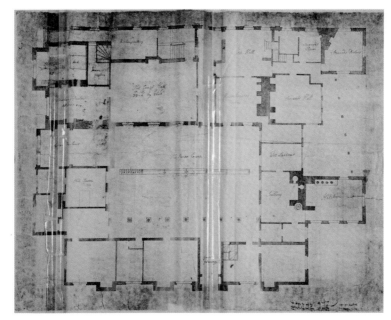

A plan of
Blithfield Hall
c.1750

a green lattice wall paper with rush matting, and his firm covered a sofa with 'Ivy leaf chintz material', to resemble the one Eleanor Bagot was sitting on with her little dog 'Trip' beside her. Next to the Conservatory is the 'L' shaped Drawing Room, and as I intended putting the yellow painted Sheraton chairs which we had bought at the sale of heirlooms in this room, John suggested a soft, but glowing yellow, for the walls, which had been dark red, and the doors in two tones of yellow instead of brown (see page 70). The honey coloured curtains, embroidered with white needlework, already in the house, looked perfect in this room. Next to the 'L' shaped Drawing Room was a room with windows looking into the Inner Courtyard – it had been used as a book room for more modern books. Here the woodwork and fireplace date from Charles II and when the empty book cases were removed the half-timbered construction of the walls was visible, also part of an eighteenth-century flock wallpaper, which John got Coles to copy. As the room was marked as a bedroom on the eighteenth-century plan of the house, John thought it would be a good idea to furnish it as a bedroom again (see page 72), so, the wartime utility divan we had bought from Peter Jones in 1942 was sent to Colefax and Fowler to be transformed into an eighteenth-century four poster, amid cries of horror 'this can't be Lady Bagot's bed!' – and it still is my bed!

John Buckler's 1823 view of the west end of The Orangery

The Orangery showing the rose garden and church

The Orangery before WWII

Lord and Lady Bagot at the main entrance to Blithfield

Between the 'L' shaped Drawing Room and the New Drawing Room is a charming small Vestibule, the walls and doors are decorated in lilac – a lovely colour as a background for flowers, especially hydrangeas, which have always done well in the garden here. John supplied the Bowood chintz curtains.

As three of the first Lord's children died of a 'malignant fever', the last remaining portion of the Moat was filled in and the New Drawing Room, with Quality Cockloft Bedroom and Dressing Room above, were built in 1769 over where the last remaining part of the Moat had been. The New Drawing Room is a large, oblong room with a high ceiling and plenty of wall space for hanging pictures. These walls were coloured a misty aquamarine. On a summer's afternoon, gazing through this series of yellow, lilac and aquamarine rooms gave one a feeling of delight, especially remembering how dark they had been before. By putting a platform, covered with gold material, in the middle of the New Drawing Room, an excellent viewing area was made for our Coronation robes, also Sir Charles Bagot's crimson Order of the Bath Robe, the implements Sir

The New
Drawing Room

Charles used when, as Governor General of Canada, he laid the foundation stone of King's College, Toronto are to be seen here. The splendid
eighteenth-century suit, with its mulberry coloured coat, canary yellow
waistcoat, heavily embroidered with silver, had belonged to Sir Walter
Wagstaffe Bagot, as had the neat black leather shoes with red leather
heels. The two later eighteenth-century suits had belonged to the First
Lord Bagot – one dark navy, the jacket liberally embroidered with bright
flowers in silk, the other, very smart, coat and breeches made from corded
silk, fine stripes in bronze, pale blue and olive green, general colour
bronze. This suit was much admired by John Fowler.

All the rooms I have described are on the ground floor and I once saw
the peacock, 'Ferdinand' gliding out of the New Drawing Room. He must
have come in from the garden and gone on a tour of inspection!

From the west wing one enters the Cloisters, added to the sixteenth-
century south front of the house in 1820. Before the Second Lord Bagot

Sir Walter Wagstaffe's
elaborate suit c.1750 and
others

added the Cloister, with Gallery above, to the Elizabethan brick front
(built by Richard Bagot as lodgings), access to the small rooms here was
by an open colonnade. As I have mentioned, the small room 'Paradise'
needed a new oak floor, and when John suggested an aquamarine colour
for the white panelling in this room, I commented on his good memory
(it was three years since he visited Blithfield). He said he had a photo-
graphic memory. I put the ivy leaf chintz curtains in this room, the green
had turned to blue, and John had remarked about them, 'Look at this –
this is something money can't buy'.

'Paradise' – said to have been the room of a beautiful Miss Bagot and
called 'Paradise' by an admirer – was the ideal room for the children's toys.
There was a display of fans, lent by Olave Brooke, and a charming little

Blithfield Hall. Paradise Room.

'Paradise', the start of Nancy's toy collection

girl's dress, given to me by John, which was displayed on a figure with a pink beribboned straw hat. Next to this figure was a small boy, wearing a blue and white page boy's costume and a tricorne hat with 'H. Bagot' written on an inside label. All the spinning tops, books and music boxes in this room had belonged to Bagot children, and the dancing dolls music box, which had made me feel I was needed at Blithfield on my first visit, was in this room.

The next small room between 'Paradise' and the Gun Room was known as Paradise Bedroom – dark, with sixteenth-century oak panelling – rush matting covered the new concrete floor and carnation chintz curtains, stiff with their last calender, hung at the window. It seemed the perfect place for the heavy oak four poster bed which was then in 'Lady Bagot's Bedroom', upstairs in the apartment which we were using – it necessitated a new bed for Lady Bagot's Bedroom and re-decoration by Colefax and Fowler. This was done most successfully by using camellia patterned chintz curtains already in the house.

The last room in this Elizabethan south front, next to the front entrance, was the Gun Room, the obvious place for the uniforms and collection of swords, so without hesitation, John advised red walls. Between the Staffordshire Yeomanry uniforms stood a drum with the Bagot Coat of Arms on it, which used to be beaten to announce meals. It is said the 'Call to Arms' was beaten. This caused some confusion when Sir Walter Wagstaffe Bagot invited the Hanovarian Garrison from Lichfield, for a meal – he was known to have Jacobite sympathies – Sir Walter hurriedly explained that the 'Arms' were knives and forks! The Staffordshire Deputy Lieutenant's uniform and a Royal Household uniform belonged to the Fourth Lord Bagot, Lord in Waiting to Queen Victoria. J Day, in livery, mustard yellow coat and dark blue breeches, stood by the door, his highly polished silver buttons shining, with a coronet above the family goat's head crest. A neat shop counter was fitted into this room, where guide books, post cards, etc could be bought. Visitors entered and left by the front entrance marked on the 1750 plan as the 'Great Gateway'.

Until we got the grant for repairs, only the part of the house where we were living had electricity, so, now the west and south fronts needed wiring for lighting and heating. No plumbing was contemplated for this part of the house, so we didn't have to worry about pipes freezing in winter. Cloakrooms were made in the old Stables, where several horse-drawn vehicles could be seen, including the Second Lord's handsome travelling coach, which had taken him over the Alps.

Having our house at No 16 The Gateways, London, was a great help, especially when getting ready to open the house to visitors. I was able to visit suppliers, where figures, used in clothes shops, could be bought. However, it soon became apparent that rather than costumes being made to fit the figure, in this case the figure had to fit the costume and the other difficulty was, modern faces just didn't look right. Mr Charles H Wood, General Editor of English Life Publications Ltd, was a great help. He suggested the artist, Harold Barklam, who was painting a picture of the south front of Blithfield for the guide book, might have a solution, which he had. He made papier mâché heads! Caryl and I were able to 'sit' for ours, which were to go on the figures for our Coronation robes.

I was busy writing about the family history for the guide book (printed by English Life Publications Ltd) which I couldn't have done had it not been for the *Memorials of the Bagot Family*, compiled by the Second Lord

The Gun room: Staffordshire Yeomanry Uniforms. John Day in livery

Bagot (after he had given Blithfield its Gothic dress). It was printed at Blithfield in 1824. The Second Lord's folio copy includes a set of water-colour drawings made by John Buckler, this fine copy is now in the William Salt Library, as is the Bagot Family Tree, drawn up by the College of Arms.

I was delighted by our first guide book, and proud to read, at the front 'History and description of contents by The Lady Bagot'. When Caryl saw it he said, 'They might have put spelling by Lord Bagot!'

The Second Lord Bagot's *Memorials of the Bagot Family* and the *Country Life* articles – Blithfield, Staffordshire, 28 October 1954; 4 November 1954, and 11 November 1954 – all trace the previous family history so well. My aim is to tell the story since Caryl inherited Blithfield in 1946, only a few weeks after the last sale of heirlooms was held.

Auberon Waugh said, 'The life of the English Country House has been England's great gift to world civilisation' and there is no doubt the far-seeing Gowers Report saved a great many country houses.

It was in 1946 that John Harris started his country house crusade and in 1955 said in his book, *No Voice from the Hall*, 'One Country House was demolished in Britain every two and a half days'.[2]

However, it wasn't until 1974 that the astounding exhibition 'The Destruction of the Country House' was held at the Victoria & Albert Museum in London, when it was said 'that the loss to British architecture was as great as at the time of the dissolution of the monasteries'.

I am proud to be able to quote a sentence (written before any grant was received) from the last of Arthur Oswald's articles on Blithfield in *Country Life*:

> We have already indicated and the photographs have shown the remarkable results achieved by Lord and Lady Bagot in restoring to occupation this historic house, which, but for their gallant effort, would by now in all likelihood have been on the list of those demolished.[3]

John Fowler: Prince of Decorators

When John Fowler visited Blithfield to advise us about re-decorating the Great Hall, prior to the luncheon held for HM Queen Elizabeth the Queen Mother, after she had declared Blithfield Reservoir open, I had no idea how much he would transform Blithfield.

Owing to The Gowers Report and The Historic Buildings Council, Blithfield received a repair grant which meant opening the House to visitors – and who better to advise about re-decorating these rooms than John Fowler?

Martin Wood, in his splendid book, *John Fowler Prince of Decorators*,[4] wrote in his article entitled 'Blithfield Hall':

> John was also to become a life-long friend of Nancy Lady Bagot. Indeed, as a token of his affection in his will he left her a pair of Regency painted occasional Torcheses Tables which had once been at Blithfield, so they might return once more to their old home. Although Nancy grew up in Australia, north of Sydney, she married an English peer and devoted her life to saving Blithfield, his family seat, John greatly admired what she was, with very modest

resources, trying to do.

Nancy married Caryl Bagot, heir to the barony of Blithfield Hall, in 1940. There was a considerable age difference – he was forty years her senior – and some parental resistance, but it was to be a happy marriage and each was devoted to the other. Nancy first saw Blith-field, originally an Elizabethan courtyard house, on V.E. Day in May, 1945. The 5th Lord Bagot was in the process of selling the estate to the South Staffordshire Water Company who wished to dam the small river Blythe, from which the house derives its name, to form a new reservoir. By the time Caryl Bagot succeeded his cousin the following year the sale was so far advanced that it was impossible for him to prevent it. Blithfield had been nothing but an unwelcome burden to the 5th Lord, but Nancy took a contrary view. Captivated by this romantic house, she determined to save it, and within a year had persuaded the family trustees to buy back the house and 30 acres of land.

The interiors of Blithfield were an interesting exercise for John in that they needed to combine a living house with elements of a museum. They perhaps foreshadow his work for The National Trust, and also show his affinity for ancient and beautiful houses. Lady Bagot's bedroom was John's creation, and he designed the needlework I did for the bedspread.

Of course, I was happy to lend Martin any information I had, including very detailed lists of colours used at Blithfield – which John so generously sent me – and not only colours, but an instruction on:

To scrub the oak table
Use Caustic Soda or potash (wear rubber gloves for protection)
Well wash off & then neutralize with vinegar & water – wash off again.
Glass paper down any roughness & wax polish (Beeswax & turpentine)

———————

Bitter Apple for anti moth
Roberts – chemist

Imogen Taylor, who had been John's devoted Secretary, became a dear friend of mine, helping me with many projects here after John's death in 1977. I must have written to her in 1998, sending information about John's work here. Her letter written in reply on 13 May 1998 says 'I had a lump in my throat when I saw John's rather wild handwriting which was so familiar'. The detail of how to scrub the table showed an amazing practical side and was very typical. What other decorator would do that or even know how to? On another occasion, I had been asked to give a talk on the colours used at Blithfield, to students at Derby Technical College.

A copy of John Fowler's colours:
Blithfield colours
All colours mixed specially

Trellis wallpaper handblocked
Flock wallpaper copied from an original late-eighteenth century one found in the actual room
L-shaped drawing room yellow
Stainers mixed into white wall distemper – yellow ochre, chrome yellow and black
Vestibule lilac mauve – permanent red, cobalt blue and black into white
New drawing room blue and cobalt blue chrome, raw amber and black into white
Paradise – (paint) cobalt blue, chrome yellow and black into white
Gun room red – permanent red specially ground by manufacturers

Notes

1 *Offprint from Transactions of the South Staffordshire Archaeological and Historical Society*, Volume XXX (1990 for 1988–89), p 53.
2 *No Voice from the Hall* (John Murray (Publishers) Ltd, 50 Albemarle Street, London W1X 4BD, 1998), pp 3 and 5.
3 *Country Life*, 11 November 1954, p 1667.
4 Frances Lincoln Ltd, 4 Torriano Mews, Torriano Avenue, London NW5 2RZ, 2007.

9

Blithfield – Open to Visitors

THE FIRST AGENT WHO CAME TO HELP US WITH BLITHFIELD'S NEW ROLE was Commander Guy Bagot, RN, uncle to Flying Officer, Edward Bagot, RAAF, Pathfinder Force, who in 1943 had been sent from his base at Hixon to practise bombing in Bagot's Park. One of the first things to organise was a goat 'catch-up'.

Shortly after the *Country Life* articles about Blithfield appeared, Kenneth Whitehead, an authority on deer, who was staying with the Wallaces at Little Wyrley Hall, Pelsall, wrote to Caryl asking if he might write an article on the Bagot goats for *The Country Life Annual*, which he did, so he was obviously the person to ask to take charge of the 'catch-up'. Everything had been organised without taking into account the amount of public interest this would cause, the press were anxious to take photographs and the goats were virtually wild animals. We arrived to find the 'catch-up' had already started and some goats had been killed, and as the RSPCA was informed, this certainly was not the sort of publicity we wanted. Nevertheless, some goats were brought the two or three miles to Blithfield and put into a specially prepared paddock. They were, of course, a great attraction and I used to take them sweet chestnut leaves. Soon I found they were waiting for me, so I decided to hold on to the end of a branch and a large billy, with impressive horns, took a quick mouthful of leaves and soon they got quite used to me and the leaves. They were very fussy – if they were given crusts of bread with a trace of butter they wouldn't eat them. The luscious grass in the Park at Blithfield, after the rough feed, full of herbs, in Bagot's Park, didn't suit the goats. They had to be treated for worms and taken back 'home' at the end of September, but we loved having them here with us.

Lady Bagot feeding goats

Edward and Rose Bagot
with Hervey Bagot

The peacock, Ferdinand, considered himself to be King of Blithfield, he and the big billy stared at each other through the fence for a few minutes, then the billy walked away into his own domain.

The house

It was Whitsun 1956, when Blithfield opened to the public for the first time. On leaving the main road, the drive passed under cedars of Lebanon trees and between two small stone Lodges, looking as if they contained just one room, but decorated with Coats of Arms. Continuing along the drive the long stretch of the waters of the reservoir became more and more visible, with, in the far distance, the hills of Derbyshire. Then

Lord and Lady
Bagot by the
Gateway, 1956

following a curve in the drive, the low grey house appeared spread out in
front of one and looking as firmly rooted in the ground as any of the old
oaks nearby. The Stable block on the right with its turrets and battlements seemed to be part of the Hall on the left, and the large
battlemented Gateway appeared to join the Hall and Stables together.

After parking their cars by HM Queen Elizabeth the Queen Mother's
oak tree and near to the enclosure where the goats would be viewing them
without any alarm, we hoped, the visitors would follow a route which led
under the turreted Gateway to the entrance. When the eighteenth-
century plan of the House was made the entrance to the Hall was
recorded as the Great Gateway and there would have been a bridge over

Cedar trees and lodges

the moat which surrounded the House.

The entrance, consisting of two large oak doors, also served as an exit. For those visiting Blithfield for the first time, it would have been quite a surprise to see that the House is built around an open Courtyard with a pool in the centre, containing water lilies and goldfish, the plants in pots giving it the appearance of a garden. On the north side of the Court are the tall windows of the Great Hall, which is entered via the Screen's Passage (see page 67). This passage also leads visitors to the Great Staircase, made of Bagot oak and richly carved, some of the carved panels probably formed a Gallery at the east end of the Great Hall (see page 154). The Staircase was moved to the north side of the Hall and added to during alterations in Sir Walter Wagstaffe Bagot's time, c 1750, but it still leads to what must have originally been the Great Chamber, used in Richard Bagot's day as a private Dining Room where he entertained Walter, First Earl of Essex, who lived at Chartley Hall. Richard Bagot was Deputy Lieutenant of Staffordshire in the reign of Queen Elizabeth I. His eldest son, Walter, married Lord Burghley's niece, Elizabeth Cave, and his younger son, Anthony, was in the household of Robert, Second Earl of Essex, 'the favourite'. Anthony wrote home to his father reporting of the Queen:

> When she is abroade, noboddy neare her but my Lord of Essex; and
> at night my Lord is at cards, or one game or another with her that he
> cometh not to his owne lodginge tyll birds singe in the morning?[1]

The Cloisters

The front entrance

Chinese Room

The Great Stairs,
Charlotte Sneyd's
watercolour, 1854.
On view are portraits of
Sir Hervey Bagot with his
son Hervey, and Lord
Burghley

Colonel Richard Bagot,
Governor of the Garrison
Lichfield

Elizabeth Cave, Lord Burghley's niece

The Library. Charlotte Sneyd's watercolour, 1854

The Sealed Knot Society: 'Colonel Richard Bagot's Regiment of Foote'

Colonel Willliam Salesbury

King Charles's cap given to
Colonel Salesbury

View of rose garden from
study windows

Lady Bagot's bedroom, decorated by John Fowler

Needlework on bedspread, designed by John Fowler and worked by Lady Bagot

The Gold Room, Lady Bagot's sitting room

Mrs Salesbury with her Bagot grandchildren. Portrait by Michael Wright and now in the Tate Gallery

Four generations of Bagot Ladies:

Elizabeth Cave, Lord Burghley's niece, married Walter Bagot (16th century)

Elizabeth or Mary Bagot 'a noted beauty in the Court of Charles II', married Charles Berkeley, Earl of Falmouth, and 2nd Charles Sackville, Earl of Dorset (17th century)

Hon Louisa St John of Lydyaid
Tregose, married Sir William
Bagot, 1st Lord Bagot. Portrait by
Joshua Reynolds (18th century)

Lady Louisa Legge, eldest daughter
of George, Earl of Dartmouth KG.
Married 2nd Lord Bagot as his
second wife. Portrait by Hoppner
(19th century)

North view of the Hall and Rose Garden

West view looking towards the Grove and the Bluebell Walk

The Great Stairs with the portrait of Walter Earl of Essex

Lord Essex was very anxious that his house, Chartley Hall, should not be used as a prison for Mary, Queen of Scots and wrote to Richard Bagot asking him to 'Remove all ye beddinge, hanginges and such lyke stuffe to your own house for a while'. No doubt Richard hastened to do this, and it is said some tapestries were put into a house in Abbots Bromley to make a resting place for the Queen on her way to her trial and subsequent execution at Fotheringay Castle.

The Elizabethan or Jacobean panelling in the Dining Room has been painted green, each panel picked out in gold with a gold rosette in the centre. The cornice has a vine trail pattern and the barrel ceiling gives the room height. Two windows look into the centre Court. This room has a feeling of great age, perhaps because the early sixteenth-century or late fifteenth-century oak beams, which extend the length of this north side of the Courtyard, are above the barrel ceiling. The peaceful feeling the room has, must have made it ideal for the Library it became, when the

The Library, sometimes called The Essex Chamber

First Lord Bagot put in bookcases on either side of the fireplace in 1773. Above the fireplace is a panel on which hang thirty-six Coats of Arms, giving the room a splash of colour. These were brought from Pool Park in Wales and more than adequately fill the space left by a large painting.

Some heirloom silver was displayed here, for example, a large side-board dish and jug, the gift of Sir Thomas Wagstaffe and his wife, Frances, dated 1697. Peter Archambo made the beautiful silver bread basket displayed in the centre of the dining table.

Blithfield, being a much loved family home, each generation made alterations to suit themselves, so the next room we enter after the sixteenth-century green panelled Dining Room (originally the Great Chamber) is a charming oak panelled Study. This was formed in 1740 when Sir Walter Wagstaffe Bagot built a uniform wing on the north side of the Great Hall. The Study was either copied from, or was the model for, a similar room at Chicheley Hall in Buckinghamshire, where cousins, the Bagot Chesters lived. All the panels are hinged to form cupboards, with drawers underneath, it had been used at one time as a family Chapel, but displayed here are reminders of the Welsh family of Salesbury, whose heiress Jane, had married Sir Walter Bagot during the reign of Charles II. There is a portrait of Jane's grandfather, Colonel William Salesbury, in this room. This stout-hearted Royalist was Governor of Denbigh Castle during the Civil War, the Castle being the last to surrender as a consequence of the Colonel refusing to give it up until the King told him to do so.

The following is a letter signed by King Charles I:[2]

> Newcastill 13 Sept. 1646.
> Caronel Salesbury,
> I hartely thanke you for your loyall constansie, and asseure you that whensoever it shall please God to enable me to show my thankeful-ness to my friends I will particularly remember you, as for your answer, I refer you to these messengers, to whom I have clearly declared my mynde:
> Comend me to all my friends, so I rest
> Your most assured friend
> Charles R.

The cap of crimson satin, beautifully embroidered with gold and silver thread (see page 156) was worn by Charles I. When I first saw this cap, I noticed the lining needed some repair and as I was carefully stitching it, my cousin said 'I'm sure you never thought you would be darning for Charles I!'

There is a linen money belt, with gold coins, one with the head of Queen Elizabeth I on it and a note that says:

> This is ye waist band of old governor Salesbury's breeches, comonly called Blew Stockins, which he wore constantly he was grandfather to my mother, I beg your acceptance of it desiring it may not be parted with but continue in ye family in memory of my mother & her ancestors.

Also in this room is a portrait of Colonel Richard Bagot, Governor of the Garrison at Lichfield Cathedral in 1645. He fought and was wounded at

Sir Caryl Ernest Bagot, 11th Baronet,
6th Lord Bagot, portrait by Denis Fildes

'To my dearest Nancy'... Sept 1959

the battle of Naseby, managing to return to Lichfield but dying three weeks later. There is a memorial plaque to him in the chancel at Lichfield Cathedral next to the Bishop Hacket window.

From the three windows of this little Study, there is a view across the rose garden to the eighteenth-century Athenian Stuart Orangery built by Samuel and Joseph Wyatt, with the thirteenth-century church beyond, forming a very pleasing mixture of architectural styles. Athenian Stuart's drawing of the Orangery is in The William Salt Library at Stafford, Accession Number 225/2006.

After retracing our steps down the carved oak stairs and entering the Great Hall (see page 70) with its tall south facing windows, one's spirits are always lifted. I find most Regency Gothic architecture has this effect, as long as it is not trying to look Victorian and toned down with darker colours, as the Great Hall was when I first saw it in 1939.

When the Second Lord Bagot was compiling the *Memorials of the Bagot Family* in 1824, he described the appearance of Blithfield Hall during the period when his father, the First Lord Bagot, was a boy:

> The Hall was in every respect truly Baronial; the high table at the upper end elevated by steps, a large stone bay window filled with armorial bearings, the walls hung round with twelve complete suits of armour, (parts of which as a boy, I remember having seen) the buttery-hatch, with the pantry and cellar-head, opening onto it from behind; the shuffle-board, – in short everything that could mark – 'the olden time', – was singularly perfect. The roof of oak, high and pointed, with carved crooks and rafters, supported a glazed louvre in the centre. Sir William altered the Hall in 1740 so it remained till the year 1822, when William, the 2nd Lord Bagot, entirely altered it; and under the hands of Bernasconi formed as perfect a specimen of rich Gothic architecture as has ever been executed in modern times, considering its dimensions, which are not large, though from its just proportions, it becomes one of the most agreeable and enjoyable rooms possible. The roof of oak, high and pointed, with carved crooks and rafters is there still above Bernasconi's skilful work.

The rooms are low, irregular and extraordinary; but from their all opening into each other, their irregularity becomes interesting, and their extraordinary shapes create a sort of comfort, which is frequently sought for in vain, in more magnificent abodes. The House though low covers a great space of ground.[3]

For anyone who loves history there is plenty to contemplate here, with the Bagot family tree (now in William Salt Library, Stafford) brought up to date by The College of Arms, spread out on a long oak table that used to be in the Servants' Hall.

The Coats of Arms in the windows were, at one time, in the east window of the church, and are mostly fourteenth century. One records the marriage of Ralph Bagot and Elizabeth de Blithfield. Some may contain early glass from kilns in Bagot's Park. John Fowler had the sixteenth-century Coats of Arms on a board above the fireplace so perfectly restored they didn't look 'new'.

Entering the Conservatory from the Great Hall is like another world, homely and friendly, the large doors and windows and glass roof at the far end of the room, giving it the name Conservatory, and the massed plants in pots bring the garden indoors. This is the first room in the series of rooms in the west wing.

From the Conservatory we enter the 'L' shaped Drawing Room, in Tudor times one would have entered by the blocked-up door in the Courtyard.

Mr RA Meeson in his article 'Two early roofs at Blithfield Hall, Staffordshire and their significance', says, 'The NE corner of a late medieval timber-framed first-floor open chamber once adjoined the SW corner of the hall. At ground floor and first-floor levels, much of the evidence has been built away but most of the roof survives'. Ralph and Elizabeth's son, Sir John, sued a wright, Robert Stanlowe, in 1398, for having re-built the Hall at Blithfield so negligently and unskilfully that it had fallen into ruin.

With three west facing windows in this room and its soft yellow walls it must have had a warm glow, and the large open fireplace would have kept it warm in winter. Above this chimney piece hangs the delightful portrait of Mrs Salesbury with her Bagot grandchildren, by Michael

Wright, and on either side are the portraits of the First Lord Bagot and his wife, painted by Sir Joshua Reynolds, PRA. Lady Bagot before her marriage, was the Hon Louisa St John of Lydyaid Tregose.

The room on the left of the 'L' shaped Drawing Room has windows facing east, looking into the central Courtyard. On the old plan of the House c 1740, it is marked as a Bedroom. In the Second Lord's time, it had been used as a Bookroom, but everything had been sold in 1945, and it was John Fowler's idea to turn it into a Bedroom again. The fireplace and wooden wainscoting date from the reign of Charles II.

Between the yellow 'L' shaped Drawing Room and the New Drawing Room was the small lilac Vestibule, with its Bowood chintz curtains, and 'sharp' yellow cloth over a deal table, these were decorating ideas anyone could copy in their own houses. Indeed, the then Bishop of Derby's wife, asked for the receipt for the lilac-mauve walls, as she wanted to have similar colouring in her Bedroom. Also, I am sure a number of visitors copied the white net covered dressing table in the Bedroom. We used to call Blithfield 'The Stately Home that's Homely'. However, the Adam style New Drawing Room, with its robes and eighteenth- and nineteenth-century suits displayed on figures was not homely, more a museum. To keep the costumes from fading, the Venetian blinds had to be kept drawn at all times, some friends who called once said they didn't like to disturb us, as they could see we were entertaining guests!

The 1820 Gothic Cloister, cleaned from its Victorian dull grey colouring, like the Great Hall, ran the full length of the south side of the Inner Courtyard, and from it one entered the little low ceilinged rooms of the sixteenth-century brick front, built by Richard Bagot. 'Paradise' — a great attraction with its toys, was next to the dark oak panelled 'Paradise Bedroom', and then came the Gun Room, which was beside the front door, or 'Great Gateway'. Now bereft of guns, the Gun Room was of more interest to most of our visitors, as it was transformed into a small shop where guide books, post cards and models of Bagot goats could be bought. We used to get crowds of visitors, especially on bank holidays, visitors who were so good natured and never seemed to mind queuing.

Blithfield had been more or less isolated for so long that local people enjoyed coming to help. Doreen Bexon and Sarah Jackson came from their cottage in the village of Admaston – Doreen to manage the Tea Rooms with Mrs Excell's help, and Sarah was one of the guides who stood in the rooms ready to talk to people about what they were seeing. Mrs Rowe also came from Admaston. Mrs Excell and Mrs Lucas came from Newton, also Mrs Kent, Mrs Barton and her daughter Bessie, Mrs Capewell and Miss Lane. Mrs Cope came from Colton. The guides really enjoyed coming and looked smarter and smarter. When I complimented Mrs Cope about her blond hair she said 'My husband said I look just as I did when he married me'. Mrs Cope had beautiful sky-blue eyes.

I used to take some of the guides' places so that they could go and have a cup of tea. One day when I was in 'Paradise', a lady came up to me and said knowingly 'They've all gone haven't they?', so I said, 'Well, I may be in Paradise, but I haven't gone yet!' Another time, I was in the Dining Room and Caryl was sitting on a seat in the sun in the Courtyard, watching people coming in, and smoking cigarettes, some visitors came into the room and a woman walked over to the window and seeing Caryl sitting there beckoned to her companion saying 'Ere Bert, cum over ere – that's im sitting down there – andsome old boy ain't ee?' Mrs Lucas told me when she was in the Dining Room once, a man came up to her and said 'Do you mean to say one woman owns all this house?' Mrs Lucas, incensed said, 'Yes, and if you lived here I hope your wife would like hard work!'

Miss Roch, Headmistress of the school of St Mary and St Anne, in Abbots Bromley (now Abbots Bromley School for Girls), used to allow girls from the Sixth Form to come and act as guides. They weren't supposed to take tips, but I gave money towards the school's swimming pool. They were good for the school and good for Blithfield.

Getting the house ready for opening was always a very chilly business because we only had electric heaters on the other side of the house and after 1956 we 'opened' on Good Friday afternoon as a trial run for Easter. I remember some visitors saying they had come inside as it was so cold outside, but found it even colder inside!

After walking around the House, visitors usually liked to go to Blithfield Church, where so many Bagots lie alongside many of those with whom they lived. Going back to the Domesday Book, compiled in 1086, to give William the Conqueror an idea of all he had gained by his conquest, Blithfield appears as 'Blidevelt' and was valued at 20 shillings. It was given to Roger de Montgomery, Herman held it under him, and Herman's grandson, John, took the name of 'Blithfield'.

The Domesday Book also records that Bagod held land under Robert de Stafford at Bramshall, near Uttoxeter, in Staffordshire, and his son and grandson held land under Robert de Stafford in 1166 at Bradelie, now Bagot's Bromley.

In c.1193 Hervey Bagot married his Overlord's daughter, Milicent. When her brother was killed in the Crusades with Richard I, Milicent became a great heiress. The children of Hervey and Milicent called themselves 'Stafford', inheriting the now extinct title (in the male line) of Dukes of Buckingham. Simon Bagot, probably Hervey's brother, became Lord of the Manor of Bagot's Bromley in 1195 – it was one of the largest manors in Staffordshire and has always been mostly woodland. Simon's descendants were living in the old Hall at Bagot's Bromley in 1360 when Ralph Bagot married 'the girl next door', Elizabeth de Blithfield, an heiress, then the Bagots came to Blithfield and it has been the Bagots' family home ever since.

The church

The Church of St Leonard, Blithfield, consists of a Nave of four bays and a Clerestory, north and south isles, western Tower and Chancel. The Nave is the oldest portion probably dating from the latter half of the thirteenth century. This building must have replaced an older building because mention is made in the Domesday Book of a Priest at Blithfield.

The Nave – the original thirteenth-century plan was as complete as it is now. The present Clerestory was no part of the earliest design, but the lines of the pitch of the first roof of the Nave are marked, both on the Tower wall and on the wall over the Chancel arch. The carved heads at the junctions of the head-moulding of the Nave arches have the appearance of being done from life. If so, the carvings appear as follows – beginning on each side from the east end – on the north side:

(1) Richard de Blithfield;
(2) King Henry III;

(3) a layman, architect?; and on the south side:

(1) Roger de Meyland, Bishop of Coventry and Lichfield;

(2) Queen Eleanor of Province;

(3) Rector de Verney.

The fine oak roof was erected about 1853, it being an exact copy of the original. The twenty-five carved bosses were gilded in 1966, so becoming much better appreciated.

The Font is undoubtedly as old as any part of the building. The Benches – the old oaken carved bench ends, twenty-one in number, together with some of the benches, date from the early part of the fifteenth century. The Chancel-Screen, which is in the same style as the bench ends, is probably later in date. The whole was taken down in 1881 and restored to its original design. Above the Screen was once a Rood Loft, the doorway of which can still be seen in the south wall of the Nave, also the two corbels on the east wall, on which it mainly rested. The Pulpit, designed by the elder Pugin, took the place, in 1846, of a seventeenth-century oak one. The Clerestory with its three-light windows and external parapet is of late Perpendicular character and was probably erected at the end of the fifteenth or early sixteenth century by Sir Lewis Bagot.

The Chancel – late thirteenth century: the present high pitched roof, made of oak from Bagot's Park, was a restoration in 1851 from Pugin's designs, and it was in 1851 that the east window was rebuilt after the exact pattern of the original. The plan of the Tracery of this window, in not being carried through at the quatrefoil, has been noted by archaeologists as a unique design. The east window in the Chancel was made by Goddard and Gibbs, a London firm, as a Memorial to my dear late husband, Sir Caryl Ernest Bagot, Sixth Lord Bagot and Eleventh Baronet. His Coat of Arms is on the north side and the Arms of Walter H Bagot of Adelaide, South Australia on the south side. The two Coats of Arms on either side of the lamb and flag, are the family Arms of Richard Bagot, Bishop of Bath and Wells. The earlier window was erected to the Bishop's memory in 1856 and is described by The Reverend Douglas Murray in his book *Blithfield* as representing 'The Passion of Our Lord' which was the subject of the five upper lights and in the five lower lights He is represented in His typical character as 'The Light of the World', 'The Good Shepherd', 'The Bread of Life', 'The True Vine' and 'The Corner Stone'. In the quatrefoil at the top He is figured as 'The King of Glory'. Unfortunately, like many windows of this period, all the faces had disappeared from the figures. The Goddard and Gibbs' window follows the story of the Bishop's window and allows a good deal more daylight into the Chancel. It was dedicated to Caryl's memory in 1966, by The Reverend Stanley Towlson, who was introduced to the living by Caryl in 1957. The plate on Caryl's stall in the Chancel records:

> Sir Caryl Ernest, 6th Baron Bagot, born 9th March 1877, only son of The Reverend Lewis Bagot, served in the Irish Guards during World War I, succeeded his cousin in 1946 and with Nancy his wife made Blithfield his home until his death, 5th August 1961, during which time the Hall was brought back to life and beauty.

The Memorial to Sir Charles Bagot, GCB nearby, on the north Chancel wall, has a plate and helmet and spurs above. The Insignia was above his stall in Henry VII Chapel in Westminster Abbey. Sir Charles died in 1853 in Canada, of which he was Governor General. He was the second son of the First Lord Bagot, who had spent many years as Member of Parliament for Stafford until, in 1780, he was made a Peer in Lord North's Government. The First Lord was fond of writing letters in verse and on that occasion wrote to his former tutor, Doctor Thomas Townson, 'Perhaps you will be glad to hear the King has just made me a Peer. I hope you'll think my Title comely, t'is Bagot Lord of Bagot's Bromley'. On 2 July 1997, a sale by private treaty of Lordships of the Manor was advertised, Bagot of Bagot's Bromley being amongst them. As it was part of the Bagot title, I felt I must bid for it and was able to secure it for £8,000, so becoming the Twenty-ninth Lord of the Manor of Bagot's Bromley. Unfortunately, no land or privileges go with it.

In the Nave there is a Memorial to Thomas Townson, Rector of Blithfield 1749–1759. At the foot of the inscription is this couplet:

> Let future Rectors follow, if they can,

The bright example of this holy man

which immediately gives future Rectors an inferiority complex.

Sir Charles Bagot's younger brother, the Bishop, also had a distinguished career. Besides being Rector of Blithfield and Leigh, he was Bishop of Oxford during the Oxford Movement, Dean of Canterbury, Canon of Windsor and ultimately Bishop of Bath and Wells.

The 'Altar' tomb, nearest to the east wall of the Chancel, actually with feet tucked into it, is that of the 'Elizabethan', Richard Bagot, who was twice High Sheriff of Staffordshire and Deputy Lieutenant, also Steward of the Queen's Manors in the County. A letter dated 26 August 1586, was forwarded from the Privy Council to Richard Bagot, Esq, one of the Lieutenants of the County of Stafford, signifying:

> Her Majesty's gracious acceptance of his faithful and ready service in aiding Sir Amias Powlet, Kt., from time to time, and especially in the late service done in the removal of the Scottish Queen.

In the *Memorials of the Bagot Family*, the Second Lord says:

> Richard Bagot was always being asked for advice, provisions, money, with regard to the latter article he seems to have been a very considerable sufferer, for I find many years after applications made to the Queen's Ministers by him, and his son, for repayment of money so lent, but apparently with little or no success!

Richard was asked to take armour from Roman Catholics, some of whom were friends and neighbours, as it was feared they might join forces with Spanish Armada soldiers if they should land in England.

The names of Dudley, Cecil, Knollys, Paulet, Walsingham and Stafford appear in correspondence with him, most of which is now in the Folger Shakespeare Library, Washington, USA. Richard's eldest son, Walter, married a niece of Lord Burghley, the Queen's Treasurer. There is an attractive portrait of Elizabeth Cave at Blithfield, holding a rose, signifying her engagement. Walter and Elizabeth's granddaughter, Jane Lane, was instrumental in saving the life of Charles II after the Battle of Worcester.

Richard Bagot's tomb and that of his wife, Mary, said to be of Italian workmanship, and Richard's armour, either gilded or painted, has the Italian Sallet 1480, with goat's head crest placed above it at the time of Richard's funeral. It was an earlier Richard who fought and was killed at the Battle of Bosworth.

The first alabaster table-top tomb – that of Sir Lewis Bagot – shows his three wives and nineteen children. The head of his first wife, Mistress Lucy, peeps over his shoulder. It was a case, common in those days, of an infant marriage, for in 1475 when the marriage took place, Lewis was only fourteen years of age. Lucy died young and Lewis' second wife appears on the right side of her husband, with eleven children – five males and six females at her feet. Sir Lewis was one of the Staffordshire Knights at the Field of Cloth of Gold, when Henry VIII met the French King, Francoise Premier.

An earlier Bagot, Ralph, was left a minor when his father died aged thirty-five, a victim of the Great Pestilence, 1349–1350, and it was Ralph who was to marry the Blithfield heiress, Elizabeth, which brought the Bagots from the Hall at Bagot's Bromley to Blithfield. Ralph, being a minor, was brought up by his wife's family and he and Elizabeth married c 1360.

Ralph's father, Sir John Bagot, in spite of his comparatively early death, had fought battles against the Scots in the reign of Edward III. In 1344, he was a Justice of the Peace for Staffordshire, fought at Crecy in 1346 and in 1347 and 1348, was one of the Staffordshire Members of Parliament, as was Simon de Ruggeleye.

Before leaving the church, mention must be made of the six bells, in which Hervy Charles Bagot, MSc, of Adelaide, South Australia – the only bell founder in Australia – has taken a great interest. The two newest bells were given by the Duke of Westminster in 1878, on the coming of age of his godson, William, Fourth Lord Bagot.

Mention must also be made of the splendid pipe organ, renewed in the early 1960s. If a bank holiday was wet, as quite often happened, visitors would enjoy listening to our rector, The Reverend Stanley Towlson playing the organ. He had a degree in music and played with great sensitivity.

Out in the garden, the First Lord Bagot designed part of the Grove in the eighteenth century, most of which can still be seen. The Hall lies in a hollow, to the east, but on high ground the Second Lord's Archery Ground (where the Queen Anne Rectory stood) stretches away to the west. On a fine day Stafford Castle and the Wrekin can be seen from here. A walk among the bluebells in the Grove, with a view across a river valley on either side, was one of the reasons Caryl and I felt we couldn't leave Blithfield. Only about two or three hundred yards to the north-west stands the Old Rectory amongst its terraces, built in the early 1800s by the Second Lord Bagot for his younger brother, Richard, my husband's great grandfather, and to whom the east window is dedicated.

The Museum of Childhood

In the days before the BBC production of *The Antiques Road Show* most of our visitors didn't seem to know a great deal about antiques, but everyone could relate to toys. I would hear people say 'Oh look, we used to have one of those, I wonder what became of it', and I noticed how popular the family toys were in 'Paradise'. There were several empty rooms in the West Wing and Upper Gallery, not much bigger than 'Paradise' and the Upper Gallery itself crying out to be used. I was longing to redecorate them and couldn't help collecting toys wherever we went, also people were giving me things, or lending things.

By using the Lower Gallery, above the Cloisters, the Blithfield tour could be circular instead of visitors having to cross, coming and going on the Great Staircase.

I asked Harold Barklam if he would paint murals on the bare walls of the Upper Gallery. He said he would and that his wife would help him. They hadn't painted murals before and were looking forward to it. I was thinking in terms of Kate Greenaway's children, but the Barklams asked if they could do a series of modern children's games, in the city, in the country, and at the seaside. These murals brightened up the whole place. Regency wallpapers were in fashion, so the Pink Bedroom had a Blue Dressing Room, and the Yellow Room had a Yellow Dressing Room, the curtain materials matched the lattice wallpapers. The small rooms looked charming, with children's furniture, and I was even able to buy back a child's four poster bed, bought by a friend at the 1945 sale of heirlooms! The rooms were small enough for all the contents to be seen from the Gallery.

I bought a polyphon from Mary Phillips, Pamela, Lady Wolseley's sister, who had a fascinating antiques shop at Wolseley Bridge. The polyphon, with its cheerful tunes, stood where the Gallery turned from west to the north side of the house. A collection of dolls stood in a glass fronted case here, including the Victorian Punch and Judy puppets I had found in an antiques shop at the World's End, an area I knew well from helping the WVS deliver 'meals on wheels'. It was these puppets I took to the BBC production of *The Antiques Road Show*, when it was held in Lichfield Cathedral. Dear Hilary Kay remembered my lending the puppets to an exhibition at Sothebys, in aid of the *Save the Children Fund*. Because I am disabled now, I didn't have to queue, but I thought what seemed like endless queues of people winding around the Cathedral showed the English at their best, chatting and joking, with objects of all sizes and in every sort of packaging. *The Antiques Road Show* had brought out the 'Dunkirk spirit'! I was rather fond of a toy barrel organ, with its monkey, bought in an antique shop in Chelsea Square, behind No 16 The Gateways. Peterkin had his shop in Chelsea Square, and he produced delicious food if ordered – very welcome in wartime. He said he got into his oven if there was an air-raid.

The Wolseleys lent me a well made Victorian toy with brass figures on a table-top – a spinning top won points depending on how difficult it was to spin the top through the figures' open legs. Elizabeth Hiskins lent me a beautiful dolls' house, and when Caryl and I went to Australia in 1959, John Bagot of Adelaide and his family gave me a dolls' house, which I appreciated enormously, because it was an architect's model of a house built in Adelaide in 1896. His wife and family collected all the dolls' house furniture, there was even a dog sitting on the front door mat until he disappeared.

When Caryl and I visited the National Trust property of Snowshill in Gloucestershire, I told the Curator about our 'Museum of Childhood' and he lent us a child's carriage c 1790. I found a newly restored Regency rocking horse in London, and later found out it had been repainted by someone who worked for John Fowler and she had repainted the panelling in 'Paradise'.

I was simply delighted to find four two-seater merry-go-round horses

'That is Lord Bagot and those are his three
beautiful daughters'. Lady Bagot's portraits from
Caryl, Lord Bagot's desk

The Study

in the King's Road for my Museum; however, they had to be housed at No 16 The Gateways until they could be collected. Poor Caryl said 'I do wish you'd get rid of those horses, they make me feel so restless'. These horses led the way to the Toy Museum – one stood in the Cloisters, at the foot of the neat little staircase to the Lower Gallery, and the other three horses stood in the three oriel windows of the Gallery, along which visitors passed to reach the toys in the Upper Gallery.

The Cloister, with the Gallery above, replaced a colonnade in 1820, when Blithfield received its Gothic 'dress'. Before then, the small rooms in the sixteenth-century south front of the house would not have been so comfortable.

The oriel windows in the Lower Gallery had to be replaced with the aid of a grant from The Historic Buildings Council.

Living in the house opposite to ours at No 16 The Gateways was Pam Preston, who became a great friend. She told us she had seen a most attractive child's sleigh in an antique shop at South Kensington and it had the Bagot Coat of Arms painted on it. On remarking on this to the proprietor, he said he had offered it to the family, but they were too impoverished to buy it back. When she told Caryl, he asked her to buy it, which she did, and then told the proprietor she had bought it for Lord Bagot! It was Dutch in origin, and may have been bought by Sir Charles Bagot when Ambassador to The Hague, as a present for his brother the Second Lord Bagot.

I wish to end this chapter by quoting an extract from *A Guide to English Country Houses*, by Garry Hogg:[4]

> Blithfield Hall
>
> As you approach this house from the direction of Abbots Bromley you notice a number of sheets of water: you might indeed term this a watery landscape. And as you leave the minor road that has wound its way among these sheets of water you at once begin to climb gently by way of a stretch of parkland overlooking the water to the house itself.
>
> It is a house that is some five hundred years old, and has been in the possession of one family for almost the whole of that time.

Generation after generation of Bagots have devoted time and money and imagination and skill to making this home of theirs as they would wish it to be both for themselves and for their immediate descendants. It can be said here, more truly than is usually the case, that the house has 'grown up' with its occupants, being altered here, enlarged there, adapted, restored, renovated and even on occasion reduced, at the instigation of one generation or another.

For all this it has been beautifully maintained and preserved its integrity.

To pass through its gateway into the courtyard is to be swiftly conveyed into the heart of a well integrated and certainly well loved family home.

It possesses, of course, its splendid features: the noble oak Great Staircase – its treads and balusters carved from oak trees grown on the estate; the great Dining Room, with its magnificent barrel ceiling and its green and gold Elizabethan panelling: the drawingroom – L-shaped, most unusually for that period: and other impressive rooms besides. But it contains one most unusual feature perhaps unique, a feature that will delight children even more than adults: The Toy Museum – here young visitors (and their parents too, of course) can take delight in examining the toys and child's possessions of an older day: dolls'-house furniture, children's carriages, the exquisitely-wrought child's tea-services, the toy barrel-organs, Punch and Judy models, coaches and carts and much else, including treasures from abroad.

There are, too, whole rooms to be explored, including the pink, the yellow and the blue nurseries. It is these rooms, perhaps more than any other, that revive nostalgia in the elderly and wonder in the young. Here, then is a great house with something most unusual, most rewarding, to offer. It should on no account be missed.

Notes

1 Bagot Letters: LA39, Folger Shakespeare Library, Washington, DC, USA (microfilm at Stafford Record Office, Reference: MS9/LA39).

2 D.3071/1, Bagot Papers, Stafford Record Office.

3 Printed at Blithfield, Staffordshire, 1824. Copy available at Stafford Record Office.

4 *Country Life*, 1969, p 106.

10

The National Trust

▼

AFTER CHRISTMAS, CARYL'S AND MY THOUGHTS TURNED TOWARDS THE SUN
and somewhere a good deal warmer than Staffordshire. Caryl had spent
thirty years in Calcutta, and I had been born and brought up in Australia,
near to Sydney, so was used to the beautiful surfing beaches.

We had friends, who had a holiday house on the island of Tenerife, to
which they eventually retired, and our first visit there was by sea in 1955.
We sailed from Plymouth in a Norwegian ship, the *Venus*, known as the
'vomiting *Venus*' by passengers who were not good sailors. Caryl – a very
good sailor – was able to enjoy the excellent food.

Travelling in the same ship and staying in the same hotel, were
Commander Raleigh Gilbert and his wife, Joan, who became great
friends. We had the shared interest of restoring ancient family houses,
although no stones can be seen at Blithfield as old as the oldest at
Compton Castle, near Paignton in south Devon.

Raleigh (pronounced Rawleigh, like his ancestor) had been left some
money by an aunt, so he set about restoring his medieval castle to what it
would have looked like when built. To our eyes it looked completely
convincing and we enjoyed a delightful evening of lute playing in the
Great Hall. Compton Castle now belongs to The National Trust. Raleigh
and his wife had their portraits painted, with Compton in the background, and I decided, there and then, that Caryl's portrait should be
painted with Blithfield in the background.

Denis Fildes, who had painted the Gilberts' portraits, was a son of the
well-known Victorian painter, Luke Fildes. I think Caryl's portrait shows
his sweet nature; he thought he looked rather 'stuffy'!

Raleigh and Joan spent a few days with us here at Blithfield, meeting the Copelands, to whom they are related, and spending an evening at Stratford, watching Laurence Olivier and Vivien Leigh in *Titus Andronicus*. I drove there and back, but it wasn't that which caused me to feel stiff all over next day – I realised I had been sitting with muscles tensed throughout the play.

We took Jill and Wakey to see *All's Well That Ends Well* when they came to stay. Jill knew Lily Palmer, who was sitting near us with her son. Laurence Olivier joined them later – he looked older than I expected. Jill was looking very well, but was more dictatorial then ever to Wakey, who appeared to take no notice.

Caryl and I were beginning to worry about the future of Blithfield and wondered if The National Trust might not be the answer. We had been in touch with the Area Agent, Mr Colin Jones, and Charlie Brocklehurst. They were encouraging as the Hall had been restored with a number of grants from The Historic Buildings Council and we were getting between 28,000 and 34,000 visitors a year. There were still some 3,000 acres which included the historic Bagot's Park, four farms and several small-holdings. In the Hall, the heirlooms, furniture, pictures, silver, jewellery and objets d'art would all go to Harry Eric Bagot as heir presumptive when Caryl died, and as Harry wasn't born until 1893, he wasn't bound by the 1881 Settlement, nor was his brother, Reginald Walter (born in 1897) four years younger, and neither had any children.

Letters went back and forth – I said if Harry would agree to sufficient money being given to The National Trust for an endowment, I would agree to whoever held the Title living at Blithfield. As I had bought the old Rectory some years before, and had made two spacious flats – one on each of the two floors – I felt the upper floor could make a very nice Dower House.

In August 1958, Harry, who hadn't been to Blithfield since the Trustees bought the Hall back for us to live in, came to stay for a few days with his wife, Kathleen – an Australian widow, whom he married in 1951. We had a lunch party to introduce them to several of our friends, and took them for the outing on which we usually took our Australian guests. Driving through Ashbourne in Derbyshire, then the Park at Tissington, we would pass the famous wells which are 'dressed' in May (in thanksgiving for saving the village from plague and drought) with beautiful flower pictures, depicting scenes from the Bible. Driving on we would cross a ford to join the main road over the moors – Australians always love the wide-open spaces! Before long the road to Bakewell brought us to the fascinating, romantic house of the Manners family – Haddon Hall. After luncheon at The Peacock Inn in Rowsley we would travel on to Chatsworth – something quite different – apart from the fact that both houses had belonged to the Manners and Cavendish families for hundreds of years.

Unless our guests were young and strong, they usually arrived back at Blithfield asking to spend the next day quietly here. It certainly was too much for Caryl and Kathleen must have noticed him flagging. At dinner that night she asked me how old was Gerald when he died, knowing Caryl was his age. Looking at the pearl necklace I was wearing Kathleen asked me 'Are those the heirloom pearls you are wearing?' They were cultured pearls given to me by my great aunt, but it was obvious she wanted to know as much as possible about what Harry might inherit. Neither Harry nor Kathleen were very well and I gave them the name of our doctor in London.

By September, letters were going backwards and forwards between solicitors and Caryl. It seems that when Harry saw his solicitor, Elsden, after spending the weekend with us he said to him that he would never want to live at Blithfield, but the following day he rang him to say that he should not conclude that they would never consider living at Blithfield. Elsden's conclusion was that Kathleen had brought about this change of attitude and that in the event of his inheriting the title she would derive satisfaction from being Lady Bagot and the Mistress of Blithfield, even with very little to support it. Although Harry would have had very little to support Blithfield after Caryl's death, Kathleen, I was told, had a good income from her two previous husbands, but no capital.

The Historic Buildings Council and The National Trust were most helpful. In a letter dated 7 October 1958, Mr Digney of The Historic Buildings Council said 'I was very glad you came to see me about Blithfield Hall. It would have been most unfortunate if the scheme to safeguard the future of the Hall should have failed without our making every possible attempt to save it'.

I also wrote to Mr Romilly Fedden, Secretary to The National Trust,

Entrance to old rectory after it had been made into two flats

Historic Buildings Committee, who was doing all he could to help us. In December 1958, he replied 'I am very glad to be able to tell you that at their recent meeting, the Executive Committee decided that if Blithfield were acquired by the Minister and offered to the Trust, the Trust would be prepared to accept a Maintenance Grant from the Government to supplement the Endowment offered by Lord Bagot'. He went on to say 'It would be useful if we had a further meeting with Mr. Digney to discuss exactly how the property might be financed. I am sending Mr. Digney a copy of this letter. I am delighted at this development'.

That was one of the 'ups', next came a 'down'. On 12 May 1959, a letter arrived from Mr Hugh Molsen, the Minister of Works, which more or less said that as Blithfield was not in the very front rank of English country houses, and since, as time passes, the government was likely to have to take an increasingly financial responsibility for some of the most important houses in the country, he did not feel that they should now take on a permanent liability to contribute towards the maintenance of Blithfield. He added that he was very sorry.

Caryl's uncle, Charles F Henage Bagot, was the father of his cousins Harry and Reginald Bagot, and their mother, Florence Eleanor, was the sister of Gerald, Fifth Lord Bagot. When their father divorced their mother, he married again, and had another son. Harry and Reginald said they would make sure their half-brother, Heneage Charles, would not inherit anything from the estate and that is exactly what they did, although their half-brother had a son, Charles Hugh Shaun, born 1944.

Caryl and I decided to go and see a solicitor in London, who had been recommended to us, armed with the 1881 Trust, drawn up by the Third Lord Bagot. Mr Kerman said to Caryl 'You could sell Blithfield to your wife, but I don't advise that. I would suggest you putting the Hall and grounds up for auction, advertise it, let Harry's solicitors know and your wife could bid for it.' The Settlement allows you to sell anything without your heir's consent (apart from heirlooms), as long as the capital goes into the Bagot Settled Estates, after all Gerald sold to The South Staffordshire Waterworks Company, but when the Trustees bought the Hall and gardens back for us the Water Company put in restrictions. The Hall had to be offered back to the Company at the price the Trustees had paid for it. Luckily, the Company didn't want it but it could only be used as a private family home, or a school. The School of St Mary and St Anne didn't want it and we wanted to live in it and keep it open to the public.

A year previously we had planned our first visit to Australia since leaving for England from Sydney in June 1942. We would certainly have gone for a trip years ago if we hadn't been so devoted to Blithfield. 'All the better' said Mr Kerman, 'then the auction can take place when you are away'. After deciding to take Mr Kerman's advice, I wrote to Mr Molsen at the Ministry of Works on 9 July 1959, to which he replied, 'Your idea of buying the Hall yourself sounds an admirable one and it is, if I may say so very courageous of you'.

The news created a tremendous stir. If I didn't know before, I knew then what it was like to be questioned by the press. It was worst when we

Michael Read, my cousin Lucy's brother-in-law, cousin Lucy Clifford and Caryl Bagot

were at our little house at No 16 The Gateways, Chelsea. I would only say 'no comment' which made the press very angry. Now, in the end, Blithfield has become something very like The Gateways – small and larger houses surrounding two courtyards.

11

A Trip to Australia

CURIOUSLY ENOUGH, BEFORE WE SET SAIL, AND FOR THREE OR FOUR WEEKS after, Australia was the country furthest from my thoughts, which were still at Blithfield.

It was 1959 and Blithfield had never looked as lovely as it did on the day of the Horn Dance – a perfect September day, the sun as hot as summer, but mellowed by a slightly misty atmosphere. The old house, set in smooth green lawns, the trees, tipped here and there with gold, billowing towards it, everything appeared to be so serene and timeless, and yet there was doubt and sadness in everyone's mind, with the Hall advertised for sale.

Looking out over the Park we saw the misty blue waters of the reservoir, then we heard the haunting tune which heralds the Horn Dancers – it is always a thrilling moment to see them swing in through the big gateway, the curved and branching reindeer horns carried shoulder high. The ancient dance seems completely natural in such a setting, but we asked ourselves, shall we see it here again? Next morning the same question was in our minds as we left for London.

We were thankful to be joining the *Dominion Monarch* on 12 September, with Rosemary Cavenagh-Mainwaring, her son, Guy and friend Christine, soon to be his wife. It was another lovely day sailing down the Solent, away from England, the country of my forebears, towards the far distant land of my birth.

We went down to our cabin to find it full of flowers and greetings telegrams from my mother, relatives and friends in Australia, waiting to welcome us, and from relatives and friends in England, wishing us *bon voyage* and a safe return.

ESTATE OFFICES,
ASHBY-DE-LA-ZOUCH
Tel. 8

JOHN GERMAN & SON

AND AT RAMSBURY, WILTS;
BURTON-ON-TRENT, DERBY

By direction of the Trustees of the SIXTH LORD BAGOT

WITH VACANT POSSESSION ON COMPLETION

BLITHFIELD HALL, STAFFORDSHIRE

RUGELEY 5 miles, UTTOXETER 7 miles

AN HISTORIC MANSION OF ARCHITECTURAL INTEREST

THE SUBJECT OF
CONSIDERABLE
EXPENDITURE ON
REPAIRS

WITH SELF-CONTAINED
PRIVATE SUITE

PRINCIPAL ROOMS,
GREAT HALL ETC.

OPEN TO THE PUBLIC

GARDEN
COTTAGE WITH 4 BEDROOMS,
BATHROOM, etc.

2 MODERNISED FLATS

PARKLAND AND GROUNDS
TOTALLING

32 ACRES
approximately

*MAINS WATER, ELECTRICITY
AND MODERN SEWERAGE
SCHEME*

TO BE OFFERED FOR SALE BY PUBLIC AUCTION BY

JOHN GERMAN & SON AT SHREWSBURY ARMS HOTEL, RUGELEY

ON FRIDAY, SEPTEMBER 18, 1959, AT 3 O'CLOCK

Further particulars from JOHN GERMAN & SON, Estate Offices, Ashby-de-la-Zouch, Burton-on-Trent and Ramsbury, Wilts; or from the Solicitors: SIMMONS & SIMMONS, 1, Threadneedle Street, London. E.C.2

The sale, September 18, 1959

On 18 September, the day of the sale, we were about four or five hundred miles from Las Palmas, in the Canary Isles, our first port of call. The sun was warm, the seas blue and I swam and sunbathed. In the afternoon I tried to visualise that sale room in Rugeley, but mercifully it all seemed a long way off. Nevertheless, we were restless. Our friends knew all about it and tried to comfort us. After dinner I went to the cabin two or three times to see if a cable had come, and about 9 o'clock there it was, on my dressing table. I looked at it a moment before tearing it open. Blithfield was mine! I rushed up to share the good news and we all drank to the future with Australian champagne. That night I wrote in my diary 'Thank God'.

It was a wonderful beginning to a wonderful trip. Time seemed to go so quickly on board ship. One of the most popular general entertainments is 'Crossing the Line Ceremony'. Those who had not already done this are called before King Neptune's Court. The officers of the Court and the protesting victims are dressed in an odd assortment of garments. After a mock trial and with a good deal of horse play, the victims are flung into

```
THE MARCONI
INTERNATIONAL MARINE
COMMUNICATION CO., LTD.,
MARCONI HOUSE,
CHELMSFORD,
ESSEX.
Member of
```

MARCONIGRAM

Prefix	Handed in at			Date Received	Time Received
P	BURTONONTRENT		5/18	18/ 9/19 59	1856Z
No.	No. of Words	Date	Time Service Instructions	Received from	By
5/5	19/18	18	1628	GKC7	W.C.

To   LADY BAGOT SS DOMINIONMONARCH

PORTISHEADRADIO

Radio Marine
Associated Companies

BLITHFIELD BOUGHT ON YOUR BEHALF BY KERMAN FOR £12000

AGAINST KEEN BIDDING.

GERMANSON.

Form 53. Printed in England.

Marconigram. Thankfully received shortly before leaving the Canary Isles

the swimming pool, much to the delight of the onlookers. However, for providing free entertainment the victims received a signed certificate stating that they had 'Crossed the Line'.

We found that going to Australia via South Africa meant far fewer days of sticky tropical heat than any other way, but there are not so many ports of call. As I mentioned, Las Palmas, the capital of the Canary Islands is the first, and the view of the dry arid looking land doesn't tempt one ashore, but it is worth going for a drive inland, the rather precipitous roads give ever-changing views across deep valleys, bright green with banana palms, to the rocky coast and glimpses of blue sea.

I had books to read, needlework to do and letters to write. The needlework consisted of doing one of the goat's head crests for the canvas work hearth rug designed by John Fowler, and Caryl would quite often read to me as I worked. One of the passengers asked Caryl if he had any hobbies. He thought for a minute, then said, 'Yes, Nancy is my hobby'.

It was early spring in Cape Town when we arrived, and a perfect day. The flat topped Table Mountain looked exactly as I expected, but the city, clustered at the foot, looked smaller and less impressive. When we actually drove through the city we found it well planned, with broad streets. Although there were modern buildings, the older ones gave the city an 'established' European air, and many showed the Dutch influence. Some of the larger private houses were set in beautiful gardens, and there were also a number of attractive modern houses, particularly along the coast road. The gardens were bright with spring flowers, little turtle doves cooed, and all seemed peaceful and serene. We drove along the coast road for a short distance past lovely bathing beaches – pale sand, blue sea and white foaming breakers on one side, with barren rocky mountains on the other. Turning inland, along a valley, we drove through villages where arum lilies grew wild and then, on to the old established wine growing district of Constancia.

The vineyards of Groot Constancia are in this district, surrounding the lovely old house, built in the gabled Dutch style, and now a museum. On the drive back to the ship we passed the Rhodes Memorial in the form of a Grecian temple, set back on the green mountainside. There was the same feeling of space here as in Australia.

The next stop was Fremantle, Australia, and I began to feel quite excited at the thought of setting foot on Australian soil again after so long. As we drew near the wharf, the red painted corrugated iron roofs looked familiar. An English friend happened to be staying in Perth and came down to the ship with her Australian host and hostess. Before we knew where we were, we were being taken for a drive, through Fremantle, over the Swan River, where black swans floated lazily, and into Perth. It was the time for wild flowers and we drove through King's Park, which is a tract of natural bush land almost in the centre of the city. It was here that we saw the curious 'kangaroo paw', among other wild flowers.

At one point the Park juts out, and from this promontory there is a magnificent view. The Swan River, broad and blue, like an inlet of the sea, wound below us, slightly to the left was the city of Perth, and beyond, in the far distance, a range of mountains. This fine sight looking down onto the river and the city was chosen for Perth's War Memorial.

It is a city of parks and gardens, but as its population is not large, they were never crowded. We saw a number of healthy looking young men and women playing tennis, hockey and netball, and girls' marching teams practising in the sports grounds in some of the parks. Sandy beaches stretched for miles up the coast, some only a mile or two from Perth. We were shown a large modern school, where education was free, provided a child could pass the exams and the same applied to the Perth University.

Attractive modern houses, in pretty fenceless gardens, surrounded the city and were rapidly spreading out on every side. The houses all seemed to have pleasant views, but the most attractive were those built along the river, with gardens running down to the water's edge. In the day time, there were always gay little yachts to watch and at night, the lights reflected in the water. With all this, and a perfect climate, who could say that the people of Perth were not fortunate. We sadly said goodbye to our friends who had travelled out from England with us, as they intended staying in this lovely city for a while before going onto Adelaide, capital city of South Australia.

After leaving Fremantle, we were soon in the Great Australian Bight. As in the Bay of Biscay, the weather can be very rough, but luckily it was kind to us, and for three days we steamed through the Bight, rolling a bit of course, blue seas and blue skies, the great continent of Australia on one side and the South Pole on the other. We watched for albatross and soon saw them gliding and wheeling around the ship just above the waves. If you're travelling to Australia from England by sea, by the time you reach the Bight you really feel you have travelled to the 'ends of the Earth'. Just as the ship was about to turn into Port Phillip, with Melbourne at its head, we came quite close to land, and it looked surprisingly like England – green fields coming down to the water's edge – and it must be one of the few parts of Australia that does look like England!

Sydney is about twenty-four hours sailing from Melbourne and the coastline is often visible. It is low and covered with dark olive green bush, occasionally lit by a stretch of shining sand. Somehow it looks forbidding and one can easily imagine the sole inhabitants being the shadowy Aboriginals.

As often happens, when you want to feel particularly well, you catch a cold and I caught a horror in Melbourne. However, I struggled on with my packing and was up on deck about 5.30 am to watch the ship turn into Sydney Heads. It was a rather disappointing morning, inclined to rain, and I always visualise the harbour sparkling in sunlight. Again, I noticed how dark the rocks and bush looked, but soon a towering city appeared and a lovely rainbow over it. My attention was distracted from this by a small Manley ferry, rushing cheekily in front of us. It brought back memories of my first sea trip, and I can still remember how frightened I was when the ferry started to roll. Soon there were familiar sights on all sides, the small rocky islet of Fort Dennison, called 'pinch gut' by the convicts, who were prisoners there, Government House, with its gardens and lawns coming down to the water's edge. Now, of course, the most arresting feature would be the Opera House, but it was not there in 1959.

Slowly we steamed under the Harbour Bridge, and for a few moments could look up at the networks of steel above our heads. We docked a few minutes after. Almost in its shadow, there were the well-remembered and loved figures on the quayside, moving and smiling. We did the same, shouting greetings as they were doing, but we were too far away to hear the words. It seemed an age before visitors were able to come on-board, but after they had, and we were standing on deck all talking at once, all asking questions at the same time, we realised the sun was shining on us and that it was a lovely morning. 'You'll see lots of changes after nearly twenty years' everyone said, but the city of Sydney didn't look very different to me, some new skyscrapers and a fine new road called an Expressway, to take traffic round the city, instead of through it. Soon we were driving across the bridge.

It took far less time than I remembered to drive through the familiar townships – Chatswood, Roseville, Killara and Pymble, to Turramurra, where we were to stay in a guest house near my mother. It had been a large private house at one time and had a pleasant old garden to sit in. It stood on high ground looking down onto the tops of gum trees, to the outskirts of Sydney beyond. The bridge could easily be seen, and in the far distance on clear days, light sand hills and blue sea. At night there was a mass of twinkling lights. I grew to love this view and I saw it at all times. It looked best I think at sunrise, when the city buildings were hidden in mist and only the tops of gum trees peeped through. That was the time to hear the noisy kookaburras laughing, magpies and curra-wongs calling and the occasional sharp crack of the whipbird. The

Nancy's brother, George John Spicer, 'Jack', his wife Jean and younger daughter Joan, with Caryl, Nancy, her mother Ida Gertrude Spicer (née Stericker) in the garden of their house, Sydney

screech of parrots always made me look up, as I loved to catch a glimpse of these bright exotic birds, but they were usually too quick as they flashed from tree to tree.

It gets light so early in Australia, people are up early and go to bed early. During the summer the sun will be shining brightly soon after 5 am, but it is quite dark as soon as the sun sets – about 6.45. We missed the twilight very much. Sydney had had a wintery spring and we were unprepared for the cold weather which greeted us. Most houses are built for hot weather and are cold and draughty, however, we were glad enough of any breath of cool air a little later, when the hot weather came with a rush.

One of the first things we did was to drive round looking at all the familiar places – one old house, my grandmother's house, the house where we lived when we were first married, all in Wahroonga, and only about a mile or two from Turramurra where we were staying. Everything looked much smaller of course, but I was most impressed by the pretty gardens – they seemed much more attractive than I remembered. Most of them were fenceless, so could be easily seen, and instead of trying to grow plants familiar in England, people were growing all sorts of sub-tropical plants more suited to the climate, such as frangipani, gardenias, hibiscus and orchids. Being spring when we arrived, there was plenty of cherry blossom and prunus, roses and azaleas, but it is too hot for rhododendrons to do well.

It was disappointing that we were a little late for the wattle, but the lovely blue flowers of the jackarandas, mingling with the scarlet of the flame trees, was a very beautiful sight. The broad bright green leaves of the banana palm added another tropical note, and I noticed how pretty suburban streets looked planted with oleandeas, poinsettias, or flowering gum. People are much more garden conscious than they used to be.

One house we visited was that of Mr and Mrs Edward Bagot in Pymble. It was designed for them about five years before by their son, who was an architect. The plot of land was small – land near Sydney is very expensive now and the whole object of the design of the house was to give an illusion of space. It was built around a tiny courtyard, and large glass windows gave views of the garden and courtyard on all sides. We had quite an adventure here one evening, only a few days after we'd bought a very nice new little Morris Minor. We were having dinner with Mr and Mrs Bagot and I parked the car in their garden, never thinking to lock it. After dinner we looked at some colour slides of Blithfield, and when we went out to go home to our utter amazement the car had disappeared – we couldn't believe it had been stolen from under our noses! I told the police and we went home feeling we'd never see the car again. Caryl was rather inclined to blame all Australians. However, next morning the police telephoned to let me know they had the car, and when I asked how they'd managed to find it so quickly, they said the thief had left it about twelve miles away, and then telephoned to let them know where it was. My husband had to admit that perhaps Australia and Australians weren't as black as he'd thought the previous evening. I never left the car unlocked again, but obviously it had only been 'borrowed'.

Of course, it was the greatest fun meeting old friends and their families, but I found it difficult to believe that the tall children belonged to Nancy Taylor – the girl I hadn't seen since we were at school together, and who hadn't really changed much since those days. 'Don't leave it so long before coming again' they said, 'or we'll all be grandmothers!'

One of the most delightful dinner parties we went to was given by a school friend (from our Eldinhope and riding days). The party was held in Jean and Peter Russell's garden in Warrawee and consisted of a series of most delicious dishes, interspersed by cigarettes in the warm scented air and unhurried conversation, full of happy reminiscences.

Prize Day at my old school, Abbotsleigh, was at the beginning of December, the prizes were still presented in a large marquee on the oval, but the marquee had got larger to accommodate the larger school. The girls no longer wore white dresses as we did, but green linen ones. The parts of the school I remembered hadn't changed at all, in fact, I could easily imagine myself back there again, but surely we were much tidier, or rather, we were made to be!

New buildings had grown up and were in the process of being built and the grounds had extended, but I think the thing I envied the present girls for was the beautiful new swimming pool. Of course, I couldn't help comparing the School of St Mary and St Anne (now Abbots Bromley School for Girls) with Abbotsleigh. They are both Church of England schools.

Everyone was tremendously interested in Blithfield, and all longing to see it. Luckily they were able to do the next best thing, which was to see the Blithfield film on television. The ABC asked if they could show the film during *Woman's Hour Programme* one afternoon, and if I'd come and speak the commentary and be interviewed afterwards. The studios are only about twenty minutes drive from Turramurra and fine new buildings. On arrival, I was directed to the make-up room, where I lay back in a sort of dentist's chair, but quite relaxed. A friendly girl brushed, patted and painted make-up on my face, explaining that unless this was done I would look ghastly under the bright lights. She did make an excellent job which gave me confidence, but it quickly began to disappear as I sat in the small stiflingly hot studio, surrounded by lights, cameras, microphones and worst of all, a mass of snake like flexes coiling in all directions over the floor. I couldn't help visualising what would happen if I were to catch my foot in one! Before my turn came there was to be an illustrated talk on some old buildings in Sydney, and the man giving it asked me if I'd ever

Caryl and Nancy
with Jim Fowell,
leader of the horn
dancers, 1959

Lord and Lady Bagot with horn
dancers shortly before leaving
for a visit to Australia

Blithfield Hall up for sale.
'Would Blithfield be ours when
we returned?'

Lord Bagot and Major O'Neill and the Blithfield Guides

Greeted by black swans at Perth

Nancy's mother at the Palm Beach house

Caryl on the verandah of the Palm Beach house

Walter Bagot with his two daughters and Caryl in the garden of Forest Lodge, in the Adelaide hills

Cara with Nancy and Caryl at Blithfield

Nancy and Caryl in the courtyard at Blithfield, at the time of Cara's baptism

Caryl's magnolia in Blithfield churchyard

Mrs Hilda Lucas by the magnolia in the Rose Garden

Colonel and Mrs John Kitson. John Kitson is one of Cara's godfathers

Mrs Kitson, Sunnie, with Melina, one of Nancy's god-daughters, and Jonathan

The East window at
Blithfield Church by
Goddard & Gibbs

The altar frontal: sixteenth-
century Italian needlework,
given by one of Cara's
godfathers, Edgar Clare
Wigan, in memory of his wi
Cecily Margaret Bagot

been on TV before. When I confessed I hadn't, and that I was feeling rather nervous, he said 'There's no need to worry', rather in the way a person giving complicated directions will say 'You can't miss it'. However, when he heard my name he said 'Well! My wife was at school with you'. So we found plenty to chat about and the waiting time soon passed. Everyone says I seemed perfectly calm and collected – I didn't feel it, but at least it wasn't difficult to know what to say about Blithfield. You can imagine my surprise and delight when a cheque for £5 arrived a few days later – my fee for a ten-minute appearance!

Another new experience was a visit to a 'drive-in cinema'. It seemed rather incongruous to see the huge asphalted circular space, with an enormous screen at one end, surrounded by the ancient dark and secretive bush land of Frenches Forest. The cars were parked in rows in front of the screen and beside each car was a post on which hung a microphone. You simply put the microphone in your car, an excellent plan, as one can easily adjust the volume. (For once, Caryl could hear perfectly.)

There was a pleasant modern restaurant, with outdoor terrace, and a sort of small fun fair for children, with swings and merry-go rounds. So families could have a very pleasant evening's entertainment at low cost. But, of course, it is the climate which makes it. The evening we went it would have been a crime to stay indoors. The soft warm darkness reminded one of black velvet, the bright stars, of diamonds, and the surrounding bush of the strangeness of Australia.

The weather changed almost overnight in November, from a cold spring to a hot summer, and as Christmas drew nearer it got hotter still. Crowded Christmas shopping in Sydney wasn't inviting and Christmas decorations, which included reindeer and cotton wool snow, although making one feel cooler, looked rather odd. We began to wonder if it would be too hot to eat plum pudding on Christmas Day!

Christmas Eve was another soft velvet night and Christmas morning dawned fresh and clear, with a gentle mist in the valley, fortunately not too hot. Everything seemed so quiet – I felt as if the church bells should be ringing, and then remembered it was only 5 am.

Our thoughts were very much at Blithfield, picturing our lovely ancient church, decorated for Christmas, and the bells ringing out joyfully across the countryside, perhaps it was snow covered! Then we reminded ourselves that Australian time was ten hours ahead, and that everyone would still be asleep. Of course, it was a great joy to be going to the Church of St James', Turramurra with my mother again. The first service was at 6.30 am. We went to the 8 o'clock service and had to queue to get into the church. The women wore bright summer dresses and the flowers on the altar looked lovely, as they always seemed to, but there was no holly with its shining red berries, and it didn't seem quite like Christmas until the old familiar service began.

That evening we drove over the Harbour Bridge to have dinner with Mr and Mrs Alec Bagot (Mr Alec Bagot is Commander Bagot's elder brother). Their house and garden overlooked the harbour at Elizabeth Bay. On Christmas night, we stood in the garden for some time, feeling the warmth and watching the twinkling light around us. Across on the farther shore were more lights, and those in the ships were reflected in the dark water – it was a fairy tale scene.

Early in the New Year we visited Miss Everett, who had been Head-mistress of Abbotsleigh when I and my two cousins had been at school there. I received the following reply to my letter of thanks from her:

> 31 Fox Valley Rd.,
> Wahroonga.
> January 5: 1960.
>
> Dear Nancy,
> Thank you for your charming letter. I am glad you liked my tiny home and its setting which was really looking its worst. Spring and Autumn are the most attractive seasons for me. The azaleas flourish here so well and the Iris.
>
> As soon as I can see how the land around is to be developed I will seriously set about getting the grounds and lawns in order again.
>
> I read with the utmost interest the delightful brochure on the history of Blithfield Hall which you produced. No wonder you love every stone of it, and what a marvellous record for it to have remained in the family for 900 years.

In Alec and Christobel Bagot's garden overlooking Sydney Harbour on Caryl and Nancy's twentieth wedding anniversary, 1 March 1960

Thank you too for your most flattering and I feel undeserved compliments to myself on the honour conferred on me by Her Majesty The Queen.

It is a tribute to Abbotsleigh, my colleagues, and the girls who have passed and are passing through the school.

I am looking forward keenly to seeing colour slides of Blithfield and am happy to accept your kind invitation to have dinner with you on Saturday 16th.

I think Lord Bagot is charming and the happiness of you both was delightful to see, it radiated warmth to our little gathering.

With love and warm wishes for a year of further health and happiness in 1960.

Yours affectionately,
Gordon Everett.

We decided to go for one or two trips inland before going to the house my mother had rented at Palm Beach. The first was to the Blue Mountains, which are about sixty miles from Sydney. Driving across the flat plain, before starting to climb, the car felt like an oven – we thought we'd melt, but by the time we reached Katoomba, where we were to spend a night, it was so much cooler we were glad of our coats. Here again, it was interesting to see familiar places – for example, the hotel my mother and I once stayed at with my grandmother, when I was quite small, and where I very well remember disgracing myself by pushing a small boy off a gate on which we'd both been forbidden to swing! We drove on to look at the famous view from Echo Point and the three rocks known as 'The Three Sisters' overlooking Jamieson Valley.

Another trip was to stay with a friend about eighty miles from Sydney. We drove through the large town of Parramatta, the early capital of New South Wales and through typical rolling dusty countryside, past Camden Park, the McArthur Onslaws property, where the famous merino sheep were first bred, to our destination Bowral, still the pleasant sleepy country town, where I had my first riding lesson, and will always connect it with people wearing corks suspended on strings around the wide brims of their hats, to keep the flies off. Although it is hot in summer, being fairly high, a number of English trees and flowers grow here and people say 'It is just like England'.

Our next trip was a stay of five weeks at Palm Beach. If I were to live near Sydney this is the place I would choose to live in. All the nicest things in Australia seem to be concentrated here. Palm Beach is at the far end of the Barrenjoey peninsula, about twenty-five miles from Sydney. On one side of the peninsula is the Pacific Ocean, a sparkling blue in the sunshine, edged with white lace where the surf breaks on the pale yellow sand. On the other side are the still greeny-blue waters of the mouth of the Hawkesbury River. Between numerous inlets the dark green bush-covered hills seem to push out into the water.

Unlike most places where new houses are springing up, here, as many gum trees as possible are left, and the beautifully curved and twisted stems are used as lawn and garden ornaments, one house being actually built around a tree. The rocky bush covered hillsides, although low, are quite steep and houses are built in all sorts of nooks and crannies, even in places where one would think only a goat could stand.

'Our' house, or rather the house rented from a friend, was built on very sloping ground only two or three years before, and it looked just right in its position. From the balcony and from the glass-sided walls of the sitting room and bedroom, we looked out over dark green bush, studded with the feathery tops of palm trees to the blue sea.

In the very early morning, before it was light, you would hear the kookaburras give a sudden burst of raucous laughter, first one and the others would quickly join in, so it would continue for a minute or two and then die away. At first light currawong birds would start their almost human yodelling note, and occasionally, there would be the broken screech of a parrot. The brilliantly coloured parrots and tropical flowers made one feel one was living on a south-sea island paradise, but when I saw a little koala walking down the road towards me one morning, I felt I must be with Alice in Wonderland. I had never seen these appealing little creatures outside a koala sanctuary before, and didn't quite believe my friend when she said she'd heard one about the previous night. 'Do they make a noise?' I said incredulously, 'Oh yes', she said, 'it's rather like a pig grunting and squealing', and when I heard just that in the middle of the night I thought our conversation must have made me dream it. But there the koalas were in the morning, two of them clinging sleepily to the branches of a tree in the garden, they looked so like toys it made one want to laugh.

The kookaburras were very friendly too and would come and sit on the balcony demanding meat. If you give them a piece which is too large to be swallowed at one gulp they will bang it on anything handy, which is large enough to break the meat, or to make it more tender. This is the way a kookaburra will kill a snake.

The first morning after we arrived at our little blue house, there was a tap on the door, quite early, it was my cousin, Lucy Clifford, who was staying further up the hill. 'Are you coming for a surf before breakfast?' she said. The years suddenly slipped away and it seemed as if we were both children again. There is always activity when you are in the surf, either you are diving under a breaker, or jumping over it, perhaps it is carrying you along swiftly to the beach or knocking you over, and battering you on the sand.

The glass-green breakers heave up endlessly in front of you, they curl over in a white crest and slip smoothly down to rush in, white and foaming, to the sandy beach, and disappear in a swift second back into the sea.

The surfboard riders were much more numerous than I remembered. The newest boards are made of balsa wood or fibre glass, so are much lighter than the old, heavy wooden boards. It was very exciting to see lean brown figures, riding in on the crest of a foaming breaker. The experts made it look so easy, as experts always do.

We spent lazy days on the beach and February in England seemed very remote! However, when the heat wave came it was even too hot to sit on the beach, the sand grew red hot, and we would gladly have exchanged the heat for the cold. Heat makes one feel so exhausted.

Our twentieth wedding anniversary fell on 1 March, so we decided to attend the morning service at the church where we were married – St John's, Darlinghurst. Mr and Mrs Alec Bagot were in the parish of Darlinghurst, so we went with them. The church might easily have been in England, apart from the fact that it was very warm inside! We were delightfully surprised when the Rector Canon Morton mentioned we were in the congregation, and that we had been married in the church twenty years ago. (Incidentally, Caryl was rather proud of the fact that he was still able to wear the same suit.) After the service, we were again delighted when Lady Davidson came up and congratulated us. She and her late husband had been most hospitable and helpful to us before we were married, and we hadn't seen or heard of her since. So, altogether it was a very happy day.

At the beginning of March, a few days later, we were in an aeroplane bound for Adelaide, flying about twenty thousand feet above the vast Australian continent. I have flown over Spain, and the two countries are very similar in many ways. The parched land looked as if it had been clean shaven. From that height, it looked yellowish green, merging into yellow ochres, and brick reds, broken by what looked like occasional small seas or lakes with small patches of dark green bush near a river or reservoir where the country looked really green. The huge paddocks were neat squares and the little homesteads with red painted corrugated iron roofs looked very lonely. I don't know if we were flying too high, but I hardly saw a sign of life during the whole flight, and it made me realise the vastness and comparative emptiness of this strange land. Adelaide time is half

Flying Officer Edward Bagot RAAF Pathfinder Force. Missing from Air Operations over
Brarenschweiger, Germany on January 14, 1944, aged 22.
He was Alec and Christobel's only child

an hour behind Sydney. We had left Sydney in pouring rain about 10 am and reached Adelaide in brilliantly clear sunshine about 1.30 pm. Because of its clear dry atmosphere, and the hills just behind the city, Adelaide is often called the 'Athens of the South', and no sooner had we been told this than some new Australian immigrants appeared dressed in Greek national costume, I suppose to greet friends or relatives at the airport. As our friend drove us through the city we could see how well planned it was with broad streets running across each other in an orderly fashion. The first impression was of a city of solid worth, with a gracious old-world charm as well. During our short stay we grew to feel a great affection for Adelaide and to prefer it to the other State capitals.

But, our destination was not Adelaide. We were heading through the city to the hills beyond. As we began to climb, the olive trees and vineyards reminded us of the Mediterranean coast. Soon the city lay spread out on the flat plain below us, the sea on the horizon. As we climbed, the air was like wine, with a scent of resin from the pine trees.

About twenty minutes after leaving the city we were being welcomed by a dear kinsman, Walter Bagot, and his two daughters, at his house in the hills called 'Forest Lodge'. The house – about 100 years old – is old for Australia, and no matter how hot it was outside, like old English houses, it was cool indoors. The garden, unlike most Australian gardens, was full of welcome shade. The tall trees had been planted by Walter's grandfather, and as we looked out onto beeches and other bright green deciduous trees, backed by the dark green pines, we realised for the first time just how much we'd missed the English trees. There wasn't a gum tree in sight, and except when we heard the screech of parrots, we might have been back in England. The Bagot crest, in coloured glass over the front door, and other familiar things, all reminded us of home.

During our stay in the Adelaide Hills, late summer turned into early autumn, and some of the trees started to turn, first yellow and then gold. We take that for granted in England, but in Australia, where nearly all trees and shrubs are evergreen, it is a most unusual sight. It is only because the hills are studded with some large private gardens, where English trees have been planted, that we saw it there.

Many of the houses follow the English style too. One particular house might have been in England, and it was even called 'Arbury'. The owner, Mr Downer, who was Australian Minister for Immigration, was a neighbour of Walter's and a friend of the Newdigates of Arbury in the English county of Warwickshire, so he called his house 'Arbury' too. He even had a herd of roe deer in the park, almost a unique sight in Australia.

South Australia is a great wine producing State, and although we didn't have time to drive to the famous Barossa Valley, where most of the big vineyards are to be found, there are acres and acres around the city itself and in the hills. The grapes were being gathered when we were there and it was quite usual to see large lorries heavily laden with produce.

There are a number of Bagots living in South Australia, their ancestors were among some of the first settlers and the township of Kapunda, where they first settled, had adopted the Bagot Coat of Arms. Bagot is a well-known and respected name throughout the State. They all went out from Ireland, but originally they came from Brittany. They are all most interested in Blithfield. When they come to England, Blithfield is one of the goals they make for and it is heart warming that they have this strong family feeling. Soon after our arrival, Mr Walter Bagot gave a large family dinner party at his house in the hills. The old house made a perfect setting for such an occasion and to emphasise the importance of it the house was floodlit. Set among its tall trees and dark pines, it looked very romantic. I had taken a herd of china and plastic goats as presents for Walter's grandchildren and these were used to decorate the long table, and very handsome they looked. When dinner was over and the Queen's health drunk, Caryl proposed a toast to '*antiquum obtinens*' (possessing the ancient virtues) and said how pleased we were to be visiting the Bagot stronghold in the southern hemisphere. It was a great success and we began to realise just how strong the clan feeling is among the Bagots and were greatly touched by all the thoughtful kindnesses that were showered upon us.

We spent a very pleasant evening with Mr and Mrs John N Bagot and their family. Mr John Bagot had a fascinating antique shop in the centre of Adelaide and he had also visited Blithfield in the previous year. After dinner we were shown some photographs of the shop and in one I noticed a large dolls' house, just what I wanted for Blithfield, so I asked John if he still had it, and felt very disappointed when he said he no longer owned it. Later on, after I had shown them all the photographs of Blithfield, and we were about to leave, John suggested we all went to see his shop. As we entered he took my arm and led me to the far end of the showroom, where I was amazed to see the dolls' house, looking more lovely than I had imagined and as I examined it with delight he handed me a torch so that I could look at the tiny furniture and fittings inside. Then, I saw a card with my name on it, written on the back were a few words asking me to accept the house with his, and his family's, best wishes. I felt quite overwhelmed and hardly liked to accept such a valuable present. However, John assured me it would give them all the greatest pleasure to know it was at Blithfield. All the time I am afraid my husband's thoughts were directed on the problem of getting it home, but this was accomplished without mishap.

One of the sights of Adelaide is to see the lights of the city from the hills. You look down on miles and miles of twinkling lights far below, which appear and disappear as the car winds round the steep hill road. Each turn brings you closer, until finally the lights are on all sides.

From Adelaide we flew via Melbourne and Sydney to Brisbane. It should only have taken seven hours, but owing to an alteration in the timetable, about which we weren't informed, we missed the connection in Melbourne and the journey took thirteen hours. You can imagine how thankfully we fell into our beds that night!

On a previous trip to Brisbane it gave us the greatest pleasure to see Lena and Colin Gesh and their little boy, Roger. (Lena (née Shipley) had been brought up on a Blithfield Farm.) They had motored over 80 miles – 160 there and back – especially to see us, and we appreciated it very much.

When they walked into the hotel in Brisbane, we recognised them at once and I thought how well they all looked. We spent a very happy afternoon together, looking at colour slides of Blithfield, although there wasn't much I could tell them that they didn't already know, in fact, they could tell us some news, which just shows what a good correspondent Mrs Shipley is. We were delighted when they told us they hoped to buy a dairy farm which they intended calling Blithfield, and although Blithfield prevented them coming down to see us on our second visit to Brisbane, it was very nice to know that the name was being perpetuated in Queensland. Before they left us they presented us with the largest and juiciest pineapple I have ever tasted – I had to cut it up in the bath!

The only sad thing about our trip was that we couldn't do much to help my sister-in-law, who was in hospital near Brisbane – one consolation was that she had some very kind and loyal friends to help her. These same friends took us for some very pleasant drives, first to what is called the 'Gold Coast', south of Brisbane, and then up the north coast to Maroochydore and Mooloolaba, which is a most beautiful surfing beach.

When we were in Australia in 1940, we stayed at Surfers' Paradise, now the heart of the Gold Coast. In those days there were miles of glorious sandy beaches, which were almost deserted. The beaches are still there, but it is difficult to see them because of all the houses, motels and hotels, which have spread along the coast. Land values have soared, hence the name 'Gold Coast'. It is rapidly being developed on American lines to attract as many tourists as possible. We thought it looked very garish and unattractive compared with twenty years before, but there is no doubt that a need is felt for these sort on holiday resorts, and that more and more will grow up along the beautiful coastline. On a later visit we found it had become quite different and most attractive. After all, Australia is very similar to America, both geographically and in the way in which the two countries have developed, so the people and their way of life are almost bound to become more and more alike. Travelling north from Brisbane, we recognised the curious Glass House Mountains – they are volcanic masses of rock, thrown up from the plain millions of years ago. The new houses being built might be new houses practically anywhere, and I suppose it won't be long before the old familiar Queensland house disappears entirely. It is always built of wood and stands up about eight or nine feet from the ground on strong wooden piles, hence the name 'houses on sticks'. This not only makes the house cooler by allowing air to circulate freely, but on hot days the coolest place is under the house. The roof is corrugated iron, painted red, and rain water is collected from it in large galvanised iron tanks standing on wooden platforms, usually full of frogs.

When we returned to Sydney, it was only for two weeks, and then we would be on our way home again. The first thing to be done was to prepare the illustrated talk I was to give on Blithfield. We had had such a wonderful holiday, we felt we would like to show our gratitude by giving a 'picture evening' to help a very worthwhile cause, for which my mother had been working for several years, Moore College. My brother agreed to show colour slides of his trip abroad, so it was quite a family affair. There were lots of people I hadn't seen for over twenty years. One lady said she used to coach me in arithmetic at school – Caryl said to her 'I am sorry I can't congratulate you on the result'. A pretty fair girl told me she came because she went to school at Abbots Bromley and was now living with her Australian husband in Roseville. The 'picture evening' was given in the fine, new church hall at Roseville. About two hundred people came, far more than we expected, and we made £56 for Moore College, which is part of The Sydney Theological Training College, so we were delighted with the result. Everyone left saying they were determined to visit Blithfield!

Our heavy luggage had to go to the docks before Easter, and we said our 'goodbyes' so as to leave Good Friday, with Easter Saturday and Sunday free to spend with my mother. We were having an Indian summer – clear, warm, sunny days, but not too hot. We thought of Blithfield opening again, and wondered how they were getting on.

On Easter Sunday evening we had a dinner party in the *Dominion Monarch.*

All partings are sad, but I think the saddest thing is to watch a ship slowly moving away from the dockside. The figures on shore gallantly waved until we could see them no more, but as I said to my mother, if we didn't have sad partings we couldn't have joyful meetings, and that is the way she felt too. We were grateful to have had all those happy months together.

The ship moved slowly under the Harbour Bridge and the thousands of lights on shore looked like glowworms. When we got out into the open sea it was still quite calm, we felt the soft warm air around us, and the large harvest moon made a shining path across the sea to our ship.

We had a wonderful home-coming to Blithfield. When we saw Blithfield again on a June day we realised that although we had travelled thousands of miles we hadn't seen anything more beautiful, and the warmth of our welcome, crowned by the church bells ringing, was something very precious and to be treasured.

12

Cara and Caryl

THE YEAR 1960 WAS ONE OF THE MOST WONDERFUL IN OUR LIVES AT Blithfield. When we were in Australia I told my mother the treatment I was receiving from my gynaecologist, Dr Sara Field-Richards, wasn't proving successful, and she suggested our adopting a baby through her. However, we could only do so if my mother would help financially, as we were living on the interest produced by the capital in the Bagot Settled Estate. All this money would go to Harry on Caryl's death.

My mother was delighted with the idea of our adopting a baby and said she would be happy to help financially, which was very unselfish of her as we would be living at opposite ends of the earth. Perhaps she had had her hopes raised by a report on our arrival in Australia that I was expecting a baby. I feel sure the press report was in retaliation for my frustrating any attempts to find out more about the sale of Blithfield before we left England.

As soon as we returned to England we told Dr Field-Richards we wanted to go ahead with the plan to adopt a baby, and in the meantime I went on with extending the small Toy Museum at Blithfield into a Museum of Childhood in the West Wing. In a most worrying, and unforeseen way, the furnishing of the museum was greatly helped by Caryl's health. Whenever he was at Blithfield he developed a maddeningly irritating rash around his eyes, so he couldn't stay for more than a few days at a time. He was all right at our little house in London. In between visiting doctors to try to find a reason for this distressing condition, I visited antique shops. Then, our friend, Kenneth Whitehead, suggested our going to see a homeopathic doctor he knew, who prescribed pills made from 'poison ivy' and 'bright eyes'. When I went to collect the pills the bottle was labelled 'Miss Caryl Bagot' – this was before 'our' baby was born. The doctor told us the rash was caused because Caryl was diabetic and his liver couldn't deal with the atmosphere (Blithfield is only about four miles from Rugeley coal-fired power station), so the poisons come out where the skin is most sensitive, around his eyes. Caryl had no more trouble at Blithfield, from what seemed to be like a miracle cure.

I asked Harold Barklam, who had painted the picture on the front of the guide book, if he would paint murals on the walls of the Upper Gallery in the West Wing of the house, and with the help of his wife, the pictures they painted of children's games in the city, the country and the seaside, brought the place alive.

The small bedrooms opening out of the Gallery, decorated in the late eighteenth century and redecorated in similar fashion, housed babies' and children's furniture and toys and became the Blue, Pink and Yellow Nurseries. I bought a polyphon from a local antique shop belonging to a friend, which when wound created a jolly atmosphere.

The Historic Buildings Council were always most helpful and encouraging. Their Secretary, R Romilly Fedden, wrote to me in September 1960:

> I enclose a copy of a letter which I have sent to Mr. Maxwell, our Curator at Snowshill. I very much hope he will be able to help. Your exhibition sounds fascinating and should be an enormous draw.

The Society for the Protection of Ancient Buildings was asking owners of country houses to give illustrated talks about their houses at The Royal Institute of British Architects. I had given talks on Blithfield several times, illustrated by slides, but never in such luxury. Olave told me afterwards she heard a man sitting behind her and Caryl say in disgust, 'Oh it's a woman lecturing!' Nevertheless, he seemed to enjoy the talk and I had many letters of congratulation, one from Mrs M Dance, Secretary, saying:

> The Committee has asked me to write to you and to thank you for the wonderful lecture you gave on Blithfield at the R.I.B.A. It was a most absorbing story of tremendous interest and the way in which you described all the details made the audience feel that a visit to Blithfield was 'a must'. We all appreciate very much the considerable

Lady Bagot giving her
illustrated talk at the
Royal Institute of
British Architects

trouble you took in putting together your talk and in providing the
lovely illustrations and we thank you most warmly.

While work on the Museum of Childhood was progressing, my agent,
John O'Neill, a retired Army Major, was arranging for a helicopter to
come to Blithfield on bank holidays to give people rides over the Hall and
Reservoir. This was probably one of the reasons why we had more than
3,000 visitors over Easter, but the goats didn't like it at all.

At the same time as buying antiques for the museum, I was buying what
was necessary for our expected baby. We knew the baby would be born
early in December, but I didn't go to see her at 27 Welbeck Street until 21
December. I had a cold and then Caryl caught it. Caryl's turned to 'flu and
slight bronchitis, so there wasn't any thought of going to Blithfield until
Caryl was better, hopefully before Christmas. We were delighted the baby
was a girl. Sara Field-Richards had engaged Sister Macfarlane to come to
Blithfield to look after our baby. Sister Macfarlane telephoned me and

said she had seen the baby and called her a 'little angel'. When Sara asked me what we were going to call her, I said Caryl Rosemary, and I thought she looked rather surprised. Later I found her mother's name was Carol Rosemary! Sara had told me both the baby's grandmother and mother had attractive natures and red/gold hair, so I shouldn't have been surprised at Cara's bright red/gold hair when I did see her. She looked tiny and fragile. We decided to call her 'Cara', so as not to confuse her with Caryl. Caryl's doctor said he would be fit to travel on Christmas Eve. At the church service, on Christmas Day, our Rector, Stanley Towlson, when asking the congregation to pray for children everywhere, mentioned the babe at Blithfield.

Caryl and I were soon vying with each other to see who could get Cara's first smile. It was Caryl, and he said 'She's going to be a flirt'. I didn't get a smile until some days later, but then I don't know who Cara thought I was as I had so much to do. I was more 'going than coming!'

As I have said, we had decided to call Cara, Caryl Rosemary, and that is how she was baptised. I have a small snapshot on which Caryl had written 'Cara rapidly becoming Carissima!' We heard from Mr and Mrs Shipley, who lived at Newton Farm, which used to belong to the Estate, that everyone was thrilled and delighted. 'Just what was needed at Blithfield' they said!

On 16 January 1961, Mr Smith came from Staffordshire County Council with his assistant, Mrs Blest, who visited us about once a month until the adoption had been granted – both very pleasant and helpful, Mrs Blest especially. I used to look forward to her visits and we kept in touch for years.

Our neighbours, the Stafford Northcotes at Bishton Hall, told me of Mrs Holmes, who had been a nannie. She lived a few miles away at Great Haywood. Mrs Holmes was a great help even though I had to collect her and take her home.

The excellent German couple, Willi and Louise, left when we went to Australia, and I was hoping to get a Spanish couple from Gibraltar. I was doing all the cooking, as well as giving illustrated talks on Blithfield and helping to get the house ready for the opening at Easter.

Early in January 1961, we received a message to say that No 16 The

Cara in christening robe with Nancy, Caryl and Roy,
the West Highland terrier

Gateways had been burgled. Our 'daily', Miss Stanton was very upset and I had to go to London for the day, so I took our West Highland terrier, Roy, for a walk by torch light and caught the 8.26 am (steam) train from Stafford, rather dreading what I would find. Sadly, the cufflinks I had given Caryl on our wedding day twenty-one years earlier had gone and my mink jacket, but the small green china dessert service Caryl had given me for Christmas for the Toy Museum was still in the cupboard under the stairs. Other more valuable items were missing and I had to meet a man from the insurance company.

The train was one hour late getting back and I arrived home to find Caryl and Sister Macfarlane standing at the front door. She apologised and said she couldn't persuade Caryl to wait inside! Next day, Sister Macfarlane had a cold, so I bathed and fed Cara and wrote in my diary 'She looks like a little cherub. There is so much to do I can't spend nearly enough time with her'. 1 March 1961 was Caryl's and my twenty-first wedding anniversary – an especially happy one.

Nannie Rowney came before Sister Macfarlane left on 7 April. She thought Nannie dreadfully old-fashioned, but I am sure Nannie was just the right person to help Cara get over Sister Macfarlane leaving.

The Spanish couple from Gibraltar, Elias and Mercedes, arrived in April. They had had to leave their small children at home with their grandparents in order to come to England for the money. A Mr and Mrs Nicholls came in April, she to help clean in the house and he as a gardener. They had a flat in the old stables.

We were in London towards the end of April and I went to the White House in Bond Street to buy Cara a very pretty white organdie christening robe. I also went to Constance Spey to choose artificial flowers to put in rooms open to visitors as I knew I wouldn't have time to arrange flowers from the garden. When we got back to Blithfield, we found poor Nannie had slipped on a flagstone in the Inner Courtyard and broken her wrist. Next day I collected Mrs Holmes, as Nannie had to go to the hospital in Burton, only to return with her wrist in plaster. Luckily, she was better well before 12 May, when we were to go to Uttoxeter Town Hall for the Adoption Order to be made by Judge Tucker. We had to wait ages in the entrance (as it was Polling Day for local elections) before the Judge asked for Caryl, Cara and me to go up to his robing room. My darling Cara was very good throughout the whole affair. The Judge kept getting up to admire her. Caryl was asked if he thought he could cope with a baby, he replied with a firm 'Yes', then the Judge made the Adoption Order. On 13 May, my mother's birthday, I wrote in my diary:

> Got up early to write to Mummy, but such a lot to tell her I didn't finish and I haven't had another minute all day. Another lovely warm day, bright sunshine and the Azalea scenting the air. Our darling Cara full of smiles. Had a very nice letter from dearest Margot. Wrote out lists for christening, it will hardly be a small one! But after all no Bagot baby has been christened at Blithfield for about 100 years, so we must make the most of it. Valerie and Stanley came to tea to discuss the christening.

Caryl had already asked our friend, Bishop William (Bishop of Shrewsbury), to baptise Cara. He told me he had written in his diary 'Baptise Bagot's baby'.

I had asked Jimmy Wigan, John Kitson, Ted Bagot, Cynthia Crawley-Boevey, Jill Chandos-Pole and Kit Stericker, also Sara Field-Richards to be godparents. Cynthia was coming over from Jersey and I had prepared rooms on the Lower Gallery as guestrooms and had arranged for a bath to be put in the Cloakroom by the front door to make an extra bathroom.

I wrote out a notice for the press about our adopting Cara as they were being such a nuisance. Mr Gee came to see about getting the big gates to close, so that people couldn't come to the front doors until we were ready for them. Mr Sinkinson, photographer from Stafford, came and took a lovely photograph of Caryl, Cara (in her new christening robe) and me. Roy, my little West Highland terrier, was the only one in the group who didn't look happy.

On 30 May, my birthday, I was up at 5 am, and made garlands of white and yellow roses around the font at Blithfield Church. Mrs Fletcher arranged beautiful flowers everywhere, including the altar vases. We had a lunch party in the Library and Stanley and the Bishop robed in the Study next door. I have a movie film of the procession to Church and our return to the Conservatory.

The church looked lovely. I asked for the *Jubilate* to be sung, and the hymn was *Loving Shepherd of Thy Sheep*. Cynthia was holding Cara and remarked afterwards on her composure. When the Bishop was about to baptise her she was looking up at him with her big blue eyes. I heard him whisper to Stanley, who was holding the book for him, 'Where is it, where is it?' Caryl was saying 'I do' with the godparents!

The procession walked back to the Hall, headed as before by the Head-master of Colton School, carrying the Colton Cross, followed by the choir, then Caryl and me (Caryl looking very smart in his Ascot outfit) the godparents, Cynthia Crawley-Boevey and Jill Chandos-Pole, then Cara, Nannie and Sister Macfarlane, the church wardens, Stanley and lastly the Bishop. We all gathered by the Conservatory door while the very pretty little choir girl, June Sargeant, presented me with a Bible – the gift to Cara from the Parish of Blithfield. Then we went through into the Great Hall for tea.

Cara's christening cake came from Elkes' Bakery in Uttoxeter and was decorated with yellow rosebuds and blue ribbon around the words 'Caryl Rosemary 30th May, 1961'. The Bishop proposed Cara's health in a touching short speech and Nannie, who was rather deaf and didn't like all the fuss and attention, soon took Cara off into her domain upstairs.

Peter Rogers from Stafford, who took the movie film of the procession to and from the church, asked Caryl and me to be photographed in the centre courtyard. It is a photograph I will always treasure. Lucy Cooper told me afterwards that her small choirboy son Max had said, 'Mummy, doesn't Lord Bagot look spiffing?'

That night my darling Caryl asked me if I was happy. How could I be otherwise? It was our last really happy day together, as it was as much Caryl's day as mine. As Blithfield Church didn't have a Processional Cross, Caryl asked the firm of Bridgman, in Lichfield, to make one in wood (there was already more than enough brass to clean) and to put a Bagot Crest on one side with the following inscription on the reverse:

Presented by Lord & Lady Bagot on the occasion of the Baptism
of their Adopted Daughter Caryl Rosemary on May 30th 1961.

13

Caryl and Cara

NANNIE FOUND BLITHFIELD DIFFICULT TO COPE WITH. FIRST, HALF THE house was open to the public, then she had to walk quite a distance before she could get outside, so she decided to go to another family with a baby daughter, who lived in Derbyshire. Wally and Jackie Johnson and baby Rebecca later became great friends of Cara's and mine. Mrs Lucas, who had been a Nannie, was living in the village of Newton, not far away, and came in to help. Nannie Rowney left in June and was in tears at leaving Cara and Cara was also in tears at her going.

Caryl and I took Cara, Elias and Mercedes, and also Roy, the West Highland terrier, to No 16 The Gateways. Elias and Mercedes went to stay with his sister, but came from time to time to help us. Sara Field-Richards telephoned, hoping to persuade us to adopt a baby boy one week old. Caryl was very against it, he said 'You will be over sixty before he is earning anything'. I asked the Kitsons, who had recently adopted a baby boy, what they thought. John said he thought a one week old baby would be too near Cara in age. Caryl was very wise – I couldn't possibly have coped.

Visitors came to see us all the time. I was especially happy to welcome Nancy MacDougall's mother, Miriam Grumett and her sister, from Australia. I had known them since childhood and had spent many happy holidays with the family in their house at the seaside.

My father's younger sister, Aunt Dora, of whom I was very fond, came, also Arden Haworth-Booth, bringing some charming little summer dresses for Cara (we were having a heat wave). Cara's godmother, Kit Stericker, came up for a day from Cobham, and Peggy Bagot Chester came from her flat nearby. (Aunt Dora's husband had been Curate to the Fourth

Lord Bagot's brother-in-law.)

In the beginning of July, Jimmy Wigan had his garden, Bradstone Brook, near Guildford, open for charity and we took Cara there with us. It was Jimmy's first view of his goddaughter.

The Kulczycki family came to see us on the evening before we left for Blithfield. Unfortunately, there was a terrific storm so they couldn't leave for some time, which made us late starting for Blithfield, with Elias and Mercedes, the next day.

Having been in London for a month, Caryl, walking into the Bell Passage (the entrance we used when the house was 'open' to visitors), seemed to be especially happy and relieved to be home. Cara had sat on Mercedes' lap in the car, which was packed to capacity, and because I was looking after Cara, Caryl and I decided to use the Day Nursery and sleep in the Oak Panelled Old Study, next to Cara's room. The next day, 18 July, I longed to go out into the garden with Caryl, Cara and Roy, but I had to work on a talk I had promised to give the following day at the Imperial Hotel in Birmingham.

The following day Caryl wasn't well. Dr Abbott came and diagnosed shingles. The O'Neills went off on their summer holiday. Dr John Salter and Mrs Salter, who had been very helpful with the Museum of Childhood, came to help with the guides. As I was sitting with Caryl next day he said 'I will never go out in the garden again'. To which I replied, 'of course you will'. Audrey came to tell me a pigeon had got into the New Drawing Room and knocked the head off Caryl's figure (dressed in his Coronation robes). I was cross with her for disturbing us, for which I was sorry afterwards.

There was to be a meeting of Trustees on 24 July and James Skelton, Caryl's solicitor, who had arrived the night before, came over from Abbots Bromley at 11.30 am, then it was nearly time to feed Cara again. The Barklams came to finish the murals on the Upper Gallery. Mr Carder, Colonel Guy German, Lord Hazlerigg and Mr Stewart, all Trustees, arrived. I wasn't much use, except as a dispenser of tea.

Next day, Dr Abbott thought Caryl better and gave me a prescription for a tonic for him. I thought him rather depressed. I went to Boots' Chemist in Rugeley for the tonic and nappies for Cara, and got back just in time to greet the 'Darby and Joan' Club from Sutton Coldfield. I took Cara to see them at tea time. She waved her hand and said 'ola, ola, ola', as Mercedes had taught her.

On 26 July, Caryl had a sudden seizure and started to lose consciousness. He kissed my hand and I rushed to telephone Dr Abbott, who came and said he thought Caryl ought to go to Stafford Infirmary. I went in the ambulance with him and telephoned Dr Goldman in London from the hospital. I then telephoned Stanley as I hoped Caryl and I might be able to have Communion together. Stanley and Valerie had been away and had only just come back.

I returned to Blithfield, but I don't know how, and spent the night in Cara's room. Mercedes was looking after her. I felt terribly frightened at the thought of life without Caryl.

Next day the Towlsons took me to the hospital. Stanley knew the doctor who was looking after Caryl, and for the next ten days Caryl appeared to be unconscious. I sat beside him and Stanley said prayers, and encouraged me to arrange the flowers that had been sent. I was sure Caryl knew I was there, and at one point I felt that the prayer of Mother Julian of Norwich – 'All will be well' – was being said to me. John Salter said he thought I shouldn't go to the hospital each day, but I said – 'Caryl would if it was me'.

The O'Neills were back at Blithfield and I was staying at Colton Rectory with Valerie and Stanley, and Valerie's parents – Nance and Harry Main. I don't know what I would have done without them. Mercedes and Mrs Lucas were looking after Cara. I didn't go to the hospital at the end because I knew Caryl wasn't there, and when Nance came to tell me Stanley had heard from the hospital that Caryl was dead I said 'we meant everything to each other'.

Stanley was very sensitive and understanding. He must have made a good Chaplain in the Missions to Seamen. Valerie, kind and sympathetic, sat patiently outside while Stanley and I were with Caryl. She fed me with baby food when I didn't feel like eating. Nance was motherly and a good cook, whilst Harry kept the press away. When Harry died, not many years later, Nance said to me, 'I feel the same as you did about Caryl – we meant everything to each other'.

Caryl had said to me once that he would like to be cremated, so Stanley arranged everything. He also arranged for dear Bishop William, who had so recently taken Cara's baptism service, to take Caryl's funeral service on 5 August.

When my mother heard Caryl had been taken to hospital, she asked if I would like her to come over here and I said 'Yes'. She had never flown before and had to get ready in a terrific hurry. She arrived on the day Caryl died, suffering from 'jet lag' and not too well herself, so it must have been very upsetting for her to find me so close to the Rector and his family. Stanley and Valerie, my mother and I went to Caryl's cremation at the Crematorium near Derby. Afterwards we had a picnic tea looking at a very splendid view in the Derbyshire Peak District. For some time after Caryl's death I wanted to be out of doors in the open country as much as possible.

On 5 August, the day of the funeral at Blithfield, Mr Hammersley of Abbots Bromley brought Caryl's ashes in a box made from the begger's oak (an ancient oak tree in Bagot's Park). It was placed on a table in the middle of the Chancel and later buried by the west-end of the Orangery, in the Churchyard, where only a few years before a huge beech tree had stood. All the guides gave money and I bought a light fitting for the Memorial Chapel – now used as a Vestry. I received masses of letters, all of which I answered in the end. One of the nicest came from my cousin, who had been a bridesmaid twenty-one years before. She said 'No-one could have loved you more'.

Another letter I received, written by a school friend, Paddy Love (née Hemphill), who was in the WRNS during the war (so we had met in London), wrote about a mutual friend, who did not have a happy marriage:

> I guess it is to be expected as she is so much younger, but then I think of you and Caryl. Not many people had such a relationship in a marriage, you were lucky to have that companionship and adoration, I always thought, and think it is wonderful that you two did so many things together, you were always doing things and meeting people, and it was beautiful the way he supported you, and was interested in your friends, and the things you wanted to do, and did, and the places you went to.

Calligraphy by
Gena Jonas

When my cousin, Michael Read, came with his wife, Gena Jonas, to be with me for my ninetieth birthday, Gena asked if I would like her to inscribe something for me in her beautiful calligraphy. I chose the following for Caryl. It comes from a book collected by Lady Elizabeth Basset née Legge (her family and the Bagot family are connected by marriage):

> Youth is not a time of life; it is a state of mind. It is the
> freshness of the deep springs of life. No one grows old
> merely by living a number of years. People grow old by
> deserting their ideals. Whether they are sixty or sixteen,
> every human being may experience wonder – the undaunted
> challenge of events, the unfailing appetite for the future, the
> joy in living. For you are as young as your faith, or as old
> as your doubts.

> As long as your heart receives messages of beauty, hope,
> cheer, courage, and power from God and your fellow men,
> you are young.[1]

Note

1 From *Interpreted by Love. An Anthology of Praise*, Collected by Elizabeth Basset (published by Darton Longman & Todd, Ltd, 140–142 Wandsworth High Street, London, SW18 4JJ, 1994), p 63).

14

Life after Caryl

MY WAY OF DEALING WITH THE DIFFERENCE BETWEEN CARYL'S AGE AND mine was to ignore it, as far as possible, so I was completely unprepared for his death.

Stanley and Valerie Towlson, Valerie's parents, my mother, Cara and Blithfield, kept me going. It was a terrible time. Each morning when I awoke I felt that I wouldn't be able to get through the day, and looked forward to bedtime, when I could take a strong sleeping pill and drift off into unconsciousness. My poor mother, having taken her first flight, was suffering from 'jet lag' and fragile health, so things were not at all happy under the strain. However, she was happy for me to go on a trip to the far north of Scotland with Valerie and Stanley after the funeral. It was soothing to be in such an environment and when I remarked how much Caryl would have enjoyed it, Stanley said 'He's much more alive than we are'. We stayed wherever we could at bed and breakfasts, once at a post office.

1961 was Cara's first conscious Christmas, and she had so many presents I only gave her a very few at a time, but she was more interested in the paper they were wrapped in. After Christmas, my mother went to stay with her cousin, Dorothy Bushby, at Portland House in Weymouth.

My mother made a Settlement for Cara – I was to have the interest during my lifetime and Cara the capital upon my death. Also, to help me over the heirlooms which would go to Harry, and the mortgage I had on the Estate after buying the Hall, my mother left money for me in the care of Colonel Guy German, an old friend of Caryl's and mine.

In January 1962, John O'Neill, the agent who ran Blithfield's opening to visitors, telephoned to tell me that there was 'a bit of a fire' at the Old Rectory, but the fire brigade was there. When I looked out of the Gold Room, I could see the fire. Stanley, who was Priest-in-Charge of Blithfield

Church, and his wife, Valerie, had seen it and came to the Hall. We walked in the garden to where we could see the Rectory, it was burning like an enormous torch.

Just before I bought the Rectory all the lead had been stolen from the roof and I had had it replaced with bitumen. The Gees were in the ground floor flat, Fred Gee, a director of Sandy of Stafford, the building firm, who had done all the work here at the Hall when we received the first grant in 1955, was an ideal tenant – a good Christian and always willing to help. Bob Gee, Fred's son, had been in the flat alone, and telephoned John O'Neill to tell him he thought there was someone in the flat upstairs. He could hear footsteps and he knew the tenant was away. John went across, and as soon as he opened the door at the top of the stairs, he was met by a wall of flame.

The first floor flat was tenanted by Mr and Mrs Cornforth, whose son, John, wrote for *Country Life*. Mr Cornforth had died not long after Caryl and Mrs Cornforth had gone to stay in the south of England. Before coming home, she had asked a former gardener to go and light the kitchen stove (like an Aga) for her. We think a coal must have fallen onto the wooden floor and the fire was probably burning for some time before Bob Gee heard the sounds. The Gees managed to get all their things out, but the Cornforths must have lost a lot of furniture. I received £11,000 insurance money and immediately paid off the mortgage on Blithfield. I have always said 'My good angel was looking after me' and that 'Anyone would think I had set fire to the Rectory to pay off the mortgage on the Hall'. Apparently, that was exactly what Harry did say at the time. Caryl used to call The Old Rectory 'Nancy's folly', but it saved Blithfield twice, the second time in 1986 after a court case with Friary Construction Company. When Caryl died I had three houses and wasn't sure which one I ought to live in. Now there was no question of living in The Old Rectory and No 16 The Gateways was too small and only rented. Blithfield was where Cara and I would live.

There was so much to do, I asked Nannie Rowney to come back, which thank heavens she did. I knew Cara would be safe and happy in her hands. Mrs Lucas came too, to help and although they didn't see 'eye to eye' over Nannie Rowney's old-fashioned ways, they got along.

Cara smelling roses

When, in the following spring, Valerie, Stanley and I went for a holiday in Ireland, Valerie's parents came and stayed at Blithfield to help look after Cara. We drove around the coast from Dublin to Killarney, staying at bed and breakfasts. The weather was perfect – the air so clear it reminded me of Greece, and the fields full of the largest buttercups and violets I have ever seen and a beautiful country. On the west coast there were white sandy beaches and the roads lined in places with fuschias and hydrangeas. It was a perfect day when we rode in a jaunting car to Kate Karney's cottage and transferred to ponies to ride to the Gap of Dunloe in order to join the very large rowing boat which would take us back to the hotel in Killarney. Only rowing boats were allowed on the clear waters of the lake, which reflected the different colours of the flowering rhododendrons. That was a day never to be forgotten – I kept thinking of how much Caryl would have enjoyed it.

Daisy and Jimmy Wigan used to spend a few days with us each summer – Jimmy visited his firm's hop farm in Worcestershire and they would go

Nancy, Valerie and Stanley in a jaunting car on their way to Kate Karney's cottage

on to relatives in the Lake District, but dear Daisy had died not long before Caryl. Jimmy, who was one of Cara's godfathers, used to enjoy coming to stay when all his staff were on holiday and he had the rooms Caryl and I used to have. I was living in the Nursery Wing in the Second Lord's Oak Panelled Study, which I had made into a cosy bed-sitting room.

Dearest Jimmy's arrival always seemed to be the signal for any help I had to disappear. However, Jimmy, never having been without good staff, latterly managed by his sister-in-law, Milly Bagot, didn't understand what was going on and said one day 'Darling, I don't think anyone has cleaned my shoes'. So when he was out for his walk, I hurriedly cleaned as many as I could find. Jimmy always went for a walk morning and afternoon and after tea we played games with Cara, after dinner we played Scrabble. When Jimmy went to bed just after ten, I started on all the letters, etc, to be written. We often went out for lunch with friends, which we both enjoyed.

During the war, Daisy had met Harry Bagot, who was living in a bed-sitting room in London. She suggested he might manage Jimmy's farm, as he had been trained as a land agent, but this arrangement hadn't worked at all well, Harry was the sort of person who knew everything but couldn't

Colton Church Flower Festival

do anything. Jimmy did not like him.

After all the heirlooms were taken away, I was having to make do with photographs and copies of portraits, because Blithfield and its family go together. Jimmy wrote as usual 'Darling, can I come to stay?' To which I had to reply 'Jimmy Darling, I am afraid there is no furniture in the rooms where you stay'. To which I received a reply, which more or less said – do you mean to say that brute has taken all your furniture, then you shall have all the furniture from Daisy's rooms. Not long after a furniture van arrived with most of the furniture and some of the pictures that now furnish the rooms open to visitors at Blithfield. Sadly, dearest old Jimmy had a slight stroke and never came to stay in the rooms, but he gave a beautiful piece of early Italian needlework (The Royal School of Needlework thought it had been a Cope) as an altar frontal for Blithfield Church in Daisy's memory. However, although he didn't travel anymore, Cara and I used to visit him at Bradstone Brook. We went to his hundredth birthday party. He gave Cara the telegram he received from the Queen and he lived to be 103. I shall be forever grateful to him for his kindness.

After his death, Daisy's beautiful portrait, painted by De Laszlo, which she had left to me in her will, came to enhance Lady Bagot's Bedroom. Not only was Jimmy a wonderful help, but Ted Everett, the husband of Daisy's niece, who was a picture restorer and dealer, helped to fill in gaps with his pictures, and later, when I could afford to buy pictures, he would go to auction sales and buy family portraits for me. This was how I used some of the money my mother had given to me.

Before the House opened to visitors in 1956, the well-known picture dealer and restorer in Derby, Charles Ward, restored all the pictures, mostly portraits. After he died, his daughter, Margaret, took over the business and became a very good friend and enormous help when the heirloom pictures went. I had most of them photographed, but Margaret had an artist friend who was an expert copyist, AG McManus, who was able to copy some of the portraits from the originals, one of which was of Mrs Salesbury and her Bagot grandchildren, the former of which is now in the Tate Gallery, London. I shall be forever grateful to Margaret and her dear friend, Elsie Smithurst, they were always ready to help in any way they could, especially when life was difficult for me at Blithfield.

Caryl and I had often wished we could do something about the east window in the church. It had been installed in memory of Caryl's great grandfather, Richard Bagot, Prelate of the Order of the Garter, Dean of Canterbury, Bishop of Oxford, and Bishop of Bath and Wells. When he died in 1854, it was a bad period for stained glass windows – many lost the faces painted on the glass.

Walter Bagot in Adelaide sent me some money after Caryl died, which I had thought of using to buy an heirloom for his family. Then I was told there were some sycamore trees in the Grove, which twisted the right way to make them valuable for veneering furniture. The London firm of Goddard & Gibbs had recently put a window into nearby Colton Church, which was pleasing. I then found that if I used Walter's gift and money from the sycamore trees, I could afford to ask Goddard & Gibbs to put a new east window into Blithfield Church in memory of Richard Bagot, Caryl and Walter. The work went ahead and a most beautiful window appeared, which also gave more light to the Chancel. At the Dedication, Stanley preached a most understanding and sensitive eulogy about Caryl.

Cara and Rebecca (Johnson) in Dorothy Methuen's garden

Many in the congregation would have liked a copy, but sadly Stanley said he hadn't made any notes. I would like Blithfield Hall to be a Memorial to Caryl, which seems odd, as he was a most unacquisitive man, perhaps because he had spent the first five years of his retirement travelling with Margaret around the world.

Whilst some of the heirlooms were going to Harry and his wife, Kathleen, in Melbourne, the Australian Bagots were sending things here to display at Blithfield.

John N Bagot (whose family had given me the dolls' house for the Toy Museum) when staying at Blithfield had suggested putting an inscribed plate on Caryl's seat in the Chancel similar to the one nearby, which had been on Sir Charles Bagot's stall in Westminster Abbey as a GCB. The inscription on Caryl's plate reads:

> Sir Caryl Ernest, 6th Baron Bagot, born 9th March 1877, only son of The Reverend Lewis Bagot, served in the Irish Guards during World War I, succeeded his cousin 1946, and with Nancy his wife

made Blithfield his home until his death, 5th August 1961, during which time the Hall was brought back to life and beauty.

In 1946, Harry had written to Caryl at Blithfield 'Don't you rather dread the thought of living there and will you really have to?'

John N Bagot's eldest son, Charles Hervey, known as Harvey, a scientist, and the only bellfounder in Australia, has helped us with the Blithfield bells.

Harry's cousin, Mabel Arden Howarth-Booth, who disliked Harry, gave me a copy of a portrait of Mary Bagot, the 'Bagot Beauty' whose portrait by Sir Anthony Van Dyck, hangs amongst the 'Windsor Beauties' in Hampton Court Palace. Some years later I had the opportunity of buying back a similar portrait that had hung at Blithfield, and sold the one Arden had given me, which I am glad to say was bought by Arden's daughter. Arden was always very kind and supportive – she hated seeing all the heirlooms going, but as she was her Uncle Gerald's heiress, didn't like to protest. I was given a portrait of Sir Edward Bagot by Hugh Bagot, who had bought it here at the sale of heirlooms.

Sonia Copeland, known by her family and friends as 'Mink', was going through a bad period. Separated from her husband, and with a divorce looming, she looked so ill and thin that I suggested she went to see Dr Goldman in London. Dr Goldman told her she should either go into a nursing home or stay with me, which she did, and we became lifelong friends. Life was very difficult to begin with as she was having a nervous breakdown and couldn't stop talking. I told Stanley I couldn't get any work done and he said 'Why not put a desk in your bathroom', which I did. Of course, Mink went in there and said 'This is a wonderful house, there's a desk in every room!' However, when it came to going through the heirloom lists, I couldn't have had anyone better to help me, especially going through the china. Mink never got tired and often we would be sorting things out until 3 am!

After the heirlooms had gone, and things settled down, she helped with Cara. One day I had gone to collect Mrs Lucas, leaving Mink and Cara finishing breakfast in the Day Nursery. When I got back Cara was standing in a corner of the room looking pleased with herself. Mink said

'She defied me!' However, Cara and Mrs Lucas dearly loved each other and the white peacock created a diversion by fanning his tail on the flat roof outside the windows, so all was well.

Someone else who helped enormously was Max Cooper, the Staffordshire cabinet maker. I had known him as a small choir boy at Blithfield. I knew his parents and his grandmother – the latter had acted as a guide at Blithfield. The well-known Staffordshire naturalist, Phil Drabble, had bought Goat Lodge from Harry Bagot's brother, and knew of Bernard Jack, who trained Max, until Max got so far ahead that Bernard Jack said he couldn't teach him anymore. Max's speciality, at which he excels, is marquetry. When I asked him to copy a picture of simulated bamboo chairs for the room with late eighteenth-century Chinese wallpaper, he set to and made them using steam-bending for the first time. Amongst many other pieces of furniture, he made a beautiful Carlton House writing desk (see page 266) for me with the help of his apprentice, Tim Brown. Not only does the desk enhance the room, but I love using it.

Thus for the second time, Blithfield was kept alive!

15

Kenneth

THERE ARE SOME PEOPLE WHO SHOULD ONLY ADMIRE EACH OTHER from afar!

Ever since Kenneth Whitehead came over from his friend Frank Wallace's house, Little Wyrley Hall, to see the Bagot goats, and then write an article about them for *Country Life Annual*, 1952, he had taken an interest in them, although his great interest in life was deer and deer stalking, about which he wrote several books. Kenneth called at Blithfield from time to time, but I didn't see him for two or three years after Caryl died. When I did see him, I was able to introduce him to Phil and Jess Drabble, who had bought Goat Lodge, and had made it into a charming house for themselves. Cara and I often visited them.

The first time Kenneth invited me to go out with him, was to a car race held at the Grand National Course. During the race, to have some respite from the noise and boredom, I stayed in the ladies cloakroom, talking to the Red Cross nurse. When I got back, my fellow guests all said 'Oh you've missed the best part, a car has just crashed into the straw bales in front of our seats!'

I was very glad I wasn't there, but how foolish of me not to heed the warning – I was not going to find anyone compatible if they liked car racing or football! However, Kenneth was soon to retire from his job as manager of the Wiggins Teape Paper Mill at Chorley in Lancashire, and he had a museum there of all the specimens of animals he had shot. We decided if his museum was brought to Blithfield, and housed in the Stables, it would be a great attraction for visitors interested in that sort of thing.

Kenneth had no brothers or sisters – just a very nice mother – who I am sure must have dreaded the outcome of our marriage, when she heard what we were proposing, and poor little Cara, aged only five in 1965, must

Kenneth, Cara and Nancy in the Coach House stables, Blithfield, 1967

have wondered what it was all about. She was a bridesmaid at our large wedding in Blithfield church, conducted like her baptism by Bishop William and Stanley Towlson. Cara stayed with John and Frances O'Neill in the Garden Cottage with their five children when we went on our honeymoon – first, one week in Venice, which couldn't be anything other than delightful, but the second part in Yugoslavia with Kenneth's shooting friends was very different. Kenneth had a licence to shoot a chamoix, so we were staying in the mountains in a bed and breakfast house at Kranjska Gora. There were very few people in the small village, no one spoke English, and being a Communist country then, even the church was locked. As Kenneth left for the high mountains about 3 o'clock in the morning, and got back during the afternoon, I had plenty of time to write 'thank you' letters, but I knew I had made a mistake. I was glad he didn't shoot a chamoix and we went back to the beach on the Adriatic.

When we returned to England, Cara came with us to Chorley, and went to the little school there. Kenneth's housekeeper was looking after us. Kenneth had a great deal of work to do, and his friends around him;

whilst everything I wanted to do was at Blithfield, but I couldn't leave Cara. As a result, on Fridays after school, I drove to Blithfield, took Cara to Valerie Towlson's ballet class on Saturday morning, and worked until Sunday evening, when I drove back to Chorley.

In the New Year, in a bid to try to save our marriage, Cara went to the Girls' Boarding School in Abbots Bromley. The school of St Mary and St Anne, as it was then, had a few day girls, but was run as a boarding school. I went ahead with expert help from my friend Imogen Taylor, who was John Fowler's assistant, to decorate a suite of rooms on the south side of the Nursery. Caryl and I had been living on the north side. This meant a new bathroom suite, built-in cupboards in the Dressing Room and Daisy's bedroom furniture placed in the Yellow Bedroom. These rooms got the morning sun, unlike the rooms in the north. I used to say, had the house been furnished as it was before the sale of the heirlooms, one could have followed the sun around the house. It was work I loved doing. The upstairs kitchen was also made more up to date and useful as a breakfast room, which seemed sensible as probably I would be the cook. The room had been the Night Nursery in the nineteenth century and Caryl and I made it into a Kitchen after buying the Hall back from The South Staffordshire Waterworks Company.

Perhaps it was fortunate that our plea for a grant to help convert the Coach House in the Stables into a Museum was turned down, but it must have been about this time that The Historic Buildings Council gave me a grant to repair the oriel window in Quality Cockloft Bedroom. Although the room hadn't been used for most of the century, the window was very obvious as it was situated at the front of the house.

It wasn't as usual as it is now to have a business name, but I continued to use Nancy, Lady Bagot in connection with Blithfield, and when Kenneth and I seemed to be seeing less and less of each other, I changed my name back to Bagot by Deed Poll.

Kenneth did join us for a short time when Cara and I were in Australia with my mother and he enjoyed the surfing and wildlife, but we parted after three years. He had bought the Mill Manager's house and decided to stay there, which he did for the rest of his life. I am sure it was best for both of us.

A history lesson

Frank Bradley, a retired architect, got in touch with John O'Neill to ask if we would like to display some of his toy theatres. I had an empty room in the West Wing, where the Museum of Childhood was, and thought the toy theatres would look very well there. John O'Neill had got some mahogany showcases from The Natural History Museum in London (they now house some Copeland China at Trelissick in Cornwall). Luckily, they were most suitable for the very charming and interesting little theatres. Frank and his wife, Con, gave Cara one which could be played with. We used to visit Frank and Con most years, where they had a neat little house in Chapel-en-le-Frith. They took us for some drives in that splendid countryside and one day we visited the Moravian village in a part of Manchester, where Con's father had been an architect. It couldn't have been more different to the centre of Manchester, very neat with paved streets. I think it was close to Christmas and we went into their decorated church, everyone we met there was very kind and hospitable.

16

The Good Samaritans

THE BAGOTS FROM IRELAND WERE SOME OF THE FIRST PIONEER SETTLERS in South Australia – their properties in southern Ireland had been destroyed. They gravitated towards Blithfield when they visited England, and I like to think that the fact I had been born and brought up in Australia was an added influence, and of course, Caryl and I welcomed them.

When Edward 'Ned' Bagot and Dorothy, his wife, were staying in London after a visit to Blithfield, they brought George and Isabel 'Belle' Bagot to have dinner with us at our little house at No 16 The Gateways. We had been told George had a station at Oodnadatta (the Aboriginal meaning is yellow flower of the mulga tree). George was known for having grown a type of grass that was not killed by drought. It is not surprising a street in Alice Springs has been given the name of Bagot.

Ned had told me that George and Belle would be going for a trip on the Continent shortly, and I asked how long they expected to be away. George spoke slowly, like most country people I had met – as if they had all day, which they probably had, 'Well – I think we will be away about – seven years!'

When they got back from their caravan trip they came to see me at Blithfield. In the meantime, a lot had happened here: Caryl had died in 1961; I had married Kenneth in 1965 and we parted in 1970; and Cara was now ten years old and at The School of St Mary and St Anne in Abbots Bromley.

It was not long before Easter when the house was due to open, so I had been working hard cleaning cold rooms and also in the Chancel of Blithfield Church. One morning I was suddenly gripped by such a pain in my back that I couldn't get out of my little folding bed in the Oak Room. George and Belle arrived as expected, sized up the situation and took over. They shopped, Belle cooked, and each morning they went off with plastic buckets and cloths to clean the Toy Museum in the Upper Gallery. In the afternoon, George would go and work in the garden.

Before they left, George gave a luncheon party in a local hotel to celebrate the opening of the Hall on time. John and Frances O'Neill joined us with John Armstrong, Estates Correspondent for *The Daily Telegraph*, who had come to write about Blithfield.

Later, on one of my visits to Australia, when staying with my old friend, Nancy Whitelaw (née MacDougall) at Surfers' Paradise in Queensland, I found George and Belle had a flat there, almost on the beach, with a spectacular view from their sitting-room window across the beach to the surf. I joined them for dinner one evening, which happened to be George's birthday.

I had a letter from George and Belle, dated August, 1982. They wished to do something to help save the Bagot goats and sent me a cheque for £7,000, which was wonderfully generous of them. The letter ended 'Use the money as a gift for whatever you find necessary in the wonderful job you are doing'.

Later, when Isabel came to stay, she told me that when she went to see George in hospital, knowing he was seriously ill, she was told he had died. Poor Isabel – she just went out onto the beach and walked and walked. I could well understand how she felt, and I am so glad she felt able to come and stay with Cara and me at Blithfield. Cara took her to the Cattle Market in Uttoxeter one day, where unhappily she fell, damaging her wrist, so I took her to the Accident and Emergency Hospital in Stafford. They said she had a fractured bone and would need to have her wrist put in plaster. She protested, saying she was flying to Moscow in two days and travelling on by the Orient Express to Japan and then to Australia. Knowing her age, which was the same as the Queen Mother, one or two doctors and nurses came to look at her!

When Isabel got back to Australia she decided to go and live in a retirement home in St George, Queensland. It was called 'Warrawee', meaning 'Come here, rest a while' in Aboriginal.

Caryl's great niece, Rosemary, and her husband, Les Shackleton, live in New Zealand, but one of their sons and his family live in Brisbane. Rosemary and Les liked to escape the New Zealand winter, so usually went to

Queensland every year and travelled about the country in their camper van. I asked Rosemary to go and see Isabel at 'Warrawee'. They became the greatest of friends, exchanging news of Blithfield, of course. Two more great friends of Isabel and Rosemary were the Turnocks – Dr Pam looked after Isabel and everyone at 'Warrawee' and her husband, Dr Bill, was the financier in the bank, on the Council and administered the medical centre at St George. When they were in England they kindly came to give me first-hand news of dearest Isabel. They were lifelong friends of Rosemary and Les, and everyone remembers Isabel very affectionately.

17

The Peacock Flat

THE PEACOCK FLAT GREW FROM WHAT HAD BEEN, UNTIL CARYL AND I HAD made a kitchen upstairs, the offices, where the household work was carried out.

Most owners of Blithfield enlarged the house! We had an Edwardian Wing containing a kitchen and laundry, which we demolished, leaving only the attractive little octagonal building as the game larder. The roof of this wing was leaking like a sieve and we were afraid of dry rot penetrating into the rooms where we were living. I hasten to add that this work was done before there were any 'planners' as we know them today. Having seen and admired the peafowl in the gardens at Warwick Castle, we decided to get some, and it was in the space left by the demolition of the Edwardian Wing that a large cage was made for the first two birds, Ferdinand and Isabella, to stay until they got used to their new home, or in Ferdinand's case, his new Kingdom!

The rooms left were under where Caryl and I were living and consisted of the Steward's Room, the Housekeeper's Room and the Still-Room, also the Butler's Room. Like most empty rooms they soon filled up, and I used to feed my dogs in the Butler's Room.

The Agent who will be best remembered at Blithfield is Major John O'Neill. He had fought in the Battle of El Alamein with Monty and the Desert Rats. John arrived at Blithfield from Gibraltar, with his wife and young family early in January 1958. He spent the thirteen years he was here as a hard-working, enthusiastic, enterprising Agent who supervised the 'opening' of the house. Sadly, he died of cancer in 1971. I had given John two ten-year leases of the Garden Cottage, so now I had to get a new Agent and think about where he could live. The obvious answer would be to make a separate flat under where we were living and with the aid of an

Horace's work room

architect this was done and named The Peacock Flat. I had no idea I
would be living in it in my old age!

Phil Drabble had bought Goat Lodge from Harry Bagot's brother,
Reggie, in 1967 when Harry, now Seventh Lord Bagot, sold Bagot's Park.
Harry was then living in Melbourne, Victoria, in the house of his wife,
Kathleen.

Phil and his wife, Jess, became great friends of Cara's and mine, and
Phil found me another Agent, Mr Denham Cookes. He was generally
known as D-C, and he came to live in The Peacock Flat with his wife. Phil
had engaged a Lichfield builder to restore Goat Lodge. The builder and
his son, Horace worked together. Horace came here to alter the peacock
cage, so I could use it as a kennel for Cara's and my King Charles Spaniels,
Fitz and Roy, when they were puppies and until they were house-trained.
It wasn't long before Horace became the Blithfield builder. He loved
working on old houses and I consider he had almost as much to do with
saving Blithfield, in his own way, as Caryl and I had. Sadly, although he
had done all the hard preliminary work in The Peacock Flat, he didn't live
to see it finished, but died of a heart-attack. He had been so much a part

Horace with the face
of the stables clock

of the life of Blithfield, his death was a very great shock and I had a
plaque put in the Servants' Hall, enscribed with these words:

> Horace Deakin
> Worked in this room from 1977 until his
> death 18.3.91 during which time Blithfield
> was divided into four houses.
> He loved old buildings and was a true
> Craftsman and trusted friend.
> N.C.B.

Caryl and I couldn't have saved Blithfield without the help given to us by
The Historic Buildings Council, so it was a double blow when the

The game larder

Chairman, Lord Glendevon, came to see me and told me, as pleasantly as possible, but firmly, that the Council couldn't continue to subsidise me as they couldn't see a future for Blithfield. I happened to mention I had made a flat for an Agent under the room where we were sitting, and Lord Glendevon suggested my doing other things on those lines.

Since 1942, when we returned to England from Australia, we had been living in The Gateways – small houses in Chelsea, built around two court-yards. Number 16, where we lived, wasn't as big as The Peacock Flat. Then there was the example of Kit Stericker, who had married my cousin Charles. Kit was an Australian and Charles had been working in Australia. When they came to England at the end of the war, they bought a rather derelict building that had been the Dairy for the 'big house' – Painshill, in Cobham. The Dairy House was built as a circle and had no upper storey.

Kit Stericker with Cara in the courtyard at The Round House, Painshill

Kit and Charles inevitably called it The Round House and turned it into the most delightful house possible, both visually and as a most affectionate and heart-warming place to stay. Kit was one of Cara's godmothers and Cara loved staying at The Round House.

The other houses, such as those in the Stables and in Painshill House itself, were made into attractive houses. The Round House was surrounded by sweeping lawns, and one of the largest cedar of Lebanon trees I have ever seen graced the lawn. When Cara and I used to stay with Kit, the historic gardens created by Charles Hamilton were a wilderness, where we often wandered. Now they have been restored and become a monument to Charles Hamilton, who went on creating his gardens until his death.

18

The Bagot Costume Collection

▼

THE COLLECTION OF EIGHTEENTH-CENTURY GENTLEMAN'S SUITS STARTED AT Blithfield Hall with Sir Walter Wagstaffe Bagot, Baronet. He married Lady Barbara Legge, eldest daughter of the Earl of Dartmouth in 1724 and in the same year became Member of Parliament for Newcastle-under-Lyme in Staffordshire. After George I died in 1727, Sir Walter was elected Member of Parliament for Stafford and only resigned in favour of his eldest son, William, in 1754.

Perhaps Sir Walter was wearing his mulberry coloured suit, with canary-yellow waistcoat – coat and waistcoat heavily embroidered with silver – for his wedding to Lady Barbara! The other two suits, also eighteenth century but later, belonged to Sir Walter's son, William, one dark navy, but beautifully embroidered with brightly coloured silk flowers and the other, much admired by John Fowler, made of corded silk fine stripes in bronze, pale blue and olive green general colour bronze. Sir William, as he became, remained Member of Parliament for Stafford until created Baron Bagot by George III in 1780, in Prime Minister Lord North's government.

Also in the collection are the robes worn by my husband for our Queen's Coronation which were made for the Coronation of William IV, and some ladies' Regency dresses and children's clothes, a page boy's costume and babies' robes.

The following article (with minor amendments, 2010) was written to go into a booklet, which was published in 1983, when all these clothes, costumes and uniforms had to be removed as the Hall was to be divided. The Staffordshire Yeomanry uniforms went to a section prepared for them in The Ancient High House at Stafford. The eighteenth-century costumes and my later twentieth-century clothes were given to what is now The Potteries Museum in Stoke-on-Trent. Along with my Corona-tion robes, I also donated the following: diamond maltese cross; emerald and diamond ring; pearl bracelet with emerald and diamond clasp; floren-tine diamond earrings; silver gilt singing bird box; platinum and diamond wrist watch; my mother's silver dressing table set; a carved ivory broach; Caryl's First World War medals and Baronet's badge:

The Bagot Collection was formed quite by chance. When Lord Bagot and I first went to live at Blithfield Hall in 1946, we found a large wooden chest full of clothes, many of them had probably been used for amateur dramatic performances, some had obviously been especially made for such occasions, but some had been left, care-fully folded, either because of their beauty and elegance, or, for sentimental reasons, or both. One of the coats had a paper sewn on it with the words *'Coat worn by Sir Charles Bagot on his wedding day'*. A little pair of Regency style shoes made of a pale blue material has *'H. Bagot'* written inside. Some of the women's shoes, and most of the children's were made at Blithfield. Two of the 18th century suits have *'Lord Bagot'* written on the linings, also, inside a wig, and a rather smart Tricorne hat has *'Hon William Bagot'* written on its base. When I was getting Blithfield ready to open to the public, in 1956, all these things, previously treated with affectionate amusement, had to help illustrate a part of the history of the family and house. Blithfield Hall was open to visitors for 21 years, but, owing to the greatly increased cost of upkeep, it had to be closed in 1977, and work on dividing the house into four separate houses had been started. When this had been done, it was hoped visitors would be able to see some of the main rooms again, but there was not space to display the costumes, so I am very happy to know they now have a 'good home' where they will be cared for and appreciated. But this is not the whole of the story. A large house like Blithfield has plenty of space for hoarding things, so, when someone who is a hoarder by nature is fortunate enough to live in a large house, after a period of time you find you have a 'collection'! The interest, and value, of the collection though, depends on the ability of those who make the

THE BAGOT COLLECTION
Collections of the City Museum and Art Gallery Stoke-on-Trent

Volume 1
Female
Clothes
and
Accessories
1775–1965

The Bagot Collection. Yvonade photographs of Nancy wearing black net evening dress by Jean Partu, Paris. Bought in Nice 1938

items. In the 18th century, the amount of painstaking work needed to create Sir Walter Wagstaffe Bagot's beautiful plum coloured coat, and canary yellow waistcoat, can easily be seen, and, I know, very well, the amount of time and effort needed to make my mid-20th century clothes.

In 1952 Lilian, Lady Bagot, widow of the 4th Lord Bagot, asked me if I would like to have her Coronation Robes, which she had had made for King George V's Coronation, naturally I accepted, with the utmost gratitude. Knowing the robes would need some alteration, she then kindly gave me the name and address of her dressmaker; so began my association with Bojenna Kulczycki, which lasted until her death in 1977. The association blossomed into one of friendship and love, not only for Bojenna, but for her family as well. Her father had been Agent to a Polish nobleman, and she had studied law, in Warsaw, before the war. She was able to escape to England, and join the Polish forces here, where she met her husband, also in the Polish forces. After the war, with one little girl, and having lost everything in Poland of course, they started to make a new life in London, where Bojenna trained as a dressmaker. She was a perfectionist, it was impossible to get her to lower her standards. Sometimes she would tell me she had been up half the night to finish a garment on time. Once, only once, I said 'I wish you wouldn't tire yourself out, do you have to spend so much time finishing all the inside seams so perfectly?' Deeply offended, she said 'My work has to be perfect, it might be in a museum one day.' A very prophetic remark! If I hadn't had a large house, with plenty of attic space, I wouldn't have been able to keep so many of the clothes Mrs. Kulczycki made for me, and if she hadn't made them so exquisitely, I might have been tempted to have some of them altered. She made almost everything I wore during the 25 years of our association, and I still enjoy wearing many of the lovely clothes she made for me. I miss Bojenna more than I can say, no one will ever say to me again 'You know every stitch is put in with love.' So, it gives me enormous pleasure that dear Mrs.Kulczycki's work will be admired, and appreciated. She put all her creative ability into it.

Some of my earliest memories are of watching my grandmother working a Singer sewing machine, then I remember my mother taking lessons in dressmaking, and how I had to stand on a table, for what seemed like hours, while the hem of my dress was straightened and pinned up. I have always enjoyed sewing and embroidery, and took dressmaking as a subject in my Australian Intermediate Exam (the equivalent of 'O' Level). After acquiring a wardrobe of French and English clothes on my first trip to Europe in 1938-1939, I used to enjoy altering them during the war years, when there never seemed to be enough clothing coupons, and it was a pleasant change to get out of uniform occasionally. Not very long after the war ended, Dior's 'New Look' gave women the chance to discard the 'Military Look', with well padded shoulders, and the short tight skirts patriotically saving material, and to look feminine again. But, to set the scene for the 1950s, I must go back into the 1940s, because, the fact that my husband and I lived in a small house in Chelsea, during the war, and after the war spent some time there each year, until my husband's death in 1961, meant that we each had city clothes and country clothes. It wasn't until clothes rationing ended, in 1949, that I really felt free to choose clothes for a special occasion, any additions to the wardrobe, before then, needed careful consideration. My husband succeeded his cousin, as 6th Lord Bagot, in 1946, so we had plenty to do, trying to make a small part of Blithfield habitable, after years of neglect.

In 1953 my husband was lucky to get two seats in Westminster Abbey for the Queen's Coronation. I say 'lucky' because peers with no special duty to perform, had to ballot for seats in the Abbey, and those not fortunate in the ballot, sat, with their wives and families, in a specially built stand outside. I consider I was exceptionally fortunate as I was one of only two Australian born Peeresses in Westminster Abbey. Lord Bagot's Coronation Robes were made for the Coronation of George IV, and he was able to buy the velvet court dress worn under the robes. As I mentioned before, Lilian, Lady Bagot, gave me her Coronation Robes, but not including the kirtle. I had to have this made, as Lady Bagot's daughter, Barbara, had the kirtle made into an evening dress after her mother had worn it to King George VI's Coronation, probably the same thing has happened to a number of Coronation robes! In December, 1952 my husband received orders, from the Earl Marshal, about dress to be worn at Queen Elizabeth II's Coronation:

> The Robe of State of a Peer is to be of crimson velvet, edged down the front with miniver fure, with a full cape, also of miniver fure with rose or bars of ermine tails, according to degree. A Baron: two rows of ermine tails. The Coronet of a Peer is to be of silver gilt, the cap of crimson velvet turned up with ermine, with a gold tassel on top, the circlet having on its rim in the case of: A Baron: six silver balls on the rim of equal size at equal distances. Peeresses attending will be expected to wear, if possible, Robes of State and Coronets, according to their respective ranks, together with Kirtles and Coronation Dress. The Robe of State of a Peeress consists of a mantle of crimson velvet, with a train, the whole edged with a band of miniver fure and having a cape also of miniver fure with rows or bars of ermine tails as follows: A Baroness: the train three feet on the ground, the edging of miniver fure to be two inches and the cape to have two rows of ermine tails. The Coronet of a Peeress is to be similar in all respects to that of a Peer of the same degree, except in regard to its size, which is smaller. The Coronation Dress worn by a Peeress with her Robe consists of a Kirtle of crimson velvet, bordered all round with a narrow edging of miniver fure, scalloped, or straight in front. The Kirtle which may be fastened down the back, or front, opens from the waist widening gradually down to the ground. The sleeves should be about nine inches long, and each have two narrow bands of miniver fure and a lilac edging which may be scalloped. White lace sleeves may be added. The Kirtle is worn over the usual full Court Dress, without a train. The petticoat (or skirt) should be white, or slightly cream coloured, with lace, embroidery or brocade, in accordance with taste. Brocade is to be of gold or silver, no colour may be introduced into it. Feathers and veils will not be worn, but a tiara should be worn, if possible.

1) Jewels may be worn round the neck, on the bodice and on the petticoat.

2) Any Robes and Kirtles worn at previous Coronations may be worn.

December 1952.

In 1953 Bojenna Kulczycki made me dresses and coats to wear at Royal Ascot. On the first day of the race meeting (Tuesday), whatever the weather, something plain was worn, on the second day, something more elaborate, so that on the third day, the garden party atmosphere was all the more noticeable, because of the previous restraint. However, nothing looks elegant if it is not suitable for the changeable English climate, so it is necessary to cater for all weathers! The same applies to clothes for Royal Garden Parties. You can't look happy if you're cold and having to clutch a large hat on a windy day, or, if the heels of your shoes sink into soft turf, or, worse still, mud. My husband was President of the Staffordshire Society from 1952–1954, and long evening dresses were worn on all formal occasions, with long white gloves, but ballet length or shorter, evening dresses were often worn when going to a theatre, or small private dinner party, in London. Fashions change more slowly in the country, and I'm sure I always wore a long evening dress when going out to dine, or, for a dinner party at home. Also, something which seems very odd today, I used to wear a hat when going out to luncheon. In October, 1953 Queen Elizabeth the Queen Mother came to luncheon given in her honour, after she had opened Blithfield Reservoir. The luncheon was held in the Great Hall at Blithfield. Mrs. Kulczycki made me a suit from peacock blue velvet, and Alice Camus, who had a shop in Sloane Street, made me a small close fitting hat of peacock blue feathers, for this very special occasion. Nearly all the materials for my clothes came from Jacqmar, in Grosvenor Street. The price of materials being greatly reduced in the winter and summer sales made it difficult to resist the temptation to buy their lovely pure silks, cottons and woollens. Some of the silk, and cotton, materials, were made into hats by

Freda, and clothes, if made in a rather dateless, classic style, of plain materials, could be brightened by Freda's hats. I was, and still am, very fond of beige as a basic colour, and used to wear a lot of black in London and dark colours in the country, cool colours in summer, and warm colours in winter. Some of the clothes, handbags and gloves in the collection, dating from the 1920s and 1930s belonged to my mother. In one or two of the 1939 dresses the use of a bright coloured floral design, on a black silk ground is very noticeable. The puff sleeves, the sort Anne of Green Gables longed for, are very much of the late 1930s period, as is the fashion for Edwardian style hats, set by Princess Marina, Duchess of Kent.

The blue silk taffeta evening dress, patterned with pink roses, was bought in Paris before the war, and given to me by a relative in the early 1950s. Mrs. Kulczycki altered it, and I wore it a lot, the last time to the opening of Parliament in 1960, plus tiara, long white gloves, and a pink silk stole. Stoles and shawls are a very comfortable fashion for anyone who feels the cold, as I do. Mrs. Kulczycki often lined my dresses and jackets with silk chiffon, and jap silk, and put a wool interlining in any top coat she made for me. I always went to her home, in Fulham, for fittings; in winter she would have a cheerful fire in her sitting room; the warmth being very necessary, as I have said. Bojenna Kulczycki was a perfectionist and liked to make a garment on one, almost, you had to have great patience, and stamina! She always had a number of the latest fashion magazines such as *L'Officiel, Elle, Vogue* and *Harper's Bazaar;* usually I chose a style from one of the books and perhaps asked for it to be simplified. Mrs. Kulczycki preferred more elaborate clothes, and, when I first knew her she would persuade me to have something she liked, but, after several alterations (which she never minded doing) she realised it was better not to try to persuade me to her way of thinking. She was probably far more willing to put up with some discomfort, for the sake of fashion, than I was. My husband didn't drive, so I always drove the car, and insisted on having the back of my dresses and jackets made broader than she would have liked, and the sleeves, less skin tight. However, clothes in the 1950s were much more restricting than anyone would put up with now.

In September, 1959, my husband and I went to Australia and were away about six months. The journey by sea took five weeks, and we came back to England by the same route which meant another five weeks at sea. Most of the passengers changed into evening dress for dinner, and sports clothes were needed for deck games. Cotton materials are coolest in tropical heat, so we had a lot of cool, comfortable, clothes, as well as lightweight woollens for the not so warm spring weather in Sydney, and, autumn weather, in April. The summer was very hot. It seems incredible now, but we took three wardrobe trunks, seven suit cases, and three hat boxes between us! Mrs. Kulczycki was busy for months making me a *'trousseau'* to take on this first trip I had made back to my homeland for seventeen years.

The book which gave me an interest, and then, a fascination with the development of fashion is James Laver's *Taste and Fashion.* In it he says:

> In every period, costume has some essential line, and, when we look back over the fashions of the past we can see, quite plainly, what it is, and can see, what is surely very strange, that the forms of dresses, apparently so haphazard, so dependent on the whim of the designer, have an extraordinary relevance to the spirit of the age... The modes of the past can be plotted with scientific accuracy. The fashions of the future are incalculable precisely because fashion is an art.

It is my hope that the Bagot Collection will give pleasure, and perhaps inspiration, to those who see all, or some, of the items. I am so glad The City of Stoke-on-Trent Museum [now known as The Potteries Museum] has taken things into their care, and I would like to thank Mrs. Sheila Bradbury and her helpers for the hours of work spent on the collection, and for their enthusiasm, which has encouraged me to write this introduction.

Nancy Bagot. Blithfield Hall, January, 1983. [Minor changes 2010]

19

Cara and her Mother

CARA'S AND MY FIRST FLIGHT TOGETHER WAS A SHORT ONE, TO JERSEY, TO stay with Louise Bagot. Mary Bagot was with her mother, also Mary's sister, Cynthia Crawley-Boevey and her daughter, Susan. They lived not far from a beach, but Cara didn't like walking in the sand or bathing in the sea, however, she enjoyed walking. It is such a lovely island, I envied them living there.

When Cynthia and Susan were staying at Blithfield, the 'RATS', or Rugeley Arts Theatre Society, were producing Shakespearian plays in the centre courtyard (see page 67). Mrs Lucas was looking after Cara and Susan, who were supposed to be in bed. In spite of much 'semaphoring' by Cynthia from her seat in the audience, Susan, watching Malvolio in *Twelfth Night* in his prison behind nursery screens, called out excitedly from the Nursery corridor above, 'Oh Mummy he's reading his part!'

A Midsummer Night's Dream was delightful, especially when Valerie Towlson's ballet class danced. The peacocks liked to join in from a chimney top whenever a song was sung. The old house made such a romantic setting as the light faded and Oberon and Titania, with their train, drifted through the Great Hall, carrying candles past the tall windows and onto the steps in front of the entrance to bless the house:

> *Oberon*:
> Through the house give glimmering light,
> By the dead and drowsy fire:
> Every elf and fairy sprite
> Hop as light as bird from brier;
> And this ditty, after me,
> Sing and dance it trippingly.

Titania:

First, rehearse your song by rote,

To each word a warbling note:

Hand in hand, with fairy grace,

Will we sing, and bless this place.

One of the first visits I made with Cara and Nannie was to stay in Devon, near Bovey Tracey, with one of Cara's godfathers, Colonel John Kitson. He had married an Australian friend of mine who, before marriage, as Marcia Russell, had been at Abbotsleigh Church of England School. John already had three children by his first wife. However, he and Sunnie (as she became known) adopted a girl, my god-daughter, Melina, and a boy, Jonathan; Cara's age was between the two.

Nannie, being old-fashioned, wouldn't stay with the Kitsons as they didn't have a nursery bathroom, and Cara being separated from her wouldn't eat! Fortunately, since then, there have been a great many happy meetings, both in Devon and at Blithfield.

Cara started her schooling by going to the excellent Richard Clarke First School in Abbots Bromley. On one of my birthdays she asked me how old I was. Evidently feeling at least a hundred, I said 'one hundred and one'. Soon after, when looking at her work, her open book said 'Today is Mummy's birthday, she is one hundred and one!'

When Cara went to the school of Saint Mary and Saint Anne in Abbots Bromley it was a boarding school, with very few days girls. Having Blithfield open to visitors, and living part-time in Lancashire with Kenneth, it seemed the best thing to do, although Cara was so young. Perhaps boarding affected her more because she was so close to home. When she was about twelve, she and some friends walked to Blithfield one weekend afternoon. Cynthia and Susan happened to be staying at Blithfield (Susan having just left her school). After tea we drove them all back to school as walking with so much traffic on the road seemed to be too dangerous.

It was between Cara's going to Saint Mary and Saint Anne in Abbots Bromley and leaving to attend Saint James' in Malvern, that we twice flew to Sydney via the USA, the first time via San Francisco.

Mrs Crawley-Boevey, née Bagot and daughter Susan

We met the American Bagots, Clifton and Rey Moore at the home of our friends, Molly and Angus Holmes, in 1967 and they came to see Blithfield and stayed with us the following year. When they heard we intended to spend Christmas that year with my mother in Australia, they begged us to fly via San Francisco and be their guests. Before leaving Blithfield we had watched the Bagot goats, in a paddock in the park in front of the Hall, being caught-up and taken to the woods at Goat Lodge, where they would spend the winter months. One of our first visits in San Francisco was to the park where we found some goats had escaped from their enclosure; so, from having watched the Bagot goats being rounded up in Staffordshire, we were helping to catch goats in San Francisco!

Rey took us to the large fashionable shop of 'I Magnum' and bought Cara some very pretty dresses which were the envy of all the girls she met in Sydney. We enjoyed rides in cable cars, but I didn't at all like going in a lift to the top of one of the highest buildings on the outside!

Flying to Sydney that way seemed endless. We landed at Hawaii, Fiji and Brisbane, before Sydney, where my mother, brother and cousins, waited to greet us. I am afraid all we wanted to do was sleep. My brother drove us to my mother's flat, or unit as it was called in Roseville, which

Margot Bagot's marriage to Commander Alexander Black, RAN. North Sydney

had a view over bushland, about eight miles north of Sydney.

As Cara's birthday was on 9 December, my cousin, Lucy Clifford, suggested a birthday party in the garden of her flat at North Sydney. Unfortunately, there was a storm at 2 o'clock, so Cara's first birthday in a warm country had to be held indoors. Cara, wearing one of the attractive dresses Rey had bought her, sat at the head of the table looking rather like Queen Victoria, while all the extrovert Australian children started on the feast laid out in front of them; I have since wondered how such unruly children could turn into such nice adults.

Ted and Rose Bagot, who lived in Pymble, close to Roseville, had four daughters. Cara often stayed with them and also at their house at Palm Beach, although with her fair skin she couldn't sunbathe and didn't like the surf.

The next time we visited Australia and we were waiting at Heathrow to board the plane, I asked Cara what she would like me to buy her. She asked for a tea towel with a Union flag pattern on it, I expect to hold her own with all the Southern Cross flags!

Cara and I loved staying with the Blacks at Trafalgar Hill. Margot Black (née Bagot), was one of Caryl's and my first visitors to Blithfield, where she soon made friends with my cousin Lucy and with Marcia. When Caryl and I were at Blithfield, the three of them shared our house at No 16 The Gateways, Chelsea. Margot was a delightful person and when she returned to Sydney she married a Royal Australian Navy Commander, Alex Black. I have never seen a happier wedding photograph than theirs.

Alex wanted to build up a station after the Second World War and bought land in beautiful country on the Shoalhaven River, about eighty miles south east of Canberra. He called the property Trafalgar Hill, because, he said, it had been such a 'bloody battle'! Alex and Margot's children, and their children, are living there now. Margot and I carried on a regular correspondence over the last fifty years and it is a great sadness to me, now 'the book' I have been telling her about is nearing completion and she is no longer here to share it with me. However, Trafalgar Hill still has Alex and the Black family.

The second time Cara and I flew to Australia via the USA, we stayed in Long Beach, Los Angeles, with Rey and Clifton's daughter and son-in-law, Nini and Steve Horn. There was a large magnolia grandiflora in their garden and our bedroom window looked onto it, the creamy velvet flowers filling our room with the scent of lemon.

The Horns were so kind and hospitable. Of course, we went to Disneyland and I could see how it had grown from the film industry. We had great fun there with Rey and Clifton and their grandson, Stephen. I was especially impressed at how clean and tidy this huge place, with all its visitors, was kept. We also toured Beverley Hills and had lunch on board the *Queen Mary* in Los Angeles harbour. Steve, later to become a Congressman, took us to visit the University of Southern California, of which he was President. Cara and I were to have the pleasure of one of Rey and Clifton's granddaughters at Blithfield the following year, when she came to join Cara at St James' School in Malvern.

When Cara was about twelve she didn't read well. She would get the gist of what was written, but didn't read the exact words. Phil and Jess Drabble suggested her having a test for dyslexia, and I was told she should have been having remedial treatment. When I told Miss Roch, Headmistress of Saint Mary and Saint Anne, she said Cara was a 'slow starter' and she would get a prefect to give her extra lessons. I decided to look for a school with a teacher trained to help dyslexia pupils. Cynthia, Cara's godmother, and her daughter, Susan, my goddaughter, came with me. We visited St Mary's, Wantage and St James', Malvern. St Mary's was too far to be visited from Blithfield in a day, whereas Malvern could not only be visited in a day, but there were also several hotels where I could stay. In addition, there was a teacher trained to help girls with dyslexia. St James' had been built by Lady Howard de Walden, it was said for her nephew, in a similar style to Osborne House on the Isle of Wight. The views were magnificent. In fact, Cara always said I sent her there because I liked the views!

The father of Cara's great friend, Marie Madeleine Simon, died almost as soon as Marie Madeleine started at St James', so her mother, Jan Simon, and I as single mothers became great friends. Jan and I were delighted when Cara and Marie Madeleine told us they were to be in a school play, which was to take place in the gardens, but it turned out that all they did was to hold trees cut from cardboard! We often stayed at The Mount Pleasant Hotel, where the gardens joined the Malvern Hills, where we loved to walk with Cara's and my King Charles' spaniels, Fitz and Roy. Rey and Clifton Moore's granddaughter, Holly Pope, had joined Cara at St James'. She was older than Cara, so had a study bedroom. Nevertheless, it must have been very strange for her coming from an American co-educational school to an English girls' boarding school. She was interested in everything and never complained. It was a pleasure to have her with us, and I admired her enormously and am very fond of her.

Cara was confirmed at the church in West Malvern by Bishop Woods, whose father was Bishop of Lichfield when Caryl and I went to live at Blithfield.

After Cara had sat GCE 'O' Levels, I agreed to her leaving, provided she attended Evendine, not far from St James', and with the same Council. The first year was for general household management and the second for *cordon bleu* cooking.

Cara and I had stayed at Levens Hall in Cumbria with Robin and Annette Bagot in 1971 on our way to stay at Harden with Lord and Lady Polwarth, Harry and Jean (Jean née Cunninghame Graham is a cousin of Caryl's). The last ride I had was on the moorlands with Harry, to make sure the bonfire, ready to celebrate Sir Walter Scott's birth in 1771, was still intact.

A few years later, Cara's first job was to cook for Jean, with Melina Kitson, my goddaughter. They will be remembered for some time for having chopped up the very large marrow, which should have won first prize in the local show!

Another friend of Cara's, Frances Orme, who was at St James' (as was her mother) had been cooking for the Countess of Sutherland at the 'House of Tongue' in the far north of Scotland, but when Frances had to return to university she suggested Cara taking her place. When Lady Sutherland visited Trentham in Staffordshire to see about a sale, she came to see me at Blithfield to reassure me about Cara's wellbeing and to tell me how pleased she and her family were to have Cara with them.

Cara and I were invited to Arabella Jauncey's wedding in Scotland. She had been staying with the Bagots in Australia. Ted and Rose and one of their daughters, Tempe, were also invited. Tempe was staying with us at Blithfield and we were to meet her parents in Scotland. The night before we left, as Tempe said she didn't have a hat to wear, I brought several of mine from the attic. They were tried on amidst many reminiscences and a not very interesting black straw hat was chosen. We left very early in the morning and arrived at Levens about 8 am. Not wishing to disturb the family, I parked the car and we followed the river to the far end of the Park, where we found the Bagot goats. This was Tempe's first sight of them – they were struggling to reach the fresh looking leaves on lime trees. It was a lovely hot day for the wedding, the country church, massed with cool looking flowers, was perfect. There were lots of families, including Cunninghame Graham, Jauncey, Maudslay, Jean and Harry Polwarth (Jean, Arabella's mother) and Bagots of course. We were pleased to see Mary Pearson, who used to come to Blithfield with Olave. At the dance in the evening, Cara, having learnt Scottish dancing from Valerie Towlson, was one of the few sassenachs who could take part in the Scottish reels.

As the Sterickers came from Yorkshire and I had been told my grandfather had been a choir boy in York Minster, Kit Stericker and I went to spend a few days in York. Staying at the Dean Court Hotel close to the

Minster, we were overwhelmed by its beauty and strength. A mirror had been placed in order to see the recently replaced timbers in a part of the roof after a fire. The Stafford firm of Venables had been employed; also, I was interested to see that Francis Bernasconi had done work on the Choir Screen. We were amazed by the wonders in the Treasury held in the Undercroft.

When walking around the fascinating streets we met friends from Lichfield, Mr Dennis Birch and his wife. Mr Birch was the Diocesan solicitor. I told them what we had been doing and when I mentioned the Treasury, wondering why there was nothing like it in Lichfield, I was told something was being planned. The result is the Heritage Museum in St Mary's Church, Lichfield.

One of the highlights of our visit was an evening with George Smith, viewing his beautiful garden and dining with him and Brian Withall in the perfect Manor House and garden at Heslington. When I was President of Lichfield Flower Club, George had come to give a pre-Christmas demon-stration, after which he came to Blithfield, giving a talk and demonstration in the Great Hall, incidentally assuring everyone that he hadn't plucked the peacock tail feathers from my Ferdinand! He and Brian spent the night at Blithfield, George in the bedroom decorated by John Fowler. George kindly made some flower arrangements for me to use when I didn't have time to do the flowers.

I was so happy when my old friend, Jean Russell (née Grant), came to stay and as an artist she delighted in the gardens and countryside at Blith-field. As a 'Grant' she had stayed with her family when a teenager at Minto House. We decided to go to Scotland, staying at the Heves Hotel, near Levens on the way, Jean was amazed at the topiary garden and we were so pleased to see Dianna Taylor, Robin Bagot's sister, who was living in the Stable Cottage. We stayed in Hawick to do some shopping as the 'sales' were taking place, and I bought pullovers, cardigans and scarves, etc. We called at Harden and then went to see Minto House. We had been told it was deserted and the present Earl was living in a more modern house nearby. Jean had telephoned, but he was away. As we approached Minto House it seemed to be welcoming us − built of soft rose-red stone, with welcoming arms outstretched, with the front door in the middle, as we got nearer we saw that the handsome iron gates were hanging. The garden, where Jean had walked was quite overgrown, doors and windows open, and we could see what looked like green Chinese wall-paper in a room upstairs. We didn't dare to go upstairs, but walked into one or two rooms on the ground floor. Jean said how she disliked seeing waste and picked up a small wooden fire surround, giving it to Cara, knowing I was making a flat for her in the rooms in the attic. For herself, she picked up a small piece of cornice, and we went out feeling very sad and wondering why no one appeared to be making any effort to save such a lovely house. We were told of a story that a Lady Minto, born in Montreal, beautiful of course, had fallen from an upstairs window. Before going on to have lunch with some of Jean's relatives, I covered the little fire surround with a rug. I said, if our hosts see it they will say 'Those dreadful Australians, they've been souveniring!'

The next day we went on to Edinburgh with the intention of visiting the Palace of Holyrood and then going on to Inverary, where Mary had booked a room for us at a hotel and had a special dinner ready for us, including raspberries from the Castle. It was a hot day and Princes Street was so crowded we couldn't find anywhere for lunch, so we bought sand-wiches and drove to the car park at Holyrood. Once parked, I opened the back of the estate car in order to make coffee. There were crowds of people about and when I went to get my bag from the back of the car it wasn't there. With it had gone £25, a gold Stafford Knot and worst of all, the keys of the car! I went to tell the police, who had an office in the car park and felt very cross when all they said was 'Oh, not another one!' There were no notices warning people. A man came from a garage and told us the Peugeot garage had closed for the night. He thought we ought to spend the night in a bed and breakfast. We felt we didn't want to lose our luggage as well, so Jean said we ought to sit in the car and pretend we were flying to Australia! Then the garage man offered us the use of his caravan, which he parked beside the car; he said he and his wife had prepared it to go on holiday – we could hardly believe our luck at such kindness, also the fact that we had bought lots of woollies in Hawick. In spite of everything, we spent rather a restless night as a police car drove round every half hour or each hour. I don't think many people have spent

Cara with Nancy's aunt Dora and cousin 'KM', Katharine Mary

Cara with her godfather Jimmy Wigan (Edgar Clare Wigan) in his garden

Above: William 2nd Lord Bagot, painted by niece Charlotte Sneyd, 1852

Left: Max Cooper's Carlton House writing desk and portrait of Hervey Bagot

Below: a faux-bamboo chair made by Max Cooper for the Chinese room

White roses in a green glass vase
Patricia Machin

Cara and Jean
Russell at Levens

Nancy and her mother at Mowell village

Cara and Kelvin after their wedding

Josef and Tamara came back to Blithfield after they had retired.

They said it would 'always be their home'

The 2nd Lord Bagot's travelling coach, 1824

Putting coaches in the orangery

Friary construction firm at work including, above, a dumper truck in The Cloisters

Lady Bagot and Rachel Haynes, Jack's daughter, in 2010. 'I would never have written this book without her, full of sense and sensibility'

Jack Brown, of Colton, in 2010. A faithful friend of Blithfield for over sixty years

a night in a caravan outside the Palace of Holyrood. The public cloak-rooms were the cleanest we had visited and the kindness of the lenders of the caravan will never be forgotten. Next morning, the Peugeot garage changed the locks on the car and we set off to join Mary in Inverary, where we enjoyed salmon and raspberries.

We were staying at a hotel and enjoyed visits to the Castle, and to the Duchess' family home. Then I lost my St Christopher and began to feel the little fire surround should not have been taken from Minto House. We were booked to go further north to stay in Buckie, where Jean's mother's relatives had come from, and to my shame I said I wanted to get back to Blithfield (very selfish of me). I will always remember dear Jean picking up the fire surround and returning to put it back into the decaying house, saying 'I never knew you were superstitious'. In a way, it was rather like a strong feeling I had when the little music box started playing on my first visit to Blithfield.

I first met Pat and Arnold Machin when they came to one of the annual parties I had at Blithfield for mentally disabled children. The parties took place in the evening and were for parents, carers and friends of the children. Arnold gave a talk and showed slides of his recently completed stamp showing his beautiful model of the Queen's head and he gave Cara some stamps.

Pat invited Cara and me to tea. They were living in a small house with a large garden at Bishops Offley. It was one of the 'never to be forgotten' days! Arnold had made a cascade into a valley, where a steep path wound round red rocks to a bridge across the bottom of the valley. The bridge was not only a bridge, but a summer house too. The small stone house (christened by Cara and me 'Mrs Tiggywinkles') had no electricity – or perhaps we didn't notice it, because Pat and Arnold always liked to use candles, and on this particular evening, the candles were in a lovely big brass chandelier. I didn't know it then, but for years to come it would be my delight to take candles each Christmas for that chandelier.

Pat, Arnold and their son, Francis, were artists, and they were able to give, wherever they lived, an enchanting quality – the Georgian farm-house, still with its old-fashioned farm buildings, Arnold's grotto, the lake reflecting fireworks, Francis' boathouse and Pat's border of old-fashioned roses, which she was so happy painting. Cara and I loved being with them, especially at Christmas, and seeing their happiness in their grandchildren. They were life-enhancing. I am thankful to have a reminder of that life in the form of some of Pat's flower pictures here at Blithfield (see page 267) and thankful to have had such highly valued friends.

Cara was working for Lady Clifford at Ugbrooke Park in Devon in early 1981, they also had a property in Victoria, Australia. I felt she was under a lot of pressure to go out there, which she could afford to do as her godfather, dearest Jimmy Wigan, who had died aged 103, had left her £15,000. I was thankful it was Australia she was going to as she would have my relatives and friends to turn to if she wanted to. The sad thing was that Ted and Rose Bagot's eldest daughter, Caroline, was coming to England and would be making Blithfield her headquarters. I had hoped they might do some travelling together. Rose telephoned me one day to ask if I knew where Caroline was. I was able to tell her I knew she had gone on a tour of the Continent with some other Australians. I then asked Rose if she knew where Cara was. Her answer was 'No, but I'll find out!'

After Cara returned from Australia, Francis Machin helped her to get a job in London and she started doing business lunches for Norton Rose, a firm of solicitors in the City. We were watching the news on television one Saturday at Blithfield, when it showed a scene of devastation caused by an IRA bomb in the City. Cara said, 'That's my kitchen!' I was so thankful she was here with me – the ancient church of St Ethelberger's was destroyed, to rise again. I was pleased when not long after, Cara decided to move to Oxford. She found a one bedroom flat in a new development, which had a small garden. The result was she fell in love with her neighbour from the flat next door, Kelvin Heath, whose family live in Oxford, and they decided to get married on his birthday 8 May 2008 in the Town Hall at Woodstock. Afterwards there was a celebration tea in The Bear Hotel. I read from a letter I had recently come across when looking up past history for this book. The letter was written by Kit Stericker, in glowing terms about Cara, to my mother in Australia.

20

The Division of Blithfield

THE IDEA OF DIVIDING BLITHFIELD, ALSO THE OLD STABLES, WAS TO KEEP them looking more or less the same from outside, but to have people living here helping with the up-keep of this historic and ancient house.

I won't say it wasn't a hard decision to have to take, especially after having made a great success of the Museum of Childhood. However, that had to go, and there is now a separate house on each side of the centre Courtyard, as well as eight houses in the Old Stables, and Blithfield still looks as it has done since the Second Lord gave it its Gothic 'dress' in 1824. It took about twenty years of planning, worry, heartache and expense to achieve my aim. Planning permission would be essential.

I knew Mrs Riley, the County Planning Officer for Stafford, through my connection with The Council for the Protection of Rural England and The Society for the Protection of Ancient Buildings. She suggested my meeting Mr Wade, the Chief Planning Officer for Burton-on-Trent, in her office, which I and my architect did. She was not there. I explained what I wanted to do, and the architect showed Mr Wade the plans. Having looking at them he said, 'If you do this there won't be so much for the visitors to see'. To which I replied, 'I know there won't, but if I don't do something the place will fall into ruins'. Mr Wade replied, 'Oh well, lots of people go to see the ruins at Tintagel, what I would like to see there would be a nice leisure centre!' So I knew I would have to find someone who would like to enter the growing enterprise of dividing country houses – a developer would be more likely to get planning permission.

I am surprised I had any friends left – all I could talk about was finding someone who would be happy to convert Blithfield into several houses. I could only offer the buildings and the land they stood on. Poor Colonel Guy German was a captive and long-suffering audience, being in a wheel-

The division: 1 Blithfield Hall, 2 Oriel House, 3 Cloister House and 4 Oak House

chair after an operation. Arnold Machin, the sculptor, who had done the best loved design of the Queen's head (which is on all our postage stamps) and his talented artist wife, Pat, were always sympathetic and sensitive listeners, so too were Phil and Jess Drabble, who had converted Goat Lodge at the entrance to Bagot's Park by employing a Lichfield builder, Mr Deakin, and his son, Horace. As I have said already, Horace loved working on old buildings. He had completed a course with The Society for the Protection of Ancient Buildings and had noticed, as I had, the work in Abbots Bromley of a local man, Mr Ray Wright, Director of the Friary Construction Company. His houses in Abbots Bromley were built around a courtyard, off the main street, with just two houses on the street, on either side of the entrance to the courtyard. Horace was a great help talking to Ray Wright and persuading him that this was an opportunity to enter the field of restoring and converting old buildings into houses and apartments. In order to get planning permission, Ray said it would be necessary to have a feasibility study done. When I told my mother she said that she would pay for it. The next thing was to draw up an agreement between The Friary Construction Company and myself. I was persuaded to ask a friend of the Drabbles to act for me – their family lawyer, in fact, Mr Philip Jagger.

Mr Wright applied for planning permission on my behalf to convert the old Forge in Admaston village into a cottage and for the two little one-roomed Lodges at the entrance to the Park to be turned into cottages. He also applied for seven houses to be constructed in the Old Stables, the Coach House there being the only bungalow. The Garden Cottage, forming the north-east corner of the Stable Courtyard, was let to Mrs O'Neill, my former Agent's widow. The old Brewhouse, being used as a garage, would make an attractive cottage too. The south front of Blithfield Hall, also the West Wing of the Hall, both facing into the Inner Courtyard, would make reasonably sized and most unusual houses, just leaving the East and North Wings as 'Blithfield Hall' in my possession. The feasibility study also included rebuilding the burnt-out remains of The Old Rectory to the west of Blithfield Church. This site had splendid views across the Trent Valley to Cannock Chase in the distance. It also had a separate approach from Lea Lane. Blithfield Church also has this same approach. Planning permission was being sought for four flats to be built in the rebuilt old Rectory and for ten houses to be built in the former Stables and Kitchen Garden.

People do not like change, especially where nothing like this had happened before. Christopher Buxton and Kit Martin were busy converting historic houses, and even ruins of houses, into apartments in other parts of the country. I had already consulted Christopher Buxton; however, there was a great deal of local opposition and planning permission didn't seem to be forthcoming. One day Horace said to me, 'The planning meetings have been opened to the public. I think I'll go along to the next one'. Afterwards he said, 'There was one member of the Committee who didn't like the Chairman'.

Ray Wright had asked Mr Peter Brownhill, Architect, to draw up plans for the two Lodges. I received a message in February 1980, to say the Planning Committee members were going to pay a visit to Blithfield to inspect the whole site. As it happened, I was going to London for the day and left instructions to have coffee and biscuits ready. It was a very cold day with snow on the ground and some of the Committee members were ladies. On arrival, Horace was there to meet them, and speaking to the member he had noticed seemed to be at odds with the Chairman, said, 'Lady Bagot is sorry, but she has had to go to London today, however, when you have seen everything, if you would like to come in for a cup of coffee you would be welcome'. The Chairman, upon hearing this, immediately said, 'Oh we won't have time for that'. 'Speak for yourself' said the man to whom Horace had spoken. Horace told me all the members were only too happy to come indoors for coffee, and we got planning permission, the Chairman declaring he would never give planning permission in bulk like this again. However, I am sure the Council in Burton-on-Trent is very pleased now to have fourteen people as tax payers at Blithfield and sixteen at The Old Rectory.

The Chairman of Blithfield Parish Council was Mr George Vernon, who owned Newton Farm and was a Church Warden, so I was much encouraged and thankful when he told me the Parish Council had agreed to my plans. Planning permission was granted.

I have since heard that when the planners came indoors, Horace showed them into his workshop in the Servants' Hall, where they re-examined all the plans. They were especially impressed with the plans made by a young architect, Mr Peter Brownhill, for the two Lodges and the Stables, but once planning permission was granted, just after this meeting, Mr Brownhill was not employed. I am sure Horace persuaded Mr Wright that this was his chance to enter the rapidly growing field of country house conversion, and I am not surprised that Mr Wright tried to entice Horace to work for him!

The idea was that I would provide the buildings and Ray Wright's firm would do the work. When a property was sold I would get 10% of the price paid. This worked for the Forge, but unfortunately by the time the first Lodge was finished, there was a downturn in the market so it was some time before a buyer could be found. Instead of its being sold on a 999-year lease, I agreed to both Lodges being sold freehold, but I wouldn't agree to the land between the Lodges and the main road being sold, knowing from the experience my cousin at Painshill had when she bought one of the Lodges. One of the first things an owner is likely to do is to make his or her Lodge look very different from its twin!

Mr Wright, not having made as much money as he had hoped for from the Lodges, said he couldn't afford to go on with the Stables unless I would agree to take 5% instead of 10%, when each of the seven properties was sold. Because the first impression as one approaches Blithfield is the view of the turreted and battlemented Stables, I agreed. Mr Wright had done me a good turn when I was in Australia by going to see the solicitors of The South Staffordshire Waterworks Company and offering to buy the drive from the Company – it being the only way of approaching the Hall. The land, having been sold to The South Staffordshire Waterworks Company by Gerald Lord Bagot was later sold to a farmer, Mr Palfrey (not long after the Second World War), a new farmhouse subsequently being built to the north of Blithfield. Mr Palfrey was asking an enormous price for giving permission for the sewer pipe (which was necessary for our project) to be taken over his land to the main sewer in the village of Admaston, so now as owner of the drive I was able to say, 'Accept a sensible price or the pipe will go along the drive'.

It was now necessary to decide what to do about the coaches in the Coach House. Horace and I agreed we could put the lovely travelling coach of 1824, in which the Second Lord had travelled over the Alps, into the west-end of the Orangery, and the little carriage on rollers (so as not to cut up the lawns) could be put into the east-end. That left the Wagonette, the Victoria and the Brougham. These were bought by a man from Stoke-on-Trent, who lent out coaches for weddings. He paid in cash, and Horace, well-padded with notes, took the money to the bank. The men who helped the purchaser of the coaches helped Horace put the travelling coach and the small coach on rollers into the Orangery. Horace had to take the wheels off the big coach and tip it on its side, but it surprised the architect, who had expected to see large doors at the back of the Orangery!

All this time, the South and West Wings of the house had been bricked off from the part of the house where I was living. Ray Wright was supposed to be looking after this part. Nothing was done to protect it. Horace used to get into it to unblock the gutters and rain-water pipes, but it became so bad Horace and I felt Ray Wright wanted to rebuild rather than restore this part of the house. Because of VAT, the first option would be much cheaper and the planners didn't seem to mind.

I am sure when Ray Wright took on the challenge of converting Blithfield into houses he thought the two widows in their sixties (Mrs O'Neill and me) living there, would be the least of his worries.

When I gave my late Agent, John O'Neill, leases for the Garden Cottage (the first for ten years, and then later another for eleven years), the land to go with it included the Kitchen Garden – a section of the western part of this garden would be needed for garages. Mrs O'Neill was offered all sorts of inducements, such as a new house in Abbots Bromley, which, if she had accepted would have enabled Ray Wright to turn the Garden Cottage into two more houses, but no, all she would accept was a considerable sum of money for the area of the Kitchen Garden needed for garages. I also noticed that after my 5% was paid on the basically completed houses in the Old Stables, more elaborate kitchens and bathrooms were installed at the new owners' requests.

One afternoon, Cara and I went to have tea with Henry Harpur-Crewe at Calke Abbey in Derbyshire, which had been taken over by The National Trust after a lot of hard work by Henry, and I noticed that the staircase was bound up like an Egyptian mummy. When I got back to Blithfield there was a dumper truck in the lovely pale apricot neo-Gothic cloisters, and even though workmen were tramping up and down, the delicate little oak staircase had no form of protection.

I had asked one or two estate agency firms to come and have a look at the Hall as I was so worried, not only by the fact that Ray Wright was four years behind the date when all the work, including The Old Rectory, should have been finished, but also by the dreadful state of 'his' part of the building. Savills had no office nearer than Hereford at that time, but when Mr Christopher Lyons came from their office and saw the state of things here, he gave me the courage, with his good advice, to go and see my trusted solicitor in London, Mr Isadore Kerman. When Mr Kerman read the agreement I had with Mr Wright he said, 'What a pity *"time is of the essence"* wasn't written into it: but as Mr. Wright's Friary Construction Company is four years over the date when all the work, including The Old

Rectory, should have been finished, you can stop him working'. So when I got home, I asked Horace to shut the big oak gates in the gateway leading to the main entrance to the Hall, which Horace did with alacrity! The result was I received a letter from Ray Wright, who was a 'pillar of the church' in Abbots Bromley, saying, 'Surely we, as two good Christians should be able to sort this matter out without going to pagan solicitors!' I sent the letter to my solicitors. Later I was sued for £500,000.

About this time I met the new Bishop of Lichfield, who gave me some good advice, 'Never have anything to do with anyone who brings religion into business'.

The next months until the trial, which was set for 22 June 1987 at The Royal Courts of Justice in The Strand, London, were some of the most worrying in my life, with all the legal papers to study, and the unknown costs! I heard from Mr Middlemass of Forsyte Kerman that my counsel, Mr Steinfield, QC, having perused all the documents, thought I had a very good case. He advised asking Friary to settle, ie they drop their claim and pay their costs, and I pay my costs, nothing more. I was told the trial could go on until 25 June.

Toby and Jane, Caryl's nephew, Commander DJB Jewitt, RN, DSC (Retired) and his wife, had asked me to stay with them at Furneux Pelham, Toby having said he would accompany me to the hearing. When I arrived, having driven from Blithfield, they presented me with a lovely book of photographs, taken when I was staying with them in the south of Spain. I wrote in my diary, 'It is very good of Toby to come with me'. We were up early on 22 June and Jane cooked us a sustaining breakfast and drove us to Bishop Stortford railway station, where Toby was greeted like a long lost friend. We went to 79 New Cavendish Street, where I was given a copy of Mr Wright's statement. We had to say what we thought of each other – I said I didn't think he had the knowledge or experience to deal with an historic house like Blithfield, and he said that I was very stubborn! It was difficult to find Court No 29 and Mr Jagger arrived late. Friary's counsel was very long-winded and I was pleased to see Judge Lipfriend look irritated on occasions. My diary entry ends, 'Boring for poor Toby who couldn't hear, neither could I. Very Tired'. My diary entry for 23 June reads, 'A marvellous day! Thank God'.

Toby and I arrived at the Law Courts at 9 am. Philip Jagger, Mr Middlemass and Mr Steinfield were also there, as was Mr Wright, with his assistants. Mr Wright's counsel went bumbling on and asked the Judge to read about a point he'd raised. The Judge said, 'Well, how long is that going to take?' 'About an hour, your Honour ...' was the reply. The Judge, not looking pleased, said, 'Oh all right' – or words to that effect! We all sat there in limbo, I thinking I might be asked to answer questions when the Judge returned. Suddenly, it seemed my counsel was in front of me saying, 'The Judge thinks you ought to settle'. As soon as I realised what he had said, I just felt enormous relief. Then I got up, and smiling, advanced to Mr Wright, hand held out, he was also smiling; we shook hands, but I think we felt like hugging each other! It then fell to me to do all the negotiating on behalf of Blithfield. The result was, I got the Hall back and Mr Wright got the site of The Old Rectory, which suited us both. Once again, for the second time, The Old Rectory had saved Blithfield. I had a bill for £10,000 to be paid at once and £36,000 to be paid later. It was my Australian 'Broken Hill Proprietary Shares', given me by my mother, that paid for this settlement. Sadly, she was no longer here to join in my thankfulness. I thanked God for all the prayers of my relatives and friends and all who loved historic houses. I telephoned Horace, of course, to let him know the good news and when I returned home I lent him the statements to read. It wasn't long before Horace was repairing some of the damage done by The Friary Construction Company to the South and West Wings of the house. And so the great drama for those who had nothing to lose had come to an end!

Mr Wright had planned for two houses to be made in the West Wing, which would have meant the proposed second house in the West Wing would have a front door in the Orangery Garden, which would have spoilt the garden. Mr Lyons started drawing up plans to enable Savills to advertise the South and West Wings for sale as two separate houses.

Rodney Melville, architect for The National Trust, and a friend, had been such a great help over the court case, now drew up contracts and technical attachments for the two houses, and I gave them their names. The South Wing, to which the Second Lord had added a Cloister to what would have been 'lodgings' in the Elizabethan Hall, would obviously be Cloister

House. The West Wing, where a large room was added by the First Lord in 1769 (known as the New Drawing Room) with bedroom and dressing room above, had south facing windows. The bedroom, known as Quality Cockloft, had an oriel window and would be known as Oriel House.

Cloister House was prepared for sale first. I had meetings with Mr Jutton of Forsyte Kerman, Mr Rodney Melville, my architect, and Mr Christopher Lyons of Savills, who I cannot thank enough for giving me the courage to end the agreement with The Friary Construction Company, even though it led to the court case. I now felt sure that Blithfield had been saved as an historic house.

Several people came to look over the two houses after Savills had advertised them in the summer of 1988. The houses had the advantage of not having been 'horriblised', although a considerable amount of restoration was necessary. On 25 June 1988, Mr and Mrs John Hyde came to view one of the houses with their three children. Cara and I liked them and thought the children 'well-behaved', better still, Horace thought well of Mr Hyde.

John Hyde has told me that when he came with his builder, the latter immediately noticed that he could move the top section of the Tower above the front entrance backwards and forwards, about an inch each way, using one hand! The movement was mainly in the upper section – the tower must have been pivoting on its supports which were on the ground floor. Over the next few days, after this discovery, which was at first mystifying, the builder removed the floor boards in the Tower room and discovered there were saw cuts through the joists at the back and sides of the room. This had the effect of disconnecting the Tower from the rest of the house, allowing it to sway freely!

Almost at the same time, Professor Colin Robinson and his wife, decided to take Oriel House in the West Wing of the Hall. It has the advantage of being 'at the end of the line', so no other traffic goes past it. Both Colin Robinson and his wife were economists, he at the University of Guildford and she at Birmingham.

There was still another house to form on the east side of the Inner Courtyard. It was the Nursery Wing, where Cara and I had been living for the last eighteen years and where we were still living. In July 1990, Mr Ivor

Shaw, who lived in Derby, spoke to Josef, who was putting up iron fencing in the Park. Mr Shaw asked if there were any houses for sale at Blithfield and when told there were none, he asked to see me and wouldn't take no for an answer. I said there might be another house, but not until I had moved into an apartment on the ground floor of the North East Wing and Cara into rooms in the attic of the same wing. This wouldn't happen for at least a year. However, he was not going to be put off, so I took him over what eventually became Oak House – the name chosen because of its oak panelled Sitting Room.

Nikolaus Pevsner, in his book *The Buildings of England – Staffordshire*[1] mentions, '... Lady Bagot's study in the E range with late C17 panelling ...'. Actually, from having been the Second Lord's Study (he was painted in it by his niece, Charlotte Augusta Sneyd (1800–1882) of Keele Hall, Staffordshire), it became my snug little bed-sitting room, where sometimes I would be the only person in this rambling eighty-roomed house. It was this room that gave its name to the Oak House.

Jack Brown (who, with his wife, used to manage the village shop in Colton) has, for some time, looked after Blithfield, and their daughter, Rachel, looks after some of the Blithfield inhabitants. I feel sure I couldn't manage without her.

Ever since Caryl and I came to live at Blithfield we had lived in rooms on the first floor. Now that I am living in The Peacock Flat, my bedroom is on the ground floor and in the summer I find it so delightful to be able to walk straight out into the garden. Cara had rooms in the attic, and the rooms of historic interest are mostly on the first floor, such as the Green Room (Chinese Room as it has become now) with late eighteenth-century Chinese wallpaper; Lady Bagot's Bedroom – decorated by John Fowler; the Library – originally the Great Chamber; the eighteenth-century oak panelled Study and the Carolean carved oak Great Staircase leading to the Great Hall on the ground floor.

As the future felt more settled, once most of the work was completed, if any of the Bagot portraits appeared for sale I would try to buy them – and here James Miller at Sothebys was a great help. The portraits of Sir Walter Bagot (living in the reign of Charles II) and his wife, Jane Salesbury, 'the Salesbury heiress', were painted by Michael Wright, and were sold at Sothebys in 1945 for £15. When the portrait of Sir Walter came up for sale again at Sothebys in 1991, James bought it for me at £8,000.

The portraits of all the family members I was able to bring home looked happy to be back at Blithfield!

Note

1 Penguin Books, London, 1974; reprinted 1975 and 1990, p 73.

21

John Ford

▼

WHEN CARYL AND I WERE IN AUSTRALIA, STAYING WITH MY MOTHER IN 1959/60, she took us to see a large house with its own farm land at Castle Hill, near Parramatta. My mother had been helping, with a group of friends, to make the house into the main property of the first Church of England Retirement Village, named after Bishop Mowll. My mother said that was where she would like to retire to and it is where I would have gone to live had I not been able to save Blithfield.

My mother died at Mowll Village at the end of December 1979, and I, as her only child, inherited all her papers, one of which was of particular interest. It was the death certificate of my great great grandfather, John Ford, which showed he died at Bathurst. Bathurst was the centre of one of the oldest settled districts of New South Wales. John Ford was described as a grazier, but to my great surprise it also stated he had been born in Staffordshire. A friend of mine who lived in Stoke-on-Trent, Sandra Burgess, had BA (Hons) and MA degrees from Keele University, and being especially interested in history used to help people wishing to look up their ancestry. She kindly spent some time looking up John Ford at the Record Office in Stafford and discovered his baptism recorded at St Mary's Church, Stafford, in 1790. His mother was Ann Ford and there was no father mentioned, which seems to indicate that he was illegitimate. Then, by searching through old newspapers, she found an account of a trial held at Stafford Assizes on 24 July 1817, of John Ford, a labourer, accused by John Edmonds (who did not appear) of stealing a mare. Although John Ford pleaded 'not guilty' and no evidence to the contrary was produced, he was sentenced to be hung. However, the sentence was commuted to transportation, King George III, 'being graciously pleased to extend his Royal Mercy to the said John Ford on condition of his being

Cara, Wayne Ford and Nancy in the colonnade at Blithfield

transported to the eastern coast of New Wales or some one or other of the Islands adjacent for and during the whole term of his natural life'. (For an explanation of the court case, see Appendix F.) John Ford, aged 27, set sail in the convict transport *Neptune*, from Downs via London and the Cape of Good Hope, arriving in Sydney on 5 May 1818. His trade was listed as 'quarryman'.

Wayne R Ford, a great nephew of my grandmother, got in touch with me after my mother died, and when I told him I had inherited a number of Ford family papers, asked if he could come and stay as he was most anxious to compile a family history. He had been a detective in the New South Wales police and, being retired, was the ideal person to gather together all the information and place it in the Bathurst Museum Historical Society Office. I told Wayne that I had visited the Office in 1982,

John Ford's
house,
1 George Street,
Bathurst

when staying with Ted and Rose Bagot at their house in Orange. Mrs
Rutherford was the archivist, she told me where she thought John Ford,
senior, had lived, and I saw the house John Ford, junior, had built at 1
George Street, which had been the Historical Society Museum until 1980.
There wasn't a lot of information about the Fords, and I told Mrs Rutherford that when I got back to Blithfield I would send her some of the
information I had inherited from my mother. I also sent her a *Blithfield
Guide Book*. So, when Wayne went to the Record Office at a later date,
after Mrs Rutherford's death, he was surprised not to find any of these
papers; luckily, they were found in the Rutherford file.

Wayne subsequently compiled extensive and well-researched notes
about our ancestors and the following are items quoted from his work.

In 1819, in the *Wentworth Papers* for the period 5 January (p 241), held at
the Mitchell Library, Sydney, there appears the following entry:

> John Ford Overseer Windsor Road Party Seven Pounds Ten
> Shillings.
> 1820 On 17th January, road works overseers John Ford, Nicholas
> Delany and James Johnson petitioned The Governor Lachlan
> Macquarie to reduce the time taken in the issue of road gang
> rations, from the Government Store at Parramatta. Their request

was looked upon favourably and a reply was received by the above mentioned on 19th January.

1821 John Ford receives a Conditional Pardon, and in the same year he was an overseer at Longbottom Farm. 'The rapid influx of convicts after war had ceased in Europe induced Governor Macquarie to establish a number of farms in 1819 to employ those convicts for whom the Government had no employment, and who were not required by the settlers.

30/11/1821 John Ford principal overseer Longbottom Farm at a salary of £25 a year.

Here I don't think I can do better than quote from Wayne's 'Foreword' to his forthcoming work, which is to be entitled *The Ford Saga*, copies of which will be deposited (along with numerous photographs and certificates) at The Bathurst Historical Society with a copy going to the Mitchell Library in Sydney:

While little is known about John Ford's early days in the colony, it would seem that he had life somewhat easier than might reasonably be experienced by a convict in those times. From these notes a picture emerges of a convict who seemed to have been treated rather well. It would seem that John Ford had a 'patron', perhaps someone of the stature of Major Druitt who gets mention several times in the notes. They both arrived in the colony within a year of each other and it may be noted that Druitt was responsible, in his capacity as Engineer, for the agricultural farm of Longbottom where Ford was an overseer and before that he must have known John Ford when he was an overseer on the Windsor Road. Furthermore Ford gave evidence before the 'Inquiry into the Engineer Dept.', which was set up to enquire into the activities of Druitt and subsequently exonerated him. Ford was an Overseer on Druitt's estate about that time. It might reasonably be assumed that a relationship between Ford and Druitt would not have continued had Druitt been found to be at fault. There is evidence that labour was exchanged between Longbottom and Melville (Druitt's property) and that Ford arranged this exchange. Then in the 'All Inhabitants List' of 1825 Ford is shown being at Melville and married one of Druitt's assigned convicts, Jane Quale, and further Druitt was married in the same church as Ford within a month of Ford's wedding.

Then in 1830 only a few years later, the records show that John Ford is a responsible citizen of Parramatta with one hundred and forty head of cattle and four hundred pounds sterling. The early records show that he was a shopkeeper and later a publican and licences confirm that he had 'The Kangaroo Inn' in Church Street, Parramatta from 1832–1835 on land he obtained prior to 1827, he then moved to Bathurst in 1837. In less than fifteen years, though getting on in years, he amassed a fortune which was valued at fourteen thousand pounds at the time of his death.

His estate was approximately 3,000 acres, 'the bulk of which was left to one of the surviving sons, Thomas Daniel Ford, who obviously did not possess the same enthusiasm for work as his father. It would appear that Thomas' love of gambling and his lack of management skills led to his downfall and so all that his father had accumulated was lost with Thomas ending up in Sydney and not living with his family. One can only imagine what might have been had the original tradition been carried on after such a foundation had been laid'. Much of the land inherited by Thomas Daniel was where gold was being found.

Jane Quale (née Cowell) and her sister, Mary Cowell, were born on the Isle of Man, and according to records went on a shoplifting spree in 1822, which resulted in their being sentenced to seven years' transportation to Sydney. As Wayne Ford says, 'so as at 1825 both John and Jane were in the employment of Major Druitt, where no doubt a romance developed'. On 7 March, 1825, John Ford married Jane Quale at the Castlereagh Church in the County of Cumberland. The witnesses to the marriage were James and Isabel Evans.

John and Jane had six children (two sons and one daughter are recorded as having died). Their eldest son, John Ford junior, was baptised at Parramatta on 17 January 1830. By 1838, John Ford senior was a respected resident of Bathurst with his eldest son and namesake, John

The Ford tomb outside Holy Trinity Church, Kelso, Bathurst

Ford junior, having built No 1 George Street, which became the office of the Historical Society of Bathhurst until 1980. John Ford junior owned a coaching company, and it was a Ford coach that Frank Gardiner, the bush ranger, held up at Eugowra Rocks. I have been told that the Bathurst Historical Society has a plan to celebrate the one hundred and fiftieth anniversary of this event in 2012. John Ford (junior) is described as 'a banker and coach proprietor, pastoralist and horse breeder' in the *Bathurst Sketchbook*.[1] It is this John Ford who is mistaken for his father in the book by Rachel Henning, when she visits Bathurst. She calls him 'The richest man in the district', saying 'Many years ago he was transported for life for horse stealing. That was in the palmy days of the colony, he soon made a fortune, got first a conditional pardon, then a free one and now is a great man here!'

It is interesting to note that on 18 December 1832, John Ford senior wrote to Major Mitchell, Surveyor General, informing him that he wished to establish a 'Pottery and Glass Manufactury on leased Government land just outside the toll gate'. As John Ford was born in Stafford, not far from the Potteries, he must have felt he would be able to make pottery and glass if given leave to do so. It seems unlikely he would have asked to start a pottery and glass manufactury had he not had any prior knowledge of the work. The following is a copy of John Ford's letter to Major Mitchell:

Sydney 18th December 1832

Sir.

In consequence of a communication which I had the
honor to have with His Excellency the Governor regarding
the leasing of a portion of Government land near Sydney
on which I intend to establish a Pottery & Glass Manufactury
His Excellency having referred me to you I have therefore the
honor to inform you that the most convenient spot for the
purpose is that triangular section of ground situate about
200 yards outside the toll gate bounded on one side by the Parramatta road on another by the road to Botony Bay at its junction
with the Parramatta road and on the other side by a
proposed continuation of the present Parramatta road from
the Toll-gate to join a new line of road to Parramatta; the
great recommendation to the above spot is its climate situation,
where there will always be a free current of air so as to enable
the workmen to endure the additional heat of the climate as
well as the heat of the Glass House.
Either of the two Paddocks situated between the burial
ground and the cattle market would answer the purpose yet
other they are nearer the town the place first described has
superior advantages for this business.
As His Excellency seemed to doubt the sincerity of my
intentions as to commencing this manufactury that such
doubt may be renewed I am willing to lease the ground on
condition that if it is not in operation before a stated period
the lease will then become void. The length of lease will require

to be liberal as some considerable time will elapse before the
works can be in operation furnaces and houses must be erected
and I fear men and some materials too will require to be got
from England.
The lowness of the Rent will express the encouragement
which the Government is pleased to afford my undertaking.
I have the honor To Be Sir
Your Most Ob St
John Ford.

To Major Mitchell
Surveyor General

Apparently, he was not given the opportunity to test his skills!

A copy of the trial held at the Stafford Assizes on 24 July 1817, can be seen in Appendix F. There appear the names of several 'good and lawful Men of the said County of Stafford then and there sworn and charged to enquire for our said Lord the King and the body of the said County of Stafford'. Many of the other 'good and lawful Men', who were to sentence John Ford to be hung, had descendants who became friends of Caryl's and mine, such as the Wedgwoods, Dyotts, Littletons and Sneyd-Kynnersleys. Theophilous Levett came from the Wychnor branch of the Levett family, this being a different branch from the Levetts of Milford Hall, who are related by marriage to the Bagot family.

The following is a remark made by John Ford, taken from a letter written by Mary Ann Rotton (née Ford) to her brother, Thomas Daniel Ford, 'Do your duty to God and Man as I did all my life and I will be sure to meet you all in a better land where all enquiries as to who and what I am will matter not'.

It was on 24 May 1982 that my cousin, Monica Monkton (née Clifford), and I visited the Historical Museum in Bathurst, when staying with Ted and Rose Bagot at their house in Orange. We had often heard of the Ford family tomb in the Church at Kelso, now we were seeing it for the first time. Holy Trinity Church, Kelso, stands on a hill overlooking Bathurst. The first Rector was appointed in 1825, and it has the distinction of being the first Church in Australia to be consecrated by a Bishop – Bishop Broughton officiating in February 1836. In the *Bathurst Sketchbook*, Holy Trinity is described as 'A simple little church but, beautified by the love of generations, it offers a wealth of historic associations to those who take time to seek it out'. The Ford tomb, where John and Jane are buried along with other members of the family, is easily found near the Church. My cousin and I felt it was a happy resting place for them.

I feel the fact that my mother and her sister had a convict in their family affected their lives to some extent and it might have affected mine had I known! Now I feel sure Caryl must have known, but it obviously made no difference.

Quite a number of people in this country regard all those who were transported as criminals, if so they can't know much about how the poor were treated. If they did anything at all reprehensible they would have been hung, and not had the opportunity of going to Australia. Many of their descendants were usually the first to volunteer to go to the aid of the 'Old Country'. My mother's two cousins, John Ford's great grandsons, were killed in the Great War – Thomas Walter Ford, a student, aged 20, was killed on landing at Gallipoli on 25 April 1915 and is commemorated at Lone Pine Memorial, and Lieutenant Sydney Kelso Ford was killed at Poziers and is commemorated on the Memorial Panel No 55.26 at Villers Bretonneux in France. In the Second World War, my cousin, Sergeant Clive Edward Wigram Clifford RAAF, 44 Sqn, an Observer in a Lancaster Bomber, was shot down on 24/25 March 1942, off Lorient, France and is commemorated on the Runnymede Memorial. This was the first Lancaster reported missing from an operational sortie. I have planted a tree for Clive and the Lancaster Crew at The National Memorial Arboretum, Staffordshire.

In Australia, the convicts are regarded as pioneers and I have often heard their descendants express a wish to thank the judges who sent their ancestors to Australia! I am proud to have some Staffordshire blood in my veins.

Note

1 Stephen Pile and Judith Webb. Rigby Ltd, Adelaide, Sydney, Melbourne, Brisbane and Perth; first published 1975. National Library of Australia.

22

The Bagot Jewitt Trust and the Chancellor
2005

▼

EARLY IN 1999 I READ IN A MAGAZINE: 'IF YOU WANT TO DO ANYTHING about Inheritance Tax, in other words Death Duty, do it before the Budget.' It was March and the Budget would be 5 April, so the Lady Ingram Scheme was entered into, whereby if I lived for another seven years, my heir would not have to pay death duty and I could live in the hall for life. This scheme had already saved Lady Ingram's heir from having to pay duty on her death, so helping her historic house to survive. Obviously the scheme was quite legal without having to pay death duty. My heir was Caryl's great nephew, born four years after Caryl's death and a grandson of Caryl's youngest sister. The 'spare' was Harry Bagot, younger son of Levens Hall Bagots.

The Bagot Title cannot be inherited through a female; like so many families the young Bagot heir (the Fourth Lord's nephew) was killed in World War 1, on the Somme, aged 19, leaving four elderly men, without children, and only about ten years difference in age between them to follow. The fifth heir had a son, born in 1944, who is now Shaun, 10th Lord Bagot and 15th Baronet. He and his wife and daughter live in London. Although Caryl's great nephew couldn't inherit the title through a female, his grandmother, as he was born in 1965, he had age in his favour and I hoped Blithfield would have a long life with him.

So from 1999 until 2005 when the Chancellor Gordon Brown's guillotine fell, I felt happy enjoying Blithfield with my neighbours, and with the help of a friend, Miss Sheila Wroughton, taking small parties of interested people around my part of the Hall, then to the church and the Grove. The Grove consists of land where the seventeenth-century garden had been and where the Second Lord had made an archery ground in the nineteenth century. It is on a ridge between the valley of the River Trent, with

Charles Hugh Shaun, 10th
Baron and 15th Baronet,
head of the Blithfield
Bagot family

Cannock Chase beyond and the Blythe valley (now the reservoir) with
Bagot's Woods beyond. The views are spectacular, with glimpses of the
old house from time to time looking as if it has grown from the ground.

Unlike when Blithfield Hall was open to the public, I no longer needed
to advertise, quite enough visitors came due to 'word of mouth' and I
didn't want to get involved with running a business again, so all the money
collected from the organised parties who came was given to Blithfield
Parish Church Council.

Blithfield Old Rectory changed from a burnt-out wreck into a vision
of its former self and enhanced the view from the Grove. Sadly, Mr
Wright wasn't able to finish his work there as his firm went bankrupt, but
the work has been finished by another firm.

It is just as well we cannot see into the future. On 5 April 2005, I read
in the *Daily Telegraph*, 'Thousands hit as tax on gifts kicks in'.

I still had another year to live before the seven-year period was accomplished and I was given a year to make up my mind whether to go on with the scheme or not; but I could see that Charlie, and his wife Cosy, wouldn't be able to continue to look after Blithfield if they had to pay £600,000 on my death and a market rent for living here.

Everyone responsible for a country house, especially an ancient historic house, dreads the thought of coping with death duties. I thought I had managed to save my heir from what I knew would be crippling duties, quite legally, provided I lived for seven years after making 'The Lady Ingram Trust'. Then, in April 2005, the Chancellor Gordon Brown's legislation came into force, wiping out what had gone before, but not making things quite clear, (even lawyers weren't sure). However, we were sure what he meant was that anyone following the previous laws would be punished for thinking their heirs wouldn't have to pay thousands of pounds in duty when they died. The only way to avoid this was for the owner to hand their property over, and everything they possessed in the property and have nothing more to do with it.

A 'granny flat' could be allowed but only if it had been made before 1986. After my agent, Major O'Neill died in 1971, as I had given him a lease for the cottage his widow and children could continue to live there, so accommodation had to be found for a new agent. This was done when the housekeeper's room, still room, butler's and steward's rooms, on the ground floor were made into a separate flat. Therefore it was decided I could live there, in what was known as The Peacock Flat, paying all expenses, as the agent used to do.

Looking back I don't know how I survived the shock, certainly I was in shock at the time. Rachael Haynes and her father Jack Brown have made the flat comfortable for me to live in, for which I am eternally grateful.

John Cornforth, in his independent report on 'Country Houses in Britain – can they survive?', commissioned by the British Tourist Authority and published for them in 1974 by *Country Life*, has a chapter entitled 'The Role of the Wife'. Had it not been for my Australian blood and up-bringing: that and of course youth, together with an adoring and supportive husband, is why Blithfield is here today.

I know Australians of Italian or Greek origin like to visit the historic houses, towns and villages when they pay a visit 'home'. It is the same for the Australians of British origin, to say nothing of those from all the countries where British people have settled. If historic buildings continue to disappear from this country, as they have done over the last sixty or seventy years, it will be a sad day for Great Britain.

I often wondered if people who came to Blithfield after 2005 thought everything they saw had just grown up overnight like a mushroom! Or if there were some who understood, and were in sympathy with DH Lawrence's quotation, in Arnold Machin's book. D H Lawrence is not one of my favourite authors but I am reminded of the following quotation from his work:

> Things men have made with wakened hands and breathed soft life into, are awake through the years with transferred touch. For this reason some old things are lovely, warm, still with the lives of forgotten men who made them.[1]

Note

1 Cited by Arnold Machin in his book *The Memoirs of Arnold Machin, R. A.* Frontier Publishing, Kirstead, Norfolk, NR15 1EG. 2002, p.160.

Appendices

▼

In 1860 the Bagot Estate consisted of:
  11,000 acres in Staffordshire
  16,000 acres in Wales.

Appendix A

1860: Blithfield
Taken from *Collections for a History of Staffordshire*
(The Staffordshire Record Society 1996) p. 98

Lord Bagot's Blithfield Estate, Staffordshire

A. Initiating Report for draining, farm buildings and roads under the Lands Improvement Company's contract number. 587, 30 October 1860 (vol. v, pp. 127-35).

The Blithfield Hall Estate is one of the finest old estates in the country, and though to the eye of the practical agriculturalist, the land may at first sight be said to be groaning under a heavy load of timber, yet it is a very magnificent burden. The immense oaks being the finest I have seen anywhere and there is this consideration that in a district best adapted for pasture or dairy purposes, with only half the land under the plough, timber may with care be made profitable as well as ornamental.

Appendix B

1938: Colonel Saint's Report

The following is a copy of Colonel Saint's Assessment of The South Staffordshire Waterworks Company Reservoir, for which I am sure he must have received a 'Golden Handshake'. This Report was sent to Caryl in 1938 and reached him when we were staying in Interlaken, Switzerland.

BLITHFIELD SETTLED ESTATES

REPORT

Re: Proposed Acquisition of Land by The South
                    Staffordshire Waterworks Company

Prepared by: Foyer White Borrett & Black, 26 Essex Street, Strand, [London] W.C.2.

The South Staffordshire Waterworks Company are preparing a Scheme for impounding the River Blithe Water in the River Blithe Valley on land belonging to the Blithfield Settled Estates and have approached Lord Bagot in regard to the land required for this purpose.

The enclosed Plan marked 'A' shows an area of approximately 270 acres which the Company wish to acquire and they propose to place a Bill before Parliament in this connection.

It will be seen from Plan 'B' that the proposed Reservoir (shown by a dotted red line) will encroach on six Holdings and this cutting into parts of the Farms, may have a far reaching affect on their remaining portions, and will probably upset the balance and proper working of the holdings. Although such severance might be tolerated by the tenants for a time, it is felt that some of them will eventually want to give up their Holdings, most of which are highly rented and some losses of rent on re-letting would, I am afraid, be highly probable.

It is considered that maintaining the water level to round about the 300 ft. contour line will cause land outside the area of 270 acres to be at times either water-logged or the under drainage to be interfered with.

The proposed Reservoir (around which a road will be constructed) will run within about 330 yards of Blithfield Hall. It will destroy the shooting on the home portion of the Estate and adversely affect the amenities of the residents. The Mansion might be looked upon as being inseparable from the land, and with the amenities so affected beneficial occupation as at present enjoyed, would be impossible.

For the foregoing reasons I advise that the Waterworks Company's proposals, as they stand, be rejected and that if land is to be compulsorily acquired the Company should offer to take the whole of each Holding affected, although only part of each is required and also in view of the material detriment to the Mansion, that they should purchase this too. On the enclosed Plan 'B' the Holdings affected are differently coloured. The area which it is suggested should be taken is enclosed by a heavy purple line and set out in the schedule attached hereto. The approximate area is 1612 acres but some further small adjustments will be made when the areas of the Cottages are measured up and added.

If the sale of the area of 1612 acres is agreed to by the Trustees, the tenant for life, and the Waterworks Company, an area of 2417 acres will remain, of which 655 acres are tenanted and 1762 acres are in hand – the latter represents chiefly Bagot's Woods and Bagots Park from which practically all the marketable timber was sold in 1933, Bagot's Woods and Bagots Park are a heavy burden, as there are between 19 and 20 miles of fences to be maintained.

In the event of the suggested sale to the Waterworks Co. being affected it is not considered that the remaining lands, comprising 4 Farms, 4 Small-holdings, and 11 Cottages together with the Woods and Bagots Park can be economically maintained and I would suggest that these be ultimately offered for sale, but not of course until the sale to the Waterworks Company is completed.

Coming to the financial side of the proposals, if the recommendations materialise, a very useful increase in income from the Settled Estates will result.

It is considered that the suggested sale to the
Waterworks Company would realise a net sum of   £30,800

and that the sale of the remainder would provide a net
        sum for investment of £20,000

            Total £50,800

£50,800 invested at 3% would produce   £1,778 p.a.

Less tax @ 5/- in the £ 445   Net £1,333

The present net income (excluding income from investments) is about
£730 per annum, as shewn in the detailed statement attached, so that the
estimated increase provided by the proposals would be about
£603 per annum or just over 82%.

P.E.W. SAINT
Gloucester
9th March 1938

BLITHFIELD SETTLED ESTATES

SCHEDULE OF LANDS comprised in the suggested sale to The South Staffordshire Waterworks Co.

Tenant	Holding	Area	Rent
A.J.Smith	Bagots Bromley Farm & 4 cotts. .	392.903 903	£215. 0. 0.
F. Tavenor	Warren Lodge		£ 2. 0 . 0.
G. Pye	Land adj. Boozeland	6.039	£ 9. 0 . 0.
R.J. Holdcroft	Barn Farm & 1 cottage	256.494	£244.11. 0.
G. Pye	Dimsdale Cott & Land (Service)	2.187 187	G.A.V. £9.
In hand	Stanley Wood Saw Mills & Croft	3.031	G.A.V. £12.
E.W. Allsop	Stansley Wood House &c.	1.140	£ 19. 0. 0.
T.C. Harris	Newtonhurst Farm	115.187	£138. 0. 0.
T.C. Harris	Cottage at Yeatsall		£ 6. 0. 0.
W. Froggatt Jr.	Dairy House Farm & 2 Cotts	252.357	£275. 0. 0.
A.J. Smith	Admaston Farm & 3 Cotts.	244.615	£365. 0. 0.
In hand	Blithfield Mill G.A.V. £20	.412	
In hand	Blithfield Hall G.A.V. £179	23.178	
Mrs. Mallam	Admaston Lodge (Rent free)	.060	
R.J. Hollins	Blithmoor Lodge & Garden	.405	£ 1. 0. 0.
J.W. Cottrell	Land Yeatsall	141.630	£150. 0. 0.
J.W. Cottrell	Cottage at Yeatsall		£2.12
J.E. Stanning	Sporting Rights (apportioned)		£ 80. 0. 0.
In Hand	Woods, Pits, Watercourses &c	172.725	
	G.A.V. £11		
		A. 1612.365	£1507. 3. 0.

BLITHFIELD SETTLED ESTATES

SCHEDULE OF LANDS remaining after the suggested sale to The South Staffordshire Waterworks Company.

Tenant	Holding	Area	Rent
G. Hampson	Oakfields Farm & 2 Cotts	273.088	£400. 0. 0.
C.F. Kent	Land pt. of Rectory Farm	22.691	£ 27. 10. 0.
Mrs. Perkins	Cottage at Admaston		£ 5. 0. 0.
Mrs Stonebridge	Cottage at Admaston		£ 7. 0. 0.
F.J.T. Martin	Cottage Smithy & Land	6.080	£ 26. 0. 0.
Henry Mardell	Cottage at Admaston RentFree. G.A.V. £5.		- - -
F. Fell	Cottage at Admaston		£ 7. 16. 0.
Chas. Bevins	Cottage (Service) G.A.V. £5		- - -
Postmaster Gen.	Wayleaves		£ 5. 0.
A.W. Blood Exors	Park Lodge Farm	86.750	£105. 0. 0.
G. Brandrick	Land pt of Heatley Bank	5.575	£ 8. 0. 0.
A.W. Brown	Marsh Farm	86.631	£125. 0. 0.
R. Gadsby	House & Land Heatley	11.206	£ 24. 1. 2.
C. Hollis	Little Dunstall Farm	163.019	£182. 15. 0.
A. Brown	Cottage Abbots Bromley		£ 5. 0. 0.
E. Whitehall	Cottage at Yeatsall		£ 5. 0. 0.
J. Whitehall Reps.	Cottage at Yeatsall		£ 5. 0. 0.
Mrs. Jackson	Goats Lodge		£ 2. 12. 0.
F.J. Frost	Squitch Cottage (Service) G.A.V. £6		- - -
H.T. Rose	Thatch Lodge, Kingstone	.537	£ 7. 16. 0.
In Hand	Woods, Bagots Park &c.	1762.266	- - -

G.A.V. £229

BLITHFIELD SETTLED ESTATES
ESTIMATE of ANNUAL INCOME AND EXPENDITURE

INCOME

Rents as from Lady day next	2370
Rents of Sporting	163
Ley Stock in Bagots Park	37

EXPENDITURE

Income Tax Sch A. B. & D.	405
Land Tax	81
Tithe	170
Rates	130
Fire Insurance	68
Estate Wages	490
Garden Wages	204
Materials for Repairs	135
Workmen's Insurance	7
Agent's Salary	150
Sundries	20
	1860
ESTIMATED SURPLUS	730
2590	2590

Appendix C

Letter concerning the Blithfield Estate – the River Blythe Water
Scheme,. 25 August, 1938 (refer also to Appendix D).

Foyer White Borrett & Black Ltd.,
26 Essex Street
Tel: Central 7664
London EC2.

HMF White
25 August 1938
AM Black

Dear Sir,

Blithfield Estate
River Blythe Water Scheme

We enclose a copy Report submitted by Col: PEW Saint on the 9 March
last and a copy of a letter from him dated 3rd August.

When we received the Report we sent copies to the three Trustees and
arranged a Meeting with them. Lord Bagot and Col: Saint at this office.
At the Meeting Col: Saint explained that the South Staffordshire Waterworks Company were under the necessity of increasing the water supply
for the growing industrial areas in Staffordshire and as the bulk of the
streams and rivers in Staffordshire had been polluted because of
industrial development there were very few sources from which pure
water could be obtained. The River Blythe is one of these sources and
Col: Saint stated that it was quite certain that if an amicable
arrangement was not entered into with The Company they would
certainly obtain compulsory power from Parliament. We are sorry we
cannot send you a Plan with the lands in question marked upon it but
the area proposed to be used for a Reservoir will cover the valley to the
east of Blithfield Hall and <u>if the Scheme is carried out Blithfield Mill
will be submerged</u> in the Reservoir. The water would, as you will see
from the 1st Schedule to Col: Saint's Report, cover a part of the
Parklands surrounding Blithfield Hall and part of Dairy House Farm and
Bagot's Bromley Farms which would render the Farms unworkable as

separate units and <u>seriously affect the amenities of the Hall as a residence.</u>

At the Meeting Col: Saint stressed the point that when the Reservoir is constructed a large area of the surrounding lands will become water-logged and the value of these lands will be seriously diminished. Of course on a Compulsory purchase, compensation would be obtained for such depreciation in value.

After going into the matter very thoroughly, the Trustees decided, with the concurrence of <u>Lord Bagot</u> (Gerald, 5th Lord) that Col. Saint should open up negotiations with the Staffordshire Waterworks Co., on the lines of selling to them, not merely the land to be covered by the Reservoir, but also the adjacent lands which could be adversely affected, and containing an area of 1612 acres as mentioned in this Report.

Col. Saint accordingly approached the Waterworks Co., as directed and, after considerable negotiation, provisionally agreed with them the terms set out in this letter of the 3rd August. These terms have been submitted to Lord Bagot and the Trustees, who are all of the opinion that having regard to the price offered (£70,000) as compared with the normal value of the property as stated by Col. Saint (£30,800) and <u>the extreme improbability of Blithfield Hall ever being required as a residence,</u> this unique opportunity of improving materially the financial position of the Settled Estate should not be lost and Col: Saint has been so informed and requested to notify the Company accordingly.

Lord Bagot has, of course, an unfettered power to sell any part of the Settled Lands, except that, in the case of the Mansion-house the Consent of the Trustees must be obtained and this has now been done.

Lord Bagot has asked us to explain the position to the remainder men who are more immediately interested in the Settlement and we are accordingly writing this to notify you of what has been arranged.

Yours faithfully,
Foyer White Borrett & Black[*]
Mr. Caryl Bagot

[*]The offices of Foyer White Borrett & Black were destroyed in World War II

Appendix D

Report re: Proposed Acquisition of land on the Blithfield Estate by The South Staffordshire Waterworks Company.

When Caryl received this report with the accompanying letter (see Appendix C) dated 25th August, 1938, it must have given him a considerable shock, because when Billy, the Fourth Lord, died in 1932, Gerald, his heir, couldn't be found.

Caryl and Margaret (Caryl was heir presumptive) went to stay with Sir Francis Newdigate at Arbury in Warwickshire, one of the Trustees of the Bagot Settled Estate. No doubt they would have come over to Blithfield and seen the historic property in all its desirable beauty. So when Caryl came to me with the documents in his hand saying,: 'I've just received this document from my solicitors in London, it's such a shame, all the beautiful old houses in England being destroyed. I'd like to show this to you it might be of interest to you one day .....'. It wasn't of interest then, because we were going on a trip up the Jungfrau that day, and I had never visited an English Country House. Caryl didn't mention the documents again. He must have realised there wasn't much he could do and decided to go on enjoying life and pursuing me with a view to marriage: – something else I didn't understand and wasn't interested in at that stage.

Caryl's and my first visit to Blithfield was in early August, 1939. We were staying with Caryl's father's cousin, Prebendary Bridgeman at Blymill, and drove over for tea at Gerald's invitation. My first view of Blithfield was of a romantic 'fairy tale' Castle. As we drove across the Park and round the slope of a hill, it suddenly appeared stretched across the drive, looking as firmly rooted in the ground as any of the old oaks nearby. At first, the group of buildings, with their turrets and battlements, seemed to be one – the Stable Block on the right being joined to the house by battlemented walls and a turreted Gateway. We didn't drive through the Gateway to the front of the house, but into a cobbled Courtyard, where the back door was opened by the Butler, Henry Mardell, who had been at Blithfield for so many years he had become a part of it. Mardell took us up the back stairs to Gerald's one living room, where the walls were papered with a beautiful 18th-century Chinese wallpaper, the green background covered with flowers, birds and butterflies. I noticed that Gerald had cut out pictures of racehorses and stuck them onto the paper with drawing pins! I had not seen any Chinese wallpaper before, but I had cut out a picture of the famous Australian racehorse, Pharlap, so at that stage I could sympathise with Gerald's love of horses. Gerald's niece, Mabel Arden Howarth Booth, was with him. On this first visit I found her rather forbidding, but later we became great friends, with our joint love of Blithfield.

From the Chinese Room we were taken through the Library – rather dark with its green and gold painted panelling – down the oak Great Staircase, through a very 'uncosy' Great Hall to a delightful Conservatory, where we had tea, looking through wide open doors into the garden, with its scents and sounds.

After tea we started on a procession through the house. Most of the furniture was covered with dust sheets and the rooms were dark until the shutters were opened: but my one abiding memory is of a child's music box, made in the shape of a round dance floor – little figures, mounted on bristles, wearing gaily painted Tyrolean costumes, danced about sedately when the rather sad tinkley music started. I felt as if I was in another age, and that I was needed here! I still have that music box in my room.

Appendix E

Mr. Philippe Bagot's History of the Bagots in France copied from Caroline Miller's letter, 9 September, 2008.

When staying in the Loire Valley in France, Caroline Miller (née Bagot) got in touch with Philippe Bagot in Blois and the following is what he told her about the Bagots:

> My name is Philippe Bagot, Breton of origin, living now in Blois on the Loire Valley (200 km far from Paris). My family name comes from a little village: Gosne in the eastern part of Brittany (between Rennes and Fougieres). Historically, this part of Brittany was not celtic, but was settled by Francs (a German tribe who gave this name to France) and Normen. This territory was a quid (sic) of no man's land (une marche in French) to protect 'Francia' from Brittany. It is the reason why the name Bagot is probably Norman of origin, it means warrior from the old Norman language waggo (warrier, fighter...) We are about 1700 Bagots in France now.

Appendix F

Court Case – John Ford

The Staffordshire Advertiser of Saturday, 9 August, 1817, Volume XXIII

reported as follows:

<u>Sentence of Death</u>

Was passed on the prisoners on Tuesday evening in the following
manner etc.
John Ford, William Yardley and William Roberts You have severally been
convicted by a very attentive and discriminating Jury, of a Capital
offence of horse stealing and I have only the task of passing the sentence
of law upon you.

(Transcribed by Wayne Ford)

Also found appearing in *The Staffordshire Advertiser* on Saturday, 2
August, 1817, Volume XXIII was the following:

<u>Staffordshire Summer Assizes</u>

Our Assizes terminated on Tuesday evening, when twenty nine unfortunate prisoners, who had previously been convicted of Capital offences,
received the awful sentence of death viz. etc, etc.
John Ford aged 27 for stealing a Mare, William Yardley aged 36 for
stealing a Mare ..... and then goes on to list William Roberts aged 19 for
horse stealing.

(Transcribed by Wayne Ford)

Records at The William Salt Library, Stafford, show that Thomas Kirk-patrick Hall, Esq., was the Sheriff presenting the Calendar of Prisoners appearing at the Summer Assizes, Stafford, on 24 July, 1817, before John Hubball on the Justices' for Stafford. John Ford aged 27 was listed as prisoner number 37 and charged for stealing a black mare the property of John Edmonds of Wolverley in the County of Worcester. He was sentenced to be hanged and reprieved.

(Transcribed by Wayne Ford)

Further research carried out by Wayne Ford caused him to make the following statements:

> The convict transport *Neptune* set sail on the 20 December, 1817, with John Ford listed amongst its convicts under transportation.

> On the 5 May, 1818, John Ford arrived at Sydney on board the transport ship *Neptune* with the record showing that he was sentenced to 'Life'. His calling or Profession was listed as a Quarryman. Further information shows that he was a native of Staffordshire, his age was given as 27 and he was described as 5 feet 8-^{1}/$_2$ inches, dark complexion, dark brown hair with hazel eyes. The *Neptune* was under the Master Robert Carnes and had sailed from Downs on 20 December, 1817, via. London and the Cape of Good Hope. The prisoners were guarded by members of the 48th Regiment and the ship conveyed 170 male prisoners. Thomas Reid was the Surgeon who accompanied the voyage. The *Neptune* was built at Whitby in 1810 and was 477 tons. The sailing time for this trip amounted to 136 days.

> Source: *The Convict Indents*, Mitchell Library, Sydney, Australia.

The Conditional Pardon held at The Mitchell Library, Sydney, Australia records the following:

Date of Pardon: 28 November, 1821.

Name: John Ford

Ship & Year: *Neptune 2*

Native Place: Staffordshire

Trade or Calling: Labourer, Offence: ....

Place and Date of Trial: Stafford 24 July 1817

Sentence: Life

Year of Birth:............., Height: 5' 8-$^{1}/_{4}$"

Comp: D[a]rk ruddy, Hair: Bl[ac]k, Eyes: Dark

Upon Wayne Ford's visit to The Public Record Office, Chancery Lane, London, in 1994, he discovered that a transcript of the trial had not survived. However, the record office did give up the following Indictment, under reference **No. ASS15/137, RC 7135:**

> Staffordshire (to wit) Be it remembered ... and General Sessions of our Lord the King of Crjer and (ms. Illegible ?) holden at Stafford in and for the County of Stafford on Thursday 24th day of July in the fifty seventh year of the reign of our Sovereign Lord George the Third by the grace of God of the United Kingdom of Great Britain and Ireland King Defender of the faith before Sir James Allen Park Knight one of the Justices of our said Lord the King of his Court of Common ... Westminster Sir William Garrow Knight one of the Barons of our said Lord the King of the court of Westminster and ... their Fellow Justices of our said Lord The King under the Great Seal of the United Kingdom of Great Britain and Ireland for the said Justices and their fellow Justices aforesaid or any two or more of them directed whereof our said Lord the King willed that any of them the said, Sir James Allen Park Knight and Sir William Garrow Knight among others in the said Letters patent named/Should be one to enquire by the Oath of good and lawful men of the said

County of Stafford as well within liberties as without and by all other ways means and methods by which they should or might better know by whom the truth of the matters might be the better known and inquired into of all treasons misprisons of treasons insurrections Rebellions Couterfeitings Clippings washings false coinings and other falsities of the Money of the United Kingdom of Great Britain and Ireland and other Kingdoms or Dominions whatsoever and of all murders felonies manslaughters killings burglaries Rapes of Women unlawful meetings and conventicles Unlawful uttering of words assemblies misprisons confederaces false allegations Trespasses Riots Routs Retentions escapes contempts falsities negligences concealments maintenances oppressions champarties deceits and all other evil doings offences and injuries whatsoever and also of the accessories of the same within the said County of Stafford as well within liberties as without by whomsoever and in what manner Soever done committed or perpetrated and by whom or to whom when how and often what manner and all other Articles and circumstances concerning the Premises and according to the Laws and Customs of England for this time to hear and determine by the oath of The Right Honourable George Granville Leverson Gower commonly called Earl Gower The Honourable Edward Monckton Sir John Wrottesley Baronet Sir John Chetwode Baronet Sir Oswald Mosley Baronet Sir John Fenton Boughey Baronet Edmund Peel Esquire Edward John Littleton Esquire William Dyott Esquire John Lane Esquire William Phillips Inge Esquire Moreton Walhouse Esquire Theophilus Levett Esquire Thomas Parker Esquire Edward Grove Esquire George Tollet Esquire Thomas Sneyd Kynnersley Esquire Francis Twemlow Esquire Josiah Wedgwood Esquire Thomas Mettershaw Esquire John Phillips Esquire and Shapland Sweeny Esquire good and lawful Men of the body of the said County of Stafford then and there sworn and charged to inquire for our said Lord the King and the body of the said County of Stafford.

It is presented that John Ford late of the Parish of St Mary Borough of Stafford in the County of Stafford Labourer on the fifteenth day of May in the year of Our Lord One Thousand eight hundred and seventeen with force of arms at the parish aforesaid in the County aforesaid one mare of the price of Ten pounds of the goods and Chattels of John Edmonds then and there being found feloniously did steal take and carry away against the Peace of our said Lord the King his Crown and dignity which said Indictment the said Justices do deliver here in Court in due form of law to be determined And Afterwards that is to say at the Assizes and General delivery of the gaol of our said Lord the King holden at Stafford in and for the said County of Stafford that is to say on the said twenty fourth day of July in the fifty seventh year aforesaid before the said Sir James Allen Park Knight and Sir William Garrow Knight and others their Fellow Justices of our said Lord the King assigned by letters patent of our said Lord the King to deliver the Gaol of the said County of Stafford of the prisoners therein being comes the said John Ford under the custody of Thomas Kirkpatrick Hall Esquire Sheriff of the said County of Stafford (in whose custody in the gaol aforesaid for the cause aforesaid he was before committed) and being brought to the Bar here in his own proper person is committed to the said Sheriff and forthwith concerning the Premises in the aforesaid indictment charged upon him being asked in what he would be acquitted thereof he the said John Ford says he is not guilty thereof and concerning this for good and ill he puts himself upon the County. Therefore let a jury thereupon immediately come before the said Justices of our said Lord the King above named and others their Fellows aforesaid here by whom the truth of the matters may be better the known and inquired into who have no affinity to the said John Ford to recognise Upon their oath whether the said John Ford be guilty of the felony aforesaid or not And the Jurors of the said jury by the said Sheriff to this matter impannelled and returned to wit Richard Leake Joseph Bloor William Woodward James Birtles William Alsop Henry Foster John Olsnam John Salt Richard Arblaster William Halbert William Bickford and Thomas Brown being called come who being chosen tried and sworn to speak the truth of and concerning the premises aforesaid upon their oath say that the said John Ford is Guilty of the Felony in the aforesaid Indictment laid to his charge in manner and form as by the said Indictment is above against him supposed And that he the said John Ford at the time of the committing the said Felony or at any time since had no-good or chattels lands or tenements to the knowledge of the said Jurors And upon this it is required by the Court here of the said John Ford if he hath or knoweth anything to say for himself why the Court here ought not to proceed the judgment and execution concerning him upon the said verdict And thereupon the said John Ford Sayeth nothing but what before he had sayd Whereupon all and singular the Premises being seen and understood by the Court here It is considered by the Court here that the said John Ford be hanged by the Neck until he be dead And the said John Ford is forthwith committed And afterwards that is to say at the same General Session of the delivery of the Gaol of our said Lord the King of the County of Stafford aforesaid our said Lord the King being graciously pleased to extend His Royal Mercy to the said John Ford on condition of his being transported to the eastern coast of New Wales or some one or other of the islands adjacent for and during the whole term of his natural life And His extension of Mercy being notified in writing by the Right Honourable Henry Lord Viscount Sidmouth one of the principal Secretaries of State of our said Lord the King to the Justices of our said Lord the King above named It is therefore ordered and directed by the Court here that the said John Ford be transported accordingly to the eastern Coast of New South Wales or some one or other of the Islands adjacent for and during the whole term of his natural life pursuant to the statute in such case made and provided for.

Pugh (?)
Deputy Clerk of the Assises

(With thanks to Wayne Ford for these transcriptions made during 1994)

Appendix G

The Bagot Jewitt Trust

Address given by Lady Bagot at the sixtieth anniversary of her coming to live at Blithfield.

4 June, 2006.

The fact that Blithfield is here today is due to Caryl, 6th Lord Bagot's great love for his young wife. After all, he was 70 in 1946, when he inherited. He had worked in India for thirty years, during which time he had fought with the Irish Guards at Passchendaele and been wounded. After he retired from India, he and his first wife, Margaret, just travelled around the world. He loved the sun and warm climates. When Margaret died he was devastated and went to stay with his sister and brother-in-law in Queensland. Had he not decided to return to France we would not have met.

My mother decided to bring me to England to meet my father's relations, and Caryl happened to be travelling in the same ship. That was in 1938: between then and 1945, when we visited Blithfield, a great deal had happened – the 2nd World War, of course. Caryl and I were married in Sydney in 1940, and returned to England in 1942 where we lived in London.

Gerald, 5th Lord Bagot was living at Blithfield. He had sold the Hall and much of the Estate to The South Staffordshire Waterworks, but he had permission to live here for life. However, he needed Caryl's permission to sell the family heirlooms in the Hall. As no repairs could be done during the war, the house was in a very bad state, and I remember sitting in this room watching the contents of the Hall being sold. One could not see across the courtyard for weeds – mostly elder.

Caryl and I never dreamt that we would ever be living here, but in April, 1946, Gerald died and The South Staffordshire Waterworks gave us three months to remove any remaining contents and hand the Hall over to them. We only had a tiny house in London and could not fit any more in it.

It was too uncomfortable to stay here because there were no modern conveniences, so we stayed at The Crown in Abbots Bromley, and I must say we were very pleasantly surprised by the excellent country food – just as well because we walked to Blithfield every morning across the Park, worked all day, and walked back to Abbots Bromley in the evening. I will never forget the walk across the Park, mostly covered by water now.

After walking to the Bromley Lodges, opposite the drive to Bagot's Park, the gravel drive wound through the Duckley Woods, which were full of Rhododendrons, to the stone bridge across the Tad Brook, Kitty Fisher's Bridge, with her two small footprints on the balustrade. From there, we walked along an avenue of Beech trees, planted for Queen Victoria's Diamond Jubilee. That was in Stansley Wood, where the sawmills were. The drive wound down to the Blythe Valley, which was crossed by an avenue of Oak trees, leading to Blithfield Mill, still working then. The water meadows looked like a Constable painting – sad that they've gone; but the reservoir looks lovely and can't be carpeted by houses!

We soon realised we had inherited a very challenging job. The part of the house where Gerald had been living was still furnished, and, although there was no living accommodation in the stables, there were five coaches in the Coach House, and large copper vats in the Brew-house. The roof of the Hall seemed to be leaking everywhere, so there was a lot of dry rot. We discovered a very damp muniments' room – before it was too late, thank goodness – as it contained masses of documents, some dating back to the 12th century. There was plenty of empty floor space to spread the documents out, and when they had dried, they were taken to the Salt Library in Stafford. Gerald had died in April, and by May we were beginning to feel differently about the place. Having been brought up in Australia, I was delighted by the Bluebells, which were new to me, and I loved history – here it was living!

Caryl felt he did not want to be the first Bagot to leave Blithfield, so, after a lot of negotiations, and 'ups and downs', it was bought back, with 30 acres of garden. Then, my life's work started, very joyfully, everything we did turned out better than expected, and there was always Caryl's delightful sense of humour.

We got a Grant to restore the Hall from the Historic Buildings Council. It was realised then that if the Historic Buildings Council were not helpful, the buildings would be lost. How different from today's Labour Government!

Blithfield was open to visitors for twenty-one years, but Caryl's death in 1961 was a devastating blow to that world. If it had not been for spiritual help and help from sensitive and kind friends, I could not have carried on. Caryl knew that if I had our baby daughter, and Blithfield to care for, I would do it. Then when things got desperate financially, it was my mother who I have to thank for saving Blithfield. Blithfield as it is wouldn't be here today if it hadn't been for her.

The fate of Blithfield has hung by a thread two or three times during the last sixty years, but Bagots have lived here for over 600 years, so they must have had a special affection and respect for the old place, and I hope that will be continued by Charlie and Cosy and that they, and their daughters, Emma and Sophie, will be happy here. Of course, I hope Caryl's and my daughter, Cara, will want to live in her cottage here some time.

Lastly, I must thank Charlie and Cosy for giving me this opportunity to thank my friends and relations for being a source of support and happiness to me.
Thank you.

Index

Abbott, Dr 222, 223

Abbotsleigh, Church of England School for Girls 8, 41-45, 47, 73, 193, 202, 203, 210, 257

Adelaide 10, 11,118, 189, 206, 208-210

Agnew, Colin 98

Anson, Viscount Thomas Edward 102

Anson, Steve 113

Aix-les-Bains 10, 13, 14, 25

Arbury Hall, Warwickshire 56, 208, 307

Baden-Powell, Lady 101

Bagot
  Alec, Mr and Mrs 202, 206
  Annette 113, 261
  Anthony 152
  Barbara 247
  Betty 118
  Cara (Caryl Rosemary) 213 et seq
  Caryl, Sixth Lord Bagot 10-16, 19-30, 49 et seq
  Charles F Henage 183
  Charles Hervey (Harvey) 233
  Charles, Sir 105, 140, 171, 172, 177
  Cosy Bagot Jewitt 8, 296, 318
  Charlie Bagot Jewitt 8, 296, 318
  Emma Bagot Jewitt 318
  Sophie Bagot Jewitt 318
  Dorothy 239
  Edward (Ned) 28, 149, 219, 239
  Eleanor 138
  William, First Lord Bagot 93, 141, 162, 165, 166, 171, 173, 283
  Florence Eleanor 183
  George 239, 240
  Gerald, Fifth Lord 26, 56, 83-92, 96, 108, 181, 183, 279, 306-308, 316, 317
  Guy, Commander 141
  Harry Eric (Seventh Lord) 76, 180, 181, 183, 229, 232, 233, 243
  Hervey 169
  Hugh 81, 86, 87, 233
  Isabel ('Belle') 239-241
  John N (of Adelaide) 175, 209, 210, 232
  John, Sir 173
  Kathleen 180, 181, 232, 243
  Lewis Richard Charles, The Reverend 49
  Lilian, Lady 118, 119, 250, 251
  Louisa, Hon 20, 81, 167
  Louise 81, 256
  Margaret (née McMenemy) 16, 19, 53, 56, 57, 76, 316
  Margot see Black, Margot
  Mary 81, 86, 87, 233, 256
  Philippe 8, 309
  Milicent, Jessie Eleanor 169
  Milly 229
  Ralph 166, 169, 173
  Reginald Walter 180, 183, 243
  Richard, Colonel 163, 172, 174
  Robin 113, 261, 263
  Rose 259, 262, 274, 288, 293
  William, Second Lord 27, 90-94,100, 105, 119, 135, 141, 144, 145, 165, 177, 275, 279, 283, 284, 295
  Simon 169
  Ted, Edward M. 259, 262, 274, 288, 293
  Tempe 262
  William, Third Lord 83, 100, 105, 183
  Walter, 1st Earl of Essex 152
  Walter (from Adelaide) 115, 118, 208, 209, 231
  Walter Wagstaffe, Sir 103, 133, 141, 144, 152, 162, 247, 250, 285
  William, Fourth Lord 56, 88, 119, 144, 173, 307

Bagot Chester, Peggy 77, 221

Bagot Collection, Potteries Museum 20, 98, 119, 248-255

Bagot's Park 27, 28, 75, 77, 79, 85, 87, 90, 93, 149, 166, 180, 243, 317

Bagot's Woods 27, 28, 83, 295, 300

Barklam, Harold 144, 174, 214, 222

Barton, Mrs and Bessie 168

Beaudesert, Cannock Chase 118

Bedford, Miss 85

Bernasconi, Francis 27, 131, 136, 165, 263

Bexon, Doreen 80, 82, 87, 88, 91, 95, 96, 98, 167

Birch, Dennis 263

Birt, Bradley 103, 105

Birtsmoreton Court, near Ledbury 103, 105

Bishop William (Bishop of Shrewsbury) 219, 224, 236

Bishton Hall 7, 107, 216

Black, Alex 260

Black, Margot (née Bagot) 103, 259, 260

Blithfield Hall 26, 27, 74 et seq

Blithfield Rectory 20, 92, 174, 180, 226, 227, 277, 278, 281, 282, 295

Blithfield Park 27, 28

Blithfield Reservoir 7, 131, 146, 253

Borrett family 36, 37

Bowen, John 59, 60, 65

Bowen, Monica (née Clifford) 11, 30, 37, 38, 42-45, 58-60, 73, 94, 95, 102, 293

Bradfield, Mr 39

Bradley, Frank 238

Bridgeman, Reverend Ernest (Uncle Ernest) 25, 28, 307

Brisbane 61-63, 210, 258

Brocklehurst, Charlie 180

Brocklehurst, Sir Philip 116

Brooke, Lady (Olave) 28, 29, 74, 76, 78, 111, 112, 115, 132, 142, 214, 262

Brooke, Rear Admiral Sir Basil 28, 112, 132

Brougham, Lord 103, 105

Brown, Gordon 7, 284

Brown, Jack 8, 284

Brown, Tim 234

Brownhill, Peter 277, 278

Buller, Milicent 76-78

Burgess, Jeff 7

Burgess, Sandra Ann 7, 286

Burghley, Lord 152, 172

Burne, Mr 90

Bushby, Dorothy 17, 19, 20, 226

Bushby, Esther 16, 17, 19, 22, 36, 37, 45, 46, 78

Bushby, Geoffrey 17

Bushby, Henry North Grant 16

Buxton, Christopher 277

Cains, Cassie 43

Calke Abbey, Derbyshire 280

Capewell, Mrs 168

Cave, Elizabeth 152, 172

Cavenagh-Mainwaring, Guy 185

Cavenagh-Mainwaring, Rafe 102

Cavenagh-Mainwaring, Rosemary 102, 185

Cavenagh-Mainwaring, Tara 102

Ceylon 11, 12, 25

Chandos-Pole, Jill 108-110, 180, 219, 220

Chandos-Pole, Wakey 108-110, 180

Chartley Hall 152, 161

Chatsworth 181

Chester, Peggy Bagot 77, 221

Chicheley Hall, Buckinghamshire 162

Chillington 110, 111

Church of St Leonard, Blithfield (Blithfield Church) 91, 92, 105, 152, 169-174, 216, 219, 220, 230, 231, 236, 239, 277

Clifford, Clive Edward Wigram 37-39, 73, 294

Clifford, Lucy 37-39, 43, 45, 58, 102-105, 115, 205, 259, 260

Clifford, Monica see Bowen, Monica

Clifford, Patrick Wigram 37

Clifford, Doris 37, 44

Compton Castle 179

Cookes, Denham 243

Cooper, Lucy and son Max 220

Cooper, Max 234

Copeland, Ida 111, 112

Copeland, Ronald 111, 112

Copeland, Sonia (Mink) 233

Cornforth, Mr and Mrs 227

Cornforth, John 227, 297

Cowell, Mary 290

Cowell, Jane see Quale, Jane

Council for the Protection of Rural England, The 275

Country Life 7, 131, 134, 145, 146, 149, 227, 235, 297

Cransford Hall, Suffolk 36

Crawley-Boevey, Cynthia 219, 220, 256,257, 261

Crawley-Boevey, Susan 256, 257, 261

Cunninghame Graham, Admiral Sir Angus 29

Cunninghame Graham, Patricia 29

Cunninghame Graham, Robert 29

Cyprus 115-118

David Evelyn Nye and Partners 134

Dawnay, Sir Oliver 132

De Blithfield, Elizabeth 166, 169

De Walden, Lady Howard 261

Deakin, Horace 8, 243, 244, 276-279, 281, 283

Denbigh Castle 163

Devas, Anthony 97, 98

Drabble, Phil and Jess 234, 235, 243, 260, 276

Elias and Mercedes, from Gibraltar 218, 221, 222

Essex, Lord Robert, 2nd Earl of Essex 152, 161

Everett, Miss 41, 42, 202, 203

Everett, Ted 231

Excell, Mrs 168

Fedden, R Romilly 181, 214

Feilden, Sir William and Lady 110

Field-Richards, Doctor Sara 119, 213, 215, 219, 221

Fildes, Denis 179

Fildes, Luke 179

Finch, Winnie 64

Fitzherbert, Mrs 103

Fitzherbert, Evelyn 103

Ford, Ann 286

Ford, John 286-294

Ford, Syd 33, 34

Ford, Thomas Daniel 290

Ford, Wayne R 8, 287, 288, 290

Ford, Lieutenant Sydney Kelso 294

Fowler, John 7, 8, 109, 131, 137, 138, 141-148, 166, 167, 175, 187, 247, 263, 285

Fremantle 11, 188, 189

Gateways, The (No 16) 76, 80, 81, 85, 87, 97, 98, 111, 144, 175, 177, 184, 218, 221, 227, 239, 245, 260

Gee family 227

German, Colonel and Mrs Guy 107, 222, 226, 275

Gesh, Lena, Colin and Roger 210

Gifford, Lady at Coronation 120

Gilbert, Commander Raleigh and Joan 179

Glendevon, Lord 245

Gowers Report 134-148

Grant, Jean Beresford see Russell, Jean

Gregory, Harry 9, 48

Grumett, Miriam 221

Haddon Hall 181

Halden, Sheila 96

Hamilton, Charles 246

Harris, The Reverend Alfred 20, 81

Harris, Dora 20, 73, 81, 221

Harris, Elizabeth 81

Harris, John 145

Harpur-Crewe, Henry 280

Harrowby, Earl and Lady 101

Haszard, Dyonese 103

Hatherill-Stephenson, Mary 7

Hawke, Lady 124

Haworth-Booth, Arden 221

Hay, Ian 12-14

Hay, John Sir 12, 13

Haynes, Rachel 7, 284

Hayter, Adrian 44

Heath, Kelvin 274

Hemphill, Paddy see Love, Paddy

Hemphill, Sybil 81

HM Queen Elizabeth the Queen Mother 7, 118, 123-125, 126, 131, 133, 146, 240, 253

Hiskins, Elizabeth 175

Historic Buildings Council, The 7, 81, 91, 134, 135, 146, 177, 180-182, 214, 237, 244, 318

Hoar Cross 108

Holmes, Mrs 216, 218

Holmes, Molly and Angus 258

Horn, Nini and Steve 260

Howarth-Booth, Mabel Arden 26, 233, 308

Hussey, Christopher 7, 131, 134

Hyde, Mr and Mrs John 283

Ingestre 105-107

Italy 22-25, 79, 110

Jackson, Sarah 80, 82, 88, 90, 167, 168

Jaques, Sandra 44

Jagger, Philip 277, 282

Jauncey, Arabella 262

Jewitt, Enid (née Bagot) 49, 57, 60, 62, 63

Jewitt, Sarah 80

Jewitt, Toby 281, 282

Jodrell, The Reverend Henry 49

Johnson, Wally, Jackie and Rebecca 221

Jonas, Gena 225

Jones, Colin 180

Keddleston 109
Keele Hall, Staffordshire 7, 284
Kent, Mrs 168
Kenyon, Lady 124
Kerman, Isadore 183, 280, 281
Kerr, Sir Howard and Lady Christina 112
Kerr, Marie 112, 113
King Charles I 163
King Edward VIII 45
King Edward VII 119
King George III 286
King George V 250
King George VI 112, 115, 118 252
King William IV 247
Kitson, John 219, 257
Kitson, Jonathan 257
Kitson, Melina 257, 262
Knox, Margaret and Berta (Bunny) 38
Kulczycki, Bojenna 119, 222, 250, 253-255

Lane, Miss Jane 168
Lang, Jack 39
Leek, Gladys (née Bagot) 19, 20, 22-25, 49, 57, 68, 71
Levens Hall 261
Lichfield, Lord 102
Little Wyrley Hall, Pelsall 149, 235
London 13, 14, 25, 66, 76, 80, 81, 85,87, 91, 94, 99, 108, 118,
    130, 134, 144, 183, 185, 213, 218, 222, 253, 254, 277
Lothian, Lady 125
Love, Paddy (née Hemphill) 81, 82, 119, 224
Love, Captain Philip 82
Lucas, Reverend CA 59
Lucas, Mrs 168, 221, 223, 227, 233, 234, 256
Ludlow 49, 57
Lyons, Christopher 281, 283

MacDougall, Marjorie 30
MacDougall, Nancy 9, 12-16, 30, 47, 48, 58, 240
Macfarlane, Sister 215, 218, 220
Machin, Arnold 273, 276, 297
Machin, Francis 273, 274

Machin, Pat 273, 274, 276
Main, Nance and Harry 223, 226, 228
Manners family 181
Manor House, Heslington 263
Mardell, Mrs 106
Martin, Kit 277
Mary, Queen of Scots 29, 161
Maudslay family 262
McManus, AG 231
McMenemy, Margaret see Bagot, Margaret
Meeson, Robert 136, 166
Melbourne 10, 112, 189, 210
Melbourne Hall, Derbyshire 112, 113
Melville, Rodney 283
Meynell, Lady Dorothy 84, 108, 126
Middlemass, Mr 281, 282
Midgley, Miss 90
Miller, Caroline 8, 274
Miller, James 285
Minto House 263, 264, 273
Monkton, Monica (see also Bowen, Monica) 293
Monte Carlo 12, 20, 21, 111
Moore, Clifton and Rey 258-261
Moore, Stephen 260
Munthe, Axel 13
Murray, The Reverend Douglas 20
Murray, Donald 20
Murray, Evelyn 20
Murray family 20, 25
Murray, Pamela 20, 25
Murray, Walter 20, 25, 170

Napier, Admiral Sir Charles 49, 75
National Trust, The 17, 111, 175, 179-184, 281, 283
Newdigate, Sir Francis 56, 307
Newport, Australia 9, 12, 44, 48, 58, 59
North, Lady Frances 16
Nutting, Sir Harold 110

Oakley Park 49
O'Neill, John 215, 222, 223, 226, 227, 236, 238, 240, 242, 280
O'Neill, Frances 236, 240, 277, 280
Oliver, Mrs 8, 45

Orme, Frances 262

Oswald, Arthur 134, 146

Palfrey, Mr 279

Palmer, Lily 180

Pam, Major 19

Paris 15, 20, 25, 37, 52

Pawlowski, Josef, Tamara and family 99

Pearson, Mary 262

Perth 11, 188, 189

Polwarth, Lord and Lady (Harry and Jean) 261, 262

Pope, Holly 261

Portland House 17, 19, 226

Prall, Mr and Mrs 97

Preston, Pam 177

Quale, Jane 290

Queen Elizabeth II

    Coronation of 115-129, 247

Radburne Hall, Derbyshire 108, 110

Radley College, near Oxford 20, 21, 50-52

Ralli family 53, 56

Randall, Thea 8

Read, Michael 225

Riley, Mrs 275

Robinson, Professor Colin and Mrs 284

Roch, Miss 168

Round House, The, Painshill 110, 245, 246

Rowney, Nannie 218, 220, 221, 227, 257

Royal Family 118

    Princess Royal 126

    Duke and Duchess of Kent 126, 254

    Princess Alexandra 126

    Princess Margaret 126

    Duchess of Gloucester 126

    Princess Marie Louise 126

Russell, Jean (née Grant) 7, 41, 43, 193, 201, 263, 264, 273

Russell, Kate Minto 7

Russell, Marcia 103, 105, 257, 260

Russell, Peter 193

Salesbury, Colonel William 163

Salesbury, Jane 163, 166, 231, 285

Salter, Dr John and Mrs 222, 223

Sandy of Stafford 227

Scarsdale, Tilla 110, 125

Seymour, Lady Katharine 132

Shackleton, Rosemary and Les 240, 241

Shaw, The Reverend Bernard Douglas 20, 81

Shaw, Ivor 284

Shipley, Mr and Mrs 210, 216

Shrewsbury, John 22nd Earl of 105, 128

Shrewsbury, Nadine 106, 125

Shugborough 101

Simon, Jan 261

Simon, Marie Madeleine 261

Sitwell, Guy 109

Smith, George 263

Smithurst, Elsie 8, 231

Snell, Bertram 59, 75

Snell, Ysolde (née Bagot) 59, 75

Sneyd family 7

Sneyd, Charlotte Augusta 137, 284

Snowshill, Gloucestershire 175, 214

Society for the Protection of Ancient Buildings, The 214, 275, 276

Sothebys 86, 87, 175, 285

South Staffordshire Waterworks Company, The 7, 28, 83, 88, 91, 95, 130-132, 183, 237, 279, 299, 302, 303, 305, 307, 316

Spicer

    Francis Aldborough (father) 37, 39, 40, 46, 70

    George John (Jack) 37, 39

    Ida (née Stericker) 9-25, 29-31, 34-37, 40, 41, 44-46, 58, 60, 73, 78, 80, 120, 185, 190, 202-204, 212, 213, 224, 226, 231, 237, 251, 258, 276, 282, 286-288

    Kitty 13

Stafford Northcote, Ben 99, 216

Stafford, Lady 125

Stafford, Lord (Fitzherbert, Basil) 103

Stanton Lacy 49

Staunton Harold 112

Steinfield, Mr 281, 282

Stericker, Charles and Kit 102, 245

Stericker, Constance Maud Mary (née Ford) 13, 19, 31-35, 37, 38, 60

Stericker, Doris 37, 44

Stericker, Ida *see* Spicer, Ida

Stericker, Kit 219, 221, 245, 262, 274

Stericker, Thomas Edward 31, 35

St Mary and St Anne school, Abbots Bromley 168, 183, 193, 237, 239, 257

Suffield, Lady 124

Sydney 9, 16, 29, 30, 32, 35, 37, 47, 58, 63, 81, 183, 189-193, 202-207, 211, 257, 258, 287-290, 292

Taylor, Diana 263

Taylor, Imogen 8, 148, 237

Taylor, Nancy 192

Towlson, Stanley 171, 173, 216,223, 224, 226, 228, 231-234, 236

Towlson, Valerie 223, 224, 226, 228, 237, 256, 262

Trelissick 111, 112, 238

Trouville-sur-Mer 14, 15

Turnock, Dr Bill and Pam 241

Tyrwhitt-Drake, Sir Garrard 91

Ugbrooke Park, Devon 274

Vernon, George 278

Vernon, Lord and Lady 112

Wade, Mr 275

Wallaces 149

Walsh, John 9, 48

Ward, Charles 8, 231

Ward, Margaret 8, 231

Wedgwood, Sir John and Lady 110

Wenger, Paddy and Mary 103, 105

Whitehead, Kenneth 149, 213, 235-237, 239, 257

Wigan, Daisy 100, 115, 116, 131, 228, 229, 230, 231, 237

Wigan, Edgar Clare (Jimmy) 92, 115, 116, 219, 222, 228, 229, 230, 274

William Salt Library, Stafford 90, 145, 165, 166, 311, 317

Williams, Anne and Mary 38

Windsor Clives 49

Withall, Brian 263

Wolseley Hall 102, 107

Wolseley, Sir Edric and Lady (Clare) 102, 103, 125, 175

Wood, Martin 8, 146

Wormley Bury House, Hertfordshire 19, 36

Wright, Ray 276-283, 296

Wroughton, Sheila 8, 114, 295

Wyatt, Samuel and Joseph 165